UPDATED

Computer World 7

Windows 7 and MS Office 2010

Mohini Arora

Collins

UPDATED

Computer World 7

Windows 7 and MS Office 2010

Mohini Arora

Published by Collins India
A division of HarperCollins*Publishers* India Private Limited

HarperCollins *Publishers*
A-75, Sector 57, Noida, Uttar Pradesh 201301, India
1 London Bridge Street, London, SE1 9GF, United Kingdom
Hazelton Lanes, 55 Avenue Road, Suite 2900, Toronto, Ontario M5R 3L2
and 1995 Markham Road, Scarborough, Ontario M1B 5M8, Canada
25 Ryde Road, Pymble, Sydney, NSW 2073, Australia
195 Broadway, New York, NY 10007, USA

Browse the complete Collins catalogue at **www.collins.in**

First edition published in 2015
Updated edition published in 2016
Latest reprint edition 2017

ISBN: 978-93-5177-444-0

Artwork by **AptaraCorp Ltd.**

Layout by **Recto Graphics**

Printed and bound in India by Nutech Print Services - India

MRP:₹280

Acknowledgements

Cover: Cybrain

Title Page: Cybrain

The screens and illustrations including the literary and artistic works as well as the trademarks displayed are the sole and exclusive intellectual property of their respective owners and Collins India do not claim any right whatsoever over them. The screens, illustrations and trademarks have been displayed only for educational and instructional purposes.

Collins India does not warrant that any website/download link mentioned in this title will be provided uninterrupted, that any website will be error free, that defects will be corrected, or that website or the server that makes it available are free of viruses or bugs. For full terms and conditions, please refer to the site terms provided on the website.

The NCO paper has been printed with the permission of Science Olympiad Foundation. No part of this may be reproduced, transmitted, in any form or by any means, electronic, mechanical, photocopying, recording or otherwise, without the permission of the copyright holder. For more details on NCO, you can visit their website www.sofworld.org. Their corporate office is at Plot No. 99, Sector – 44, Gurgaon, Haryana – 122003, India.

Preface

Computer World (Updated Edition), a series of eight books for Classes 1 to 8, is an effort to familiarize and equip students with the latest trends in computer technology. This is a well-graded course that conforms to the requirements of National Curriculum Framework (2005) and complies with the syllabus requirements of various boards.

The course is based on **Windows 7** and **MS Office 2010** with updates on Windows 8 and MS Office 2013. The progression of the series ensures that the pedagogical needs of the students are met.

The course introduces computers in the primary classes in a simple and lucid manner. It strengthens programming concepts, and gives students an opportunity to explore and experiment with the latest software in higher classes. The series has the latest versions, namely MS Visual Basic 2010 Express, Windows Movie Maker 2012, HTML 5, Adobe Dreamweaver CC, Adobe Photoshop CC and Adobe Flash 8.

The course is a perfect blend of theoretical and practical topics, and is interspersed with illustrations, keyboard shortcuts and facts. The language used for concept explanation is simple and the content is supported by step-by-step explanations and well-labelled screenshots.

Sections like You Should Know, Quick Way, Quick Recap, Word Web and Teacher's Notes cover and recapitulate the concepts through each dimension. A detailed overview of the key features of the books is given in the **Key Features** spread on the next two pages.

To enable students face the challenges, and to provide them a competitive edge by developing their lateral thinking and analytical skills, following sections are given in each book:

- Worksheets and Projects
- Assessments
- Revision Questions
- National Cyber Olympiad by Science Olympiad Foundation–for Classes 3 to 8

To meet all the learning objectives and to provide a holistic form of imparting education, the questions in various sections are based on **Bloom's Taxonomy**. This ensures that the concept understanding is tested at six different levels, namely Knowledge, Comprehension, Application, Analysis, Synthesis and Evaluation.

Lab Activities and Research Projects are given with the aim of inducing curiosity and familiarizing students with practical applications of the topics. All the books in this series have relevant sections flagged with FA and SA icons, indicating that these sections can be considered as formative and summative assessments.

Collins DigiSuite is an interactive digital solution which provides an e-book with learning materials and interactive teaching tools that will help teachers to prepare additional notes and practice questions for students.

I would like to thank all the teachers who have reviewed the series and the publisher who has invested its resources in bringing out this course to inspire the learners today. I sincerely welcome constructive feedback and suggestions to improve these books further in subsequent editions.

Mohini Arora

Key Features

You Should Know

When we cut or copy a portion of text, Windows stores that portion in a temporary storage area called the **Clipboard**.

includes interesting facts about the topic

Quick Way

To open a new presentation in PowerPoint, press the **Control** key (**Ctrl** key) and the letter **N** together.

highlights all the important keyboard shortcuts for the menu commands

Word Web

Malicious: harmful and destructive

gives the meaning of all the difficult words

Practice Time 2

Use the commands to draw and write the following in MSWLogo.

1. Each side of the square is 100 units

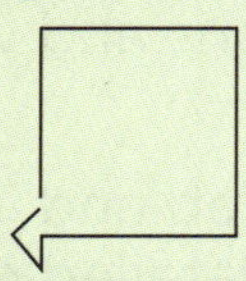

provides solution to hands-on practice questions given after covering important concepts

WINDOWS 8

UPDATES

Windows 8 is an improved version of the Windows 7 operating system. It provides all the basic features that Windows 7 has. The focus of Windows 8 is on optimizing the operating system for touchscreen-based devices (such as tablets) and cloud computing.

Unlike Windows Vista and Windows 7, there are no Starter, Home Basic, Home Premium or Ultimate editions in Windows 8. The most common editions of Windows 8 are Windows 8 Pro and Windows 8 Enterprise.

section has updates on Windows 8 and MS Office 2013 for Classes 3 to 8

Quick Recap

1. Internet is a vast computer network that connects millions of computers all over the world with one another and makes information sharing between these machines possible.
2. Internet Explorer 11 is the latest web browser from Microsoft.

recapitulates all the important points covered in the chapter

Teacher's Notes

Discussion Ideas:

- Discuss the various elements covered in this chapter and their attributes.

Demonstrations

- Demonstrate the effect of all the values of the align attribute of the <p> element.

contains interesting topic-related notes that teachers can take up in class and demonstrate to students

Research Project

FA

Vivek has collected about 20 pictures of his school and wants to share these pictures with his friends. Which program should he use for doing this?

integrates Computer Science with the other subjects and is aimed at testing the students' application skills

Lab Activity

Try the following in your computer lab.

1. Your class teacher has asked you to prepare a list of the students in your class along with their roll numbers and marks in a class test in MS Excel 2010. Do as directed by your teacher.
2. Create the worksheet shown and then make the following changes:

D7

	A	B	C	D	E
1					
2	S No.	Name	Salary	Allowance	
3	1	Asha	59000	4000	
4	2	Krishna	15000	2000	
5	3	Harsh	29000	3000	
6	4	Rita	44400	1600	
7					
8					

tests the practical application of the concepts taught

EXERCISE

A Fill in the blanks with appropriate options.

Windows Movie Maker User Interface   Video Tools Edit   Seek

1. The home page of Windows Movie Maker is known as the __________ .
2. You can start playing the movie from any place by clicking on the ________ .

assesses understanding of the concepts covered in each chapter

ASSESSMENT 1

Chapters 1 and 2

1. Write any five advantages of using a computer. (5)

FA ASSESSMENTS

facilitates the students and teachers with additional questions for Formative Assessments

NATIONAL CYBER OLYMPIAD

1. Which of the following are used to print characters by an impact printer?
   (i) An ink pen
   (ii) Electrically charged ink
   (iii) An inked ribbon
   (iv) A print head

has questions based on NCO by Science Olympiad Foundation

SA REVISION QUESTIONS

REVISION QUESTIONS

Suggested Questions for SA

1 Colour the machines you see outside the house. (6)

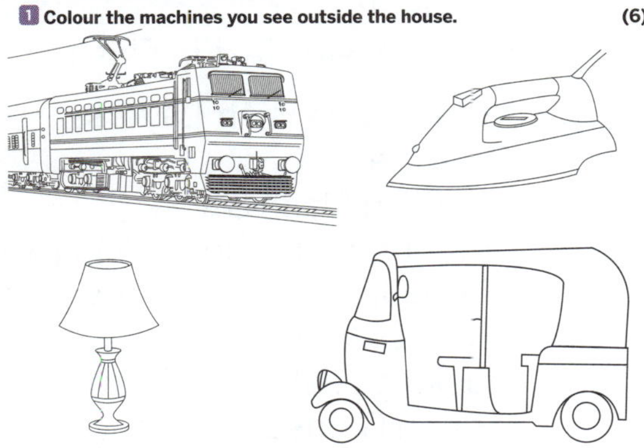

aims at testing students' understanding of the concepts taught and can be used as Summative Assessments

WORKSHEET

FA WORKSHEET AND PROJECTS–3

A Choose correct option for each of the following.

1. The Flash file is saved with an extension
   (a) .fls (c) .fla
   (b) .fll (d) None of the above

2. The Rulers option is in ______________ menu.

Projects

Your school is hosting a Christmas fair. The Principal wants to upload an animated poster on the school website giving the details of the fair. Create the same using Flash 8.

reinforces the concepts by testing students' grasping power

Collins DigiSuite is an innovative digital solution for teachers. It contains four modules delivering classroom content that can be used to effectively integrate the teaching and evaluation tools with the coursebooks.

The **e-book** includes animations, video snippets, interactive exercises, slide shows, guided tours and worksheets. The e-book reader also includes interactive teaching tools like pen tool, text highlighter, page zoom, search and bookmark.

The **Test Generator** is a question bank with a variety of questions for effective evaluation. It is an easy-to-use assessment tool for the teachers to create test papers and worksheets.

The **Teacher's Resource** consists of lesson plans, answer keys and teaching techniques for the teachers.

This module has a PDF of the **Collins dictionary** appropriate for each level with all the words and definitions one needs.

Contents

• 1 Formulas and Functions in MS Excel 2010

Learning Objectives

By the end of this chapter you should be able to
- understand cell and range references.
- learn to use formulas—text and numeric.
- understand some error results.
- learn the AutoSum feature.
- learn to use functions from Function Library.

Introduction

You have already learnt to use formulas and their applications in mathematics. In this chapter you will learn how you can use formulas in Excel 2010 to perform various calculations.

A formula is a particular method which, when used, results in a new value from an existing range of values. A formula in MS Excel always starts with an equal to sign (=) followed by one or more of the following constituents:

1. Cell addresses or range references—A4, B9:B20, C:F
2. Constant values—Numeric (423, 90.9) and Text ('Good and Bad')

3. Mathematical operators—+,-,*, %, /, etc.
4. Brackets—( )
5. Functions—Sum, Average, Min, Max, Count, etc.

CELL AND RANGE REFERENCES

The data to be used within a formula may be placed in a single cell or a range of cells in an Excel worksheet. The values in these cell references or range of cell references are used in the formulas for computation of result. Giving cell ranges in the formula saves a lot of time as there is no need to write individual references for each cell. Consider the examples of cell addresses and range references given below:

(a)	The cell in column D and row 6	D6
(b)	The range of cells in column F and rows 7 through 17	F7:F17
(c)	The range of cells in row 8 and columns A through F	A8:F8
(d)	All cells in row 8	8:8
(e)	All cells in columns A through D	A:D

You Should Know

MS Excel 2010 has 1048576 rows and 16384 columns.

USING FORMULAS

A formula may be a simple formula containing just one operator or a compound formula with multiple operators. To enter a formula for a specified set of values, type equal to (=) sign in the formula bar followed by the formula. Then click Enter or ✔ button. To understand this, consider the example given below that calculates the sum of numbers in the cells A1, A2, A3, A4 and A5.

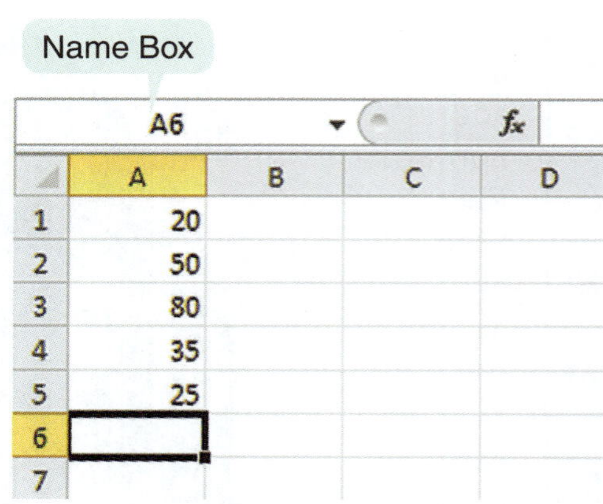

Fig. 1.1: Select the cell in which you want the result

Step 1: Click the cell in which you want the sum to be displayed. In our example, let that cell be **A6**. You will see **A6** in the **Name Box**.

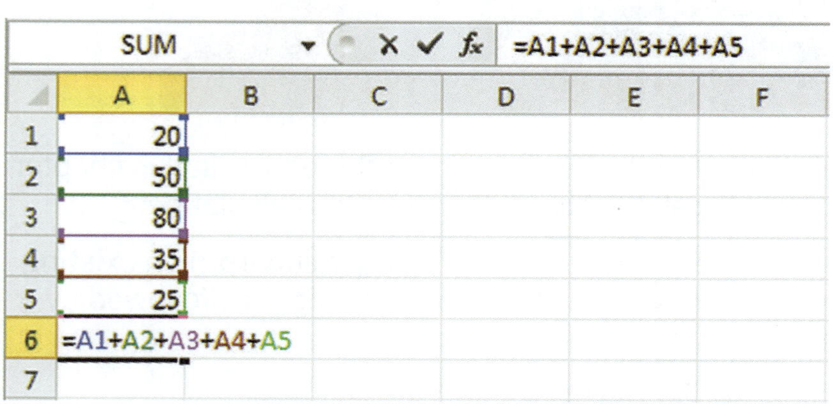

Fig. 1.2: Enter the formula

You Should Know

The formulas in MS Excel are not case-sensitive. So, A1+A2 is same as a1+a2.

Step 2: Type the formula beginning with an equal to (=) sign. As you type the formula in the cell, it is also seen in the **Formula Bar** simultaneously. You will notice that the colour of the cell name in the formula and the border colour of the corresponding cell is the same.

Step 3: Click ✓ or press the Enter key. The result will be displayed in the cell A6.

Excel gives you an advantage of **auto-editing** the result. As you change the data in the cells containing input values, the result automatically changes in the cell where formula was entered.

In the example given, if you change any of the values of cells A1:A5, then the result in the cell A6 changes automatically.

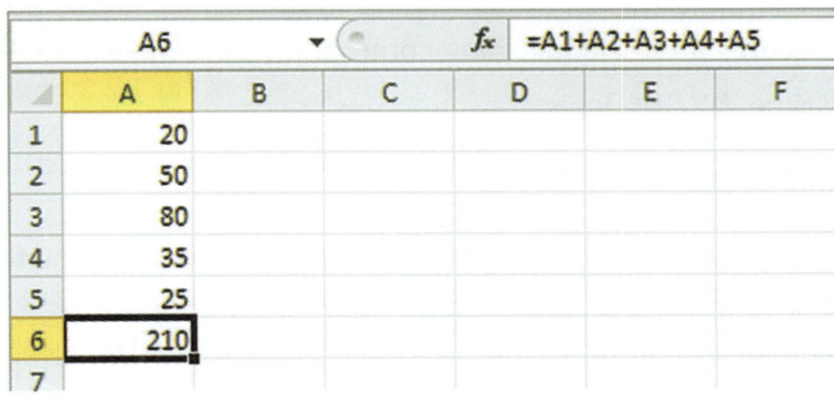

Fig. 1.3: Displaying the result

You Should Know

While writing a formula in MS Excel, you can click on the cells instead of typing the cell addresses. An animated border appears around the selected cell and **'Point'** is displayed on the Status Bar. This method is called entering a cell reference by pointing. For example, after typing '=', do not type 'A1'. Instead click on cell A1.

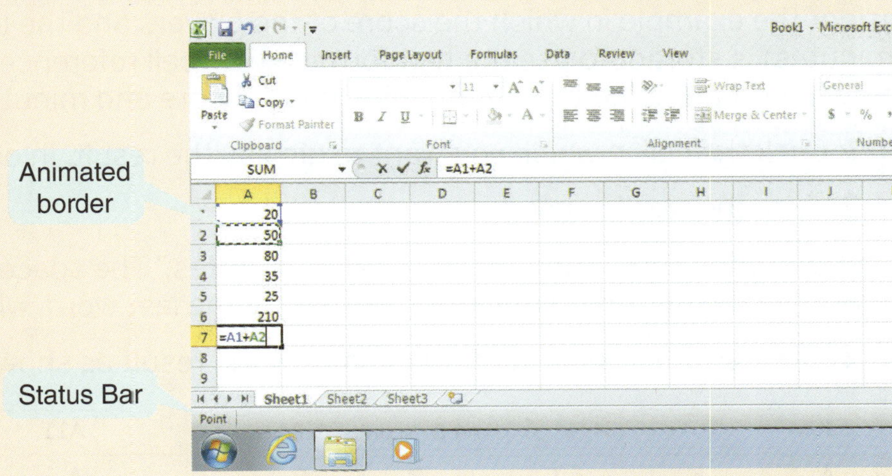

Text Formulas

A text value is a set of characters on which you cannot perform arithmetic operations such as addition, subtraction, multiplication, etc. These values are also called **strings** and they can be joined together. This process of joining one string followed by another is called **concatenation**. The **ampersand** (&) operator is used to concatenate two strings.

For example, if you type = "Blue" & "Ocean" in a cell and press the Enter key, you get BlueOcean.

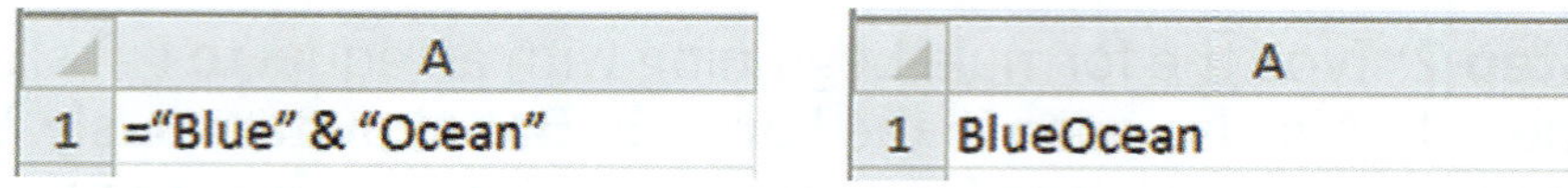

Fig. 1.4: String concatenation without space

To include a space between "Blue" and "Ocean", enter the following command:

="Blue"&" "&"Ocean"

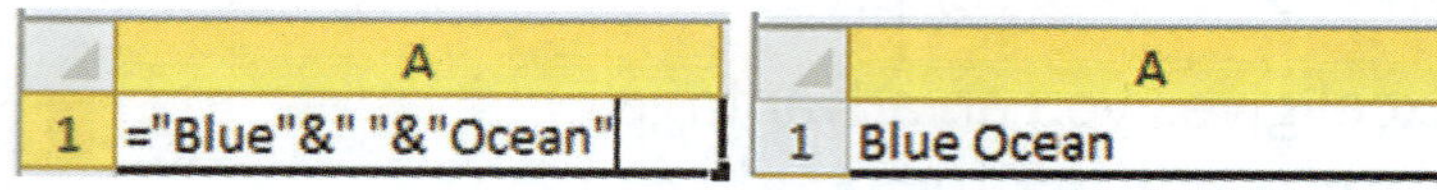

Fig. 1.5: String concatenation with a single space

Here, we have considered a single blank space also as a string and enclosed it in quotes.

Alternatively, we can also include a space either after the first string or before the second string while concatenating.

You Should Know
The string values are always entered in double quotes.

For example, both ="Blue "&"Ocean" and ="Blue"&" Ocean" will result in Blue Ocean.

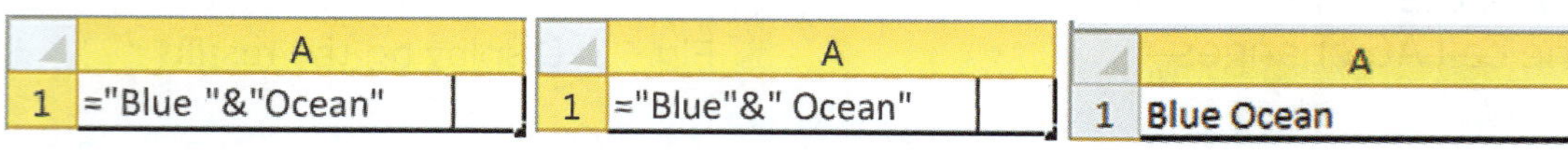

Fig. 1.6: Alternate method of adding a single space in string concatenation

You can also use cell references while concatenating the strings.

Consider the example in which the score of the players and the time for which they played (in minutes) is stored. To use the text formula with cell references, follow the steps given below after creating the table containing name, score and minutes played.

Step 1: Click the cell in which you want to display the result. In our example, it is A10.

Step 2: Type the text formula:

= A4&" scored "&B4&" runs "&" in "&C4 &" minutes." The spaces succeed and precede each word in the quotation marks except end of the last word, which uses a full stop.

Step 3: Click ✓ or press the Enter key to view the result as shown in Fig. 1.8.

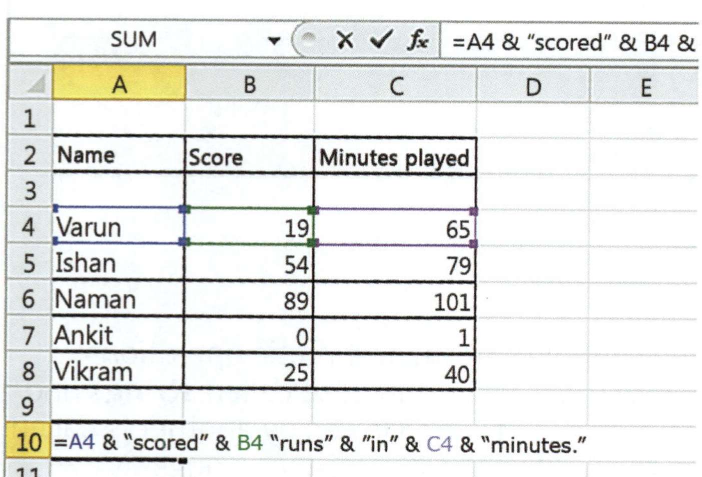

Fig. 1.7: Creating a text formula

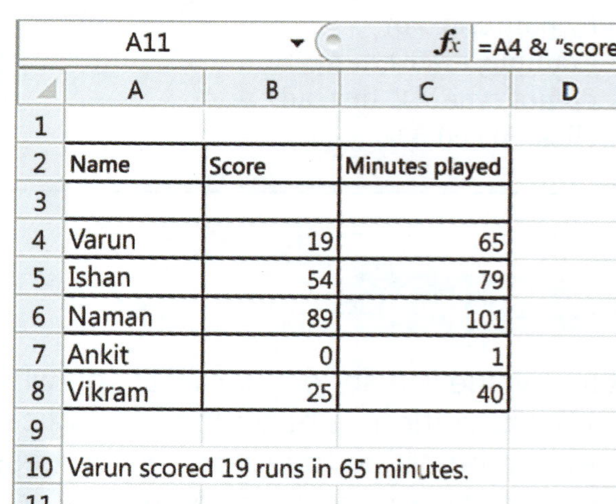

Fig. 1.8: Result of a text formula

Mathematical Operators Used in Numeric Formulas

Various mathematical operators can be used in Excel while creating and using the formulas. The following table gives the list of arithmetic operators:

Operator	Operation	Example	Result
^	Exponent	2^5	32
*	Multiplication	2*5	10
/	Division	10/5	2
+	Addition	2+5	7
–	Subtraction	10–2	8

Following points should be kept in mind while creating numeric formulas:

(a) The evaluation is always carried out from left to right.

(b) While evaluation, if multiple operators are present in a single formula, the operator having higher order of precedence will be evaluated first. The order of precedence of arithmetic operators is as follows:

- ^
- / , *
- +, –

Consider an expression: 2*5 + 3^2

In the above expression, there are three operators: *, + and ^. According to precedence rules, ^ will be evaluated first (as it has the highest precedence), then * and then +. So, the order of evaluation will be as shown below:

=2*5 + 3^2

Step 1: 2*5 + 9

Step 2: 10 + 9

Step 3: 19

(c) If two operators have the same precedence, Excel evaluates them from left to right.

(d) Any operation given in bracket will always be evaluated first.

Consider the following formula to understand the evaluation of an expression within brackets.

= (4–2*3) ^ 2

Step 1: (4–6) ^ 2 (brackets to be evaluated first)

Step 2: (–2) ^ 2

Step 3: 4

ERROR RESULTS

You may sometimes make mistakes while entering the formulas. Excel does not evaluate such formulas and display errors instead of the expected results. The table below lists some common formula errors in Excel along with their possible reasons.

Error	Reason
#DIV/0!	Division by zero (An invalid operation)
#N/A	Data is not available
#VALUE!	Formula contains invalid data

Quick Way

Press **F2** to enter or modify a formula in a cell.

You Should Know

If you see a couple of '#' in a cell, it means the column is not wide enough to display the resultant number. This is not considered as a formula error. In this case, increase the width of the column so that the complete number is displayed.

AUTOSUM FEATURE

The AutoSum feature is one of the most commonly used features of MS Excel. It automatically adds the numbers in the selected range of cells. Other than addition, the AutoSum feature can also be used to find the average, maximum value, minimum value, etc. for the selected range of cells. You can find the AutoSum button in the **Editing** group of buttons on the **Home** tab. It is also present in the **Function Library** group of buttons on the **Formulas** tab.

	A	B	C	D	E	F	G
1							
2	Household Expenditure						
3–4	Name	Grocery	Electricity Bill	LPG	Vegetables & Fruits	Misc	Total
5	Shiwali	3000	6000	2000	2000	4000	
6	Teena	2500	4500	1500	1800	3500	
7	Bhawna	4000	2900	1600	2300	4200	
8	Krishna	2700	5000	2500	2500	3800	

Fig. 1.9: List of expenses

To use the AutoSum feature, consider the following example containing the list of expenses of four homemakers.

1. Select cell G5 and click **AutoSum** (not the arrow) in the **Editing** group of buttons on the **Home** tab. You will see a formula with the **Sum** function along with a cell range. An animated border surrounds the range of cells in the formula (B5:F5). A tool tip showing the syntax of the formula also appears under the active cell.

	A	B	C	D	E	F	G	H	I
1									
2	Household Expenditure								
3–4	Name	Grocery	Electricity Bill	LPG	Vegetables & Fruits	Misc	Total		
5	Shiwali	3000	6000	2000	2000	4000	=SUM(B5:F5)		
6	Teena	2500	4500	1500	1800	3500	SUM(number1, [number2], ...)		
7	Bhawna	4000	2900	1600	2300	4200			
8	Krishna	2700	5000	2500	2500	3800			
9									

Fig. 1.10: Creating the formula using AutoSum

2. Press the Enter key or click **AutoSum** button again to view the result.

Household Expenditure						
Name	Grocery	Electricity Bill	LPG	Vegetables & Fruits	Misc	Total
Shiwali	3000	6000	2000	2000	4000	17000
Teena	2500	4500	1500	1800	3500	
Bhawna	4000	2900	1600	2300	4200	
Krishna	2700	5000	2500	2500	3800	

Fig. 1.11: Result of AutoSum

3. To further fill the range of cells G6:G8, you can use the **AutoFill** feature of MS Excel. Select cell G5. Drag the fill handle (the small black square at the lower right corner) to cell G8. While dragging, the fill handle changes to a small black cross.

Household Expenditure						
Name	Grocery	Electricity Bill	LPG	Vegetables & Fruits	Misc	Total
Shiwali	3000	6000	2000	2000	4000	17000
Teena	2500	4500	1500	1800	3500	13800
Bhawna	4000	2900	1600	2300	4200	15000
Krishna	2700	5000	2500	2500	3800	16500

Fig. 1.12: Copying the formula

4. Release the left mouse button. You will see that the AutoSum formula is copied to all the cells in the range.

Quick Way

The shortcut key for AutoSum is **Alt+=**. This shortcut key can only be used for adding adjacent cells.

Functions in Excel 2010

Functions are predefined formulas in MS Excel. Various functions are provided by MS Excel to perform various mathematical operations. One such function is Sum that adds the numbers in a given range of cells.

You have performed the addition operation in the previous section using AutoSum feature. The Sum function is inserted automatically when you click the AutoSum button.

Other functions provided by Excel 2010 are available in the options of the AutoSum feature. For using them, click on the arrow to the right of the **AutoSum** button.

The following AutoSum options are displayed:

(a) **Sum**: to calculate the sum (you have used this option by clicking directly on AutoSum). This is the default option of AutoSum feature.

(b) **Average**: to calculate the average of the values in the selected range of cells.

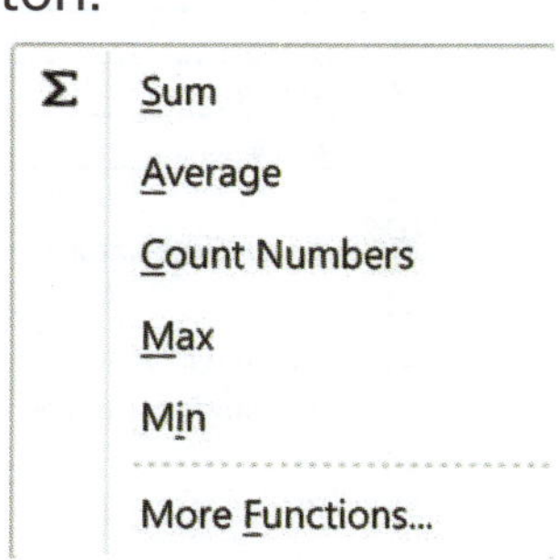

Fig. 1.13: AutoSum options

(c) **Count Numbers**: counts the number of cells containing some values.

(d) **Max**: displays the highest value from the given range of cells.

(e) **Min**: displays the lowest value from the given range of cells.

Consider an example to use the various options of the **AutoSum** button. In an Excel sheet to calculate household expenses, follow the steps given below to find the average expenditure of each category.

1. In the Excel sheet of Household Expenditure, write Average Expenditure in cell A10, Maximum Expenditure in cell A12 and Minimum Expenditure in cell A13.

	A	B	C	D	E	F	G
1							
2	Household Expenditure						
3–4	Name	Grocery	Electricity Bill	LPG	Vegetables & Fruits	Misc	Total
5	Shiwali	3000	6000	2000	2000	4000	17000
6	Teena	2500	4500	1500	1800	3500	13800
7	Bhawna	4000	2900	1600	2300	4200	15000
8	Krishna	2700	5000	2500	2500	3800	16500
9							
10	Average Expenditure						
11							
12	Maximum Expenditure						
13	Minimum Expenditure						

Fig. 1.14: Data entry in Excel

2. Select cell B10. Click the arrow to the right of **AutoSum** button. Select the **Average** option. The average function is inserted automatically.

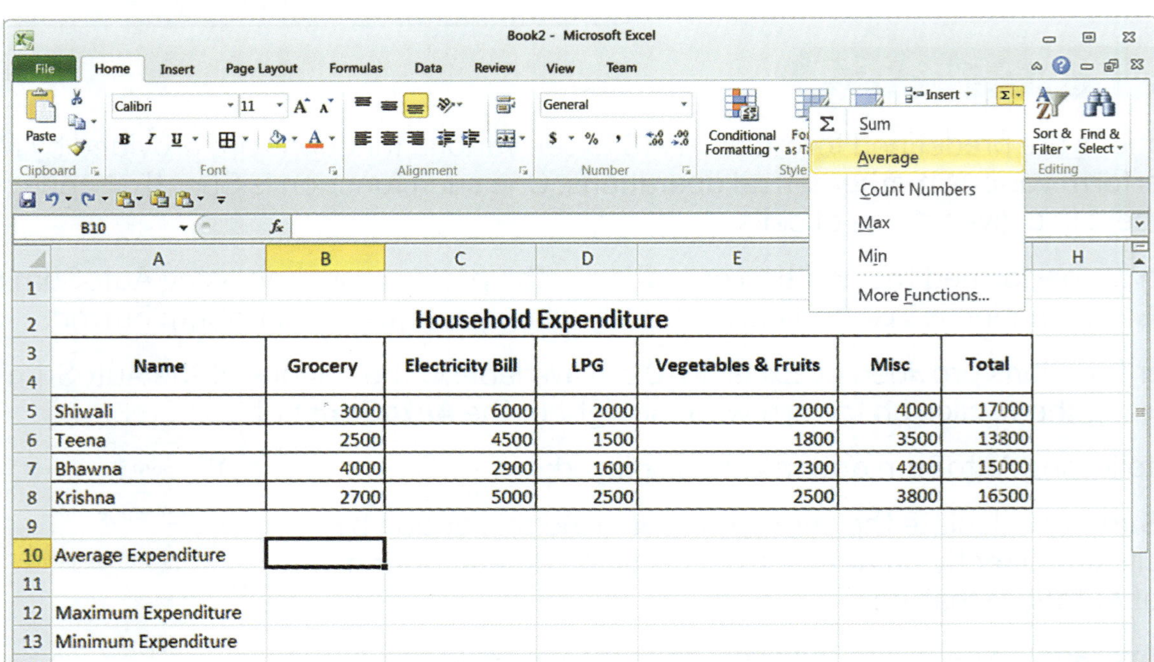

Fig. 1.15: Cell selection

3. The range in the formula is B5:B8. This range of cells will also have an animated border around it as shown in Fig. 1.16.

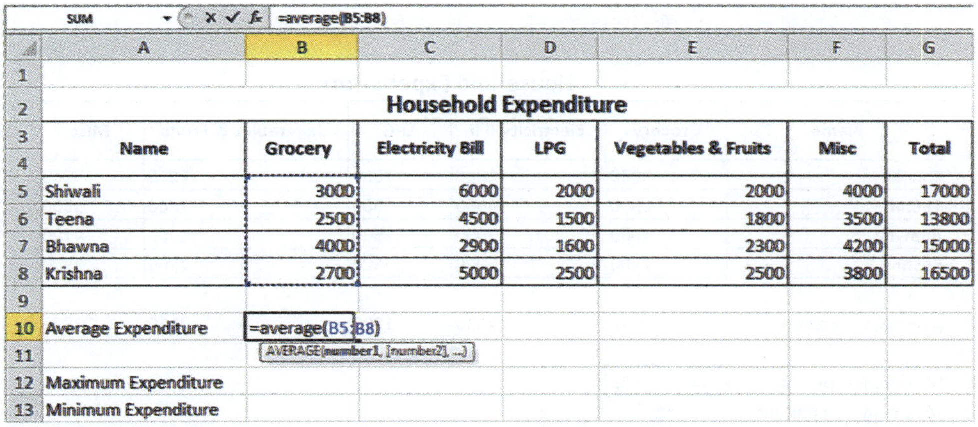

F g. 1.16: Average formula

4. Press **Enter** to view the average grocery expenditure.

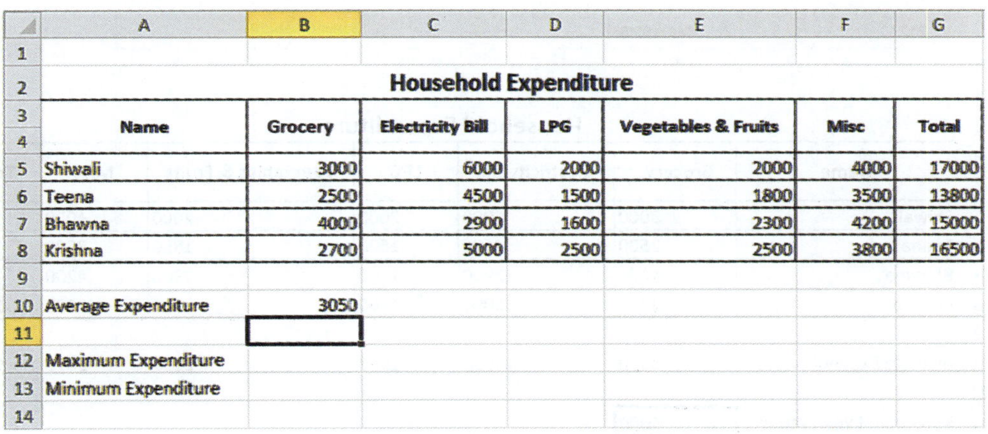

Fig. 1.17: Result of the Average formula

5. To find the average expenditure of other expense heads, use the AutoFill feature of MS Excel. Keeping the left mouse button pressed, drag the fill handle to cell G10. When you release the mouse button, the average expenditure of all the heads is displayed in the cells B10:G10.

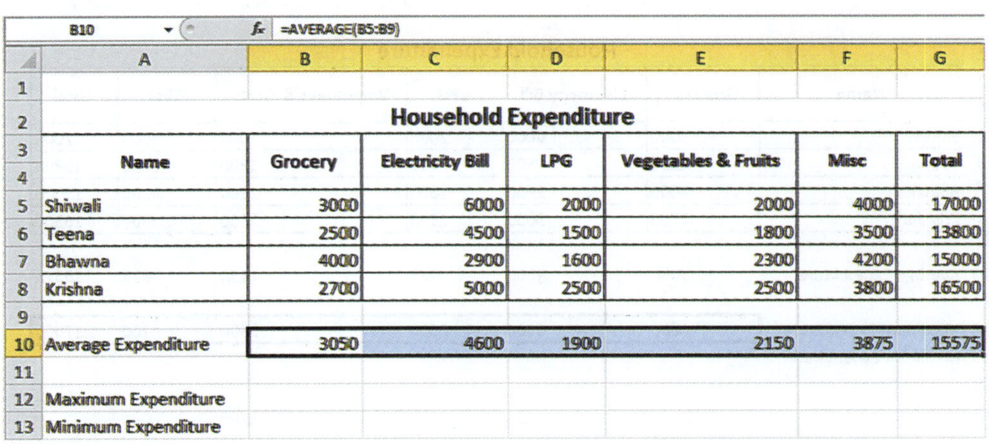

Fig. 1.18: Drag to copy the Average formula

6. To find the maximum expenditure incurred under each head, select the **Max** option from the **AutoSum** drop-down menu.

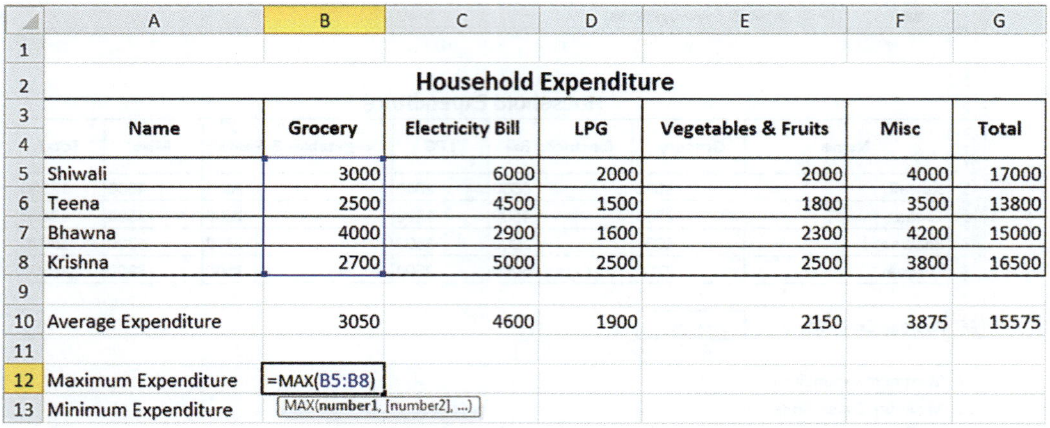

Fig. 1.19: Max formula

7. Fill the correct range (B5:B8) and press **Enter** to view the result.

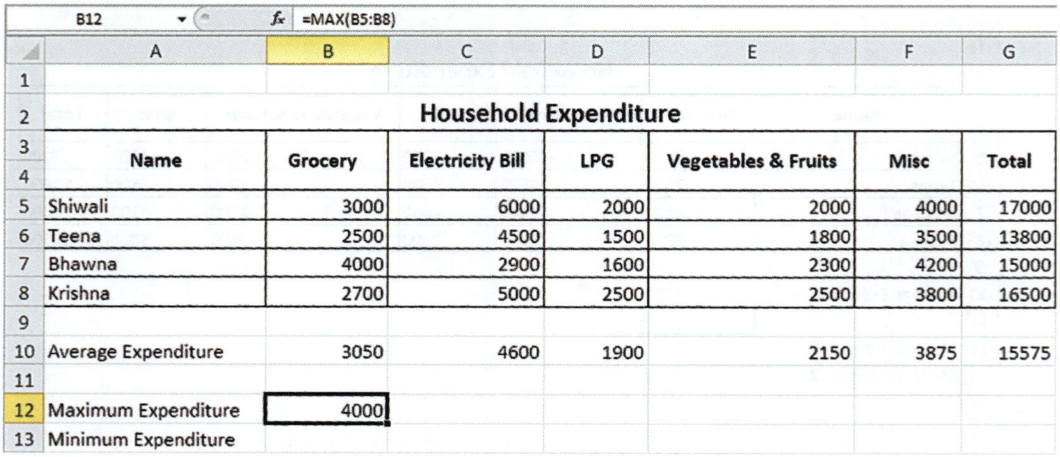

Fig. 1.20: Result of the Max formula

8. Click and drag the fill handle to view the maximum expenditure under each head.

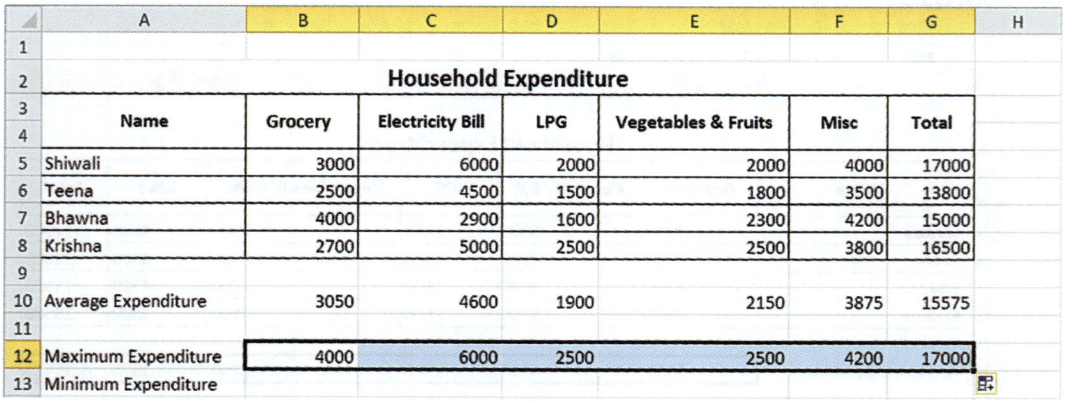

Fig. 1.21: Drag to copy the Max formula

9. Similarly, you can find out the minimum expenditure under each head by choosing the **Min** option from the **AutoSum** menu.

Household Expenditure

Name	Grocery	Electricity Bill	LPG	Vegetables & Fruits	Misc	Total
Shiwali	3000	6000	2000	2000	4000	17000
Teena	2500	4500	1500	1800	3500	13800
Bhawna	4000	2900	1600	2300	4200	15000
Krishna	2700	5000	2500	2500	3800	16500
Average Expenditure	3050	4600	1900	2150	3875	15575
Maximum Expenditure	4000	6000	2500	2500	4200	17000
Minimum Expenditure	2500	2900	1500	1800	3500	13800

Fig. 1.22: Result of the Min formula

10. The **Count Numbers** option in the AutoSum menu counts the number of numeric values in the range. To understand this, delete the contents of cell D6 under the LPG expenditure head. Now, select cell B16 and select **Count Numbers** from the **AutoSum** menu.

Household Expenditure

Name	Grocery	Electricity Bill	LPG	Vegetables & Fruits	Misc	Total
Shiwali	3000	6000	2000	2000	4000	17000
Teena	2500	4500		1800	3500	12300
Bhawna	4000	2900	1600	2300	4200	15000
Krishna	2700	5000	2500	2500	3800	16500
Average Expenditure	3050	4600	2033.3333	2150	3875	15200
Maximum Expenditure	4000	6000	2500	2500	4200	17000
Minimum Expenditure	2500	2900	1600	1800	3500	12300
Number of expenditure heads considered:						

Fig. 1.23: Count Numbers from the AutoSum menu

11. Type the correct range (B5:B8) and press the **Enter** key. You will see the result as 4.

12. Click and drag the fill handle to display the count of each expense head.

Since you deleted the contents of cell D6, the result in cell D16 will be 3 because now there are only 3 values in column D from D5 to D8.

Household Expenditure

Name	Grocery	Electricity Bill	LPG	Vegetables & Fruits	Misc	Total
Shiwali	3000	6000	2000	2000	4000	17000
Teena	2500	4500		1800	3500	12300
Bhawna	4000	2900	1600	2300	4200	15000
Krishna	2700	5000	2500	2500	3800	16500
Average Expenditure	3050	4600	2033.3333	2150	3875	15200
Maximum Expenditure	4000	6000	2500	2500	4200	17000
Minimum Expenditure	2500	2900	1600	1800	3500	12300
Number of expenditure heads considered:	4	4	3	4	4	4

Fig. 1.24: Result of Count Numbers from the AutoSum menu

You Should Know

To give a range of non-adjacent cells in a formula, separate each cell address by a **comma (,)**. For example,

=AVERAGE(A1, C5, D3, E2)

FUNCTION LIBRARY

The functions are present in the **Function Library** group of buttons on the **Formula** tab. Through these buttons you can browse and select the required formulas. Other than the **AutoSum** button, the various categories of formula buttons available are as follows:

- **Recently Used**: provides a list of recently used functions
- **Financial**: provides a list of financial functions to choose from such as INT
- **Logical**: gives a list of logical buttons such as AND, OR, NOT, etc.
- **Text**: gives a list of text functions such as LEN
- **Date and Time**: gives a list of date and time functions
- **Lookup & Reference**: gives a list of look up and reference functions
- **Math and Trig**: gives a list of mathematical and trigonometric functions
- **More Functions**: gives a list of statistical and engineering functions such as AGGREGATE, CEILING and PRECISE

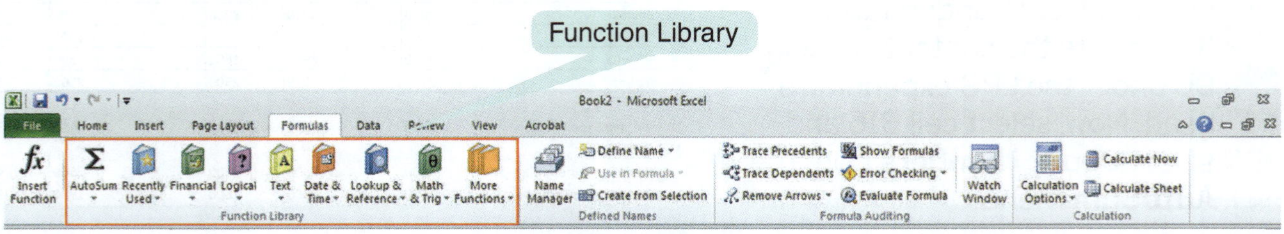

Fig. 1.25: Formulas tab

Let us use some functions from the Function Library group of buttons.

LCM

You must have calculated the Least Common Multiple (LCM) of two or more integers in mathematics. To calculate LCM in MS Excel, follow the steps given below:

1. Type the numbers in cells B1:B4.
2. Select the cell where you want to display the LCM, say B6.
3. Click Math & Trig button from Function Library group of buttons on the Formulas tab. A list of functions appears.

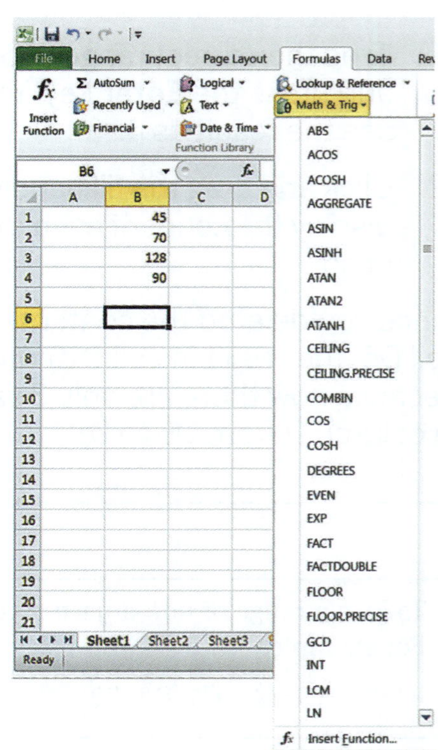

Fig. 1.26: Math & Trig drop-down list

4. Select LCM option from the drop-down list. The **Function Arguments** dialog box appears.
5. Type the cell numbers B1, B2, B3 and B4 in the Number1, Number2, Number3 and Number4 text boxes respectively. The value in each cell is displayed on the right side of the text boxes itself.
6. Click **OK**. The result is displayed in the cell B6 on the spreadsheet.

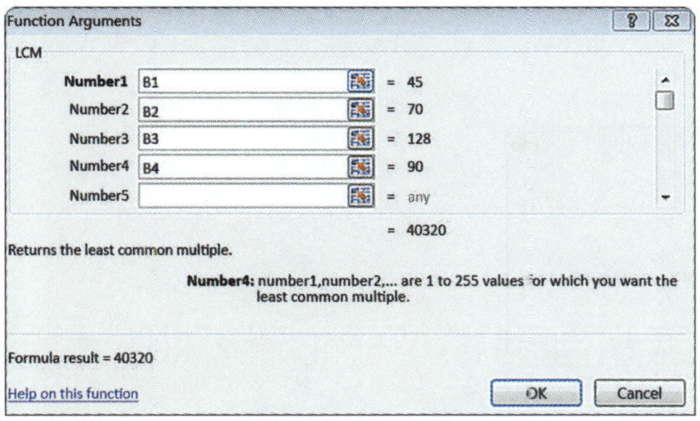

Fig. 1.27: Function Arguments dialog box

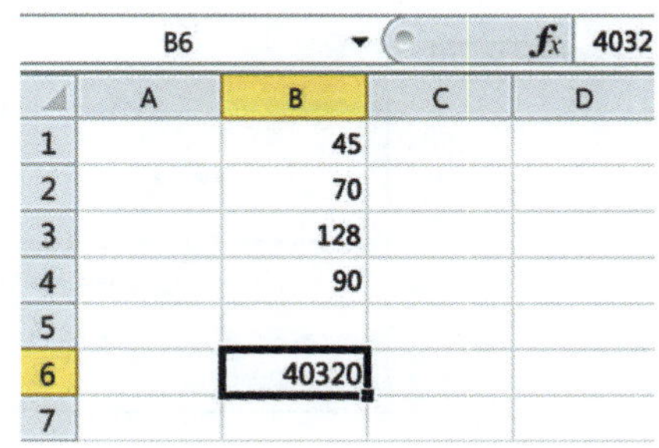

Fig. 1.28: LCM of the range of numbers

LEN

LEN is a text function which displays the number of characters in a cell. The steps are as follows:

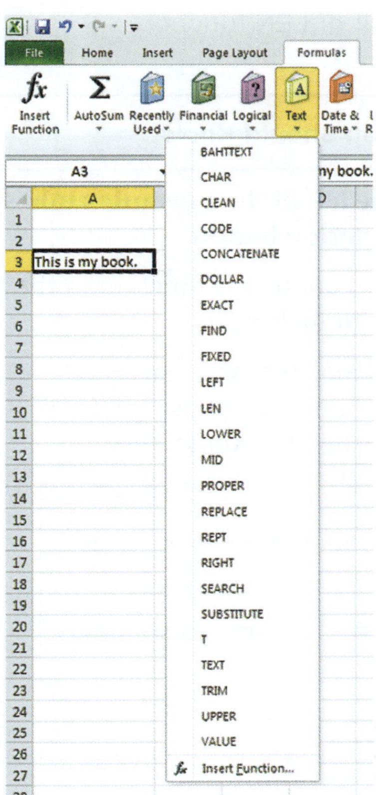

Fig. 1.29: Text drop-down list

1. Type the characters, say "This is my book." in cell A3. Increase the column width of column A to accommodate the entire string.
2. Click the cell where you want to display the string length, say B3. Click **Text** button in the **Function Library** group of buttons.

Fig. 1.30: Cell selection for result display

3. Select the **LEN** option from the drop-down list. In the **Function Arguments** dialog box, type A3. You will see the result in the dialog box.

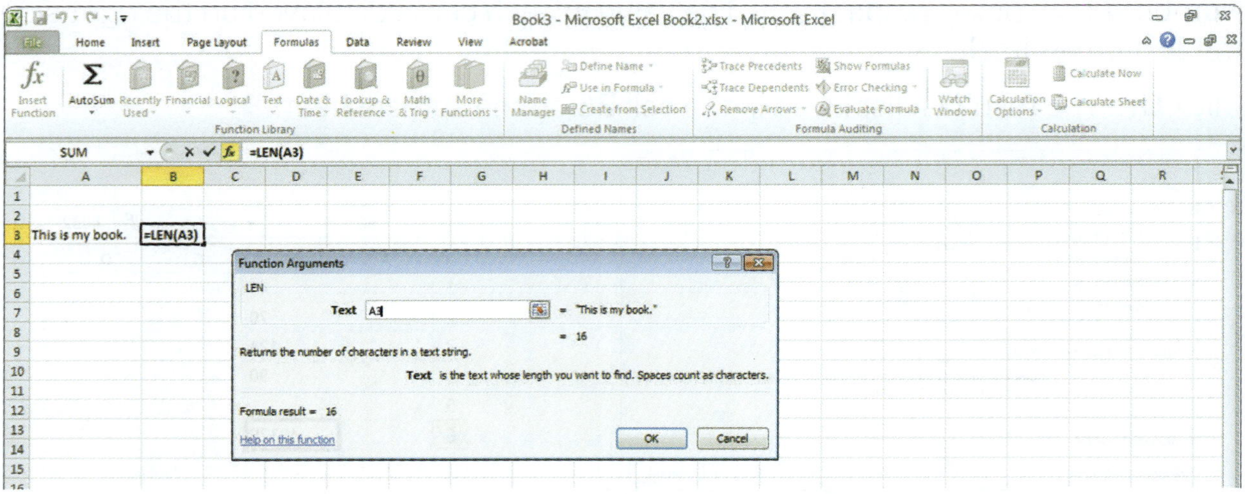

Fig. 1.31: Function Arguments dialog box

4. Click **OK**. The result is displayed in the cell B3 and the formula in the formula bar.

Fig. 1.32: Result of LEN function

Today

This is a **Date & Time** function that displays the current date. Click the cell where you want to display the current system date. From the **Date & Time** drop-down list, select **TODAY**.

The **Function Arguments** dialog box is displayed. Click **OK** and the current system date will be displayed.

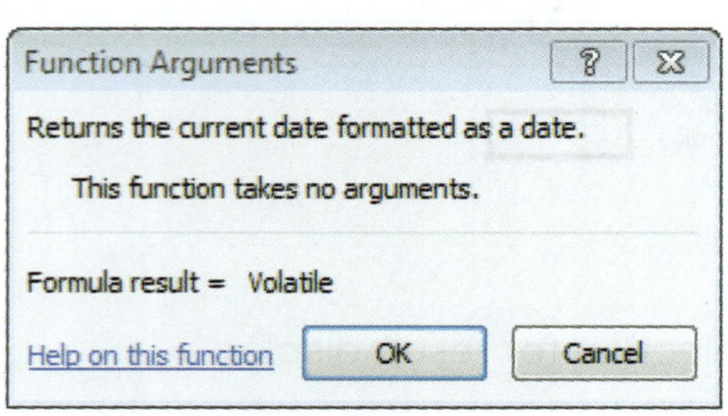

Fig. 1.33: Function Arguments dialog box

You Should Know

On the extreme left of the **Formulas tab** is the **Insert Function** button.

You can edit or choose any function in the **Insert Function** dialog box.

Through this dialog box, you can search for a particular function by giving a brief description of what you want to do.

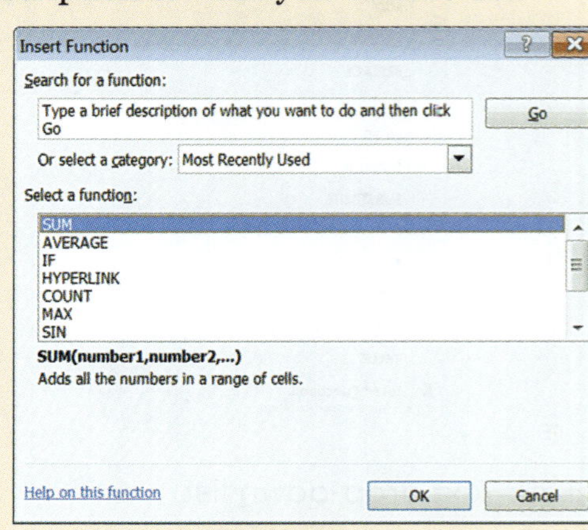

MS Office 2007 Recall

MS Excel 2007 did not have functions such as AGGREGATE, CEILING, PRECISE, etc.

Practice Time 1

The computer teacher has asked you to create a worksheet containing a list of teachers and their number of periods per week. Find out the average teaching periods and the maximum and minimum number of periods.

SOLUTION

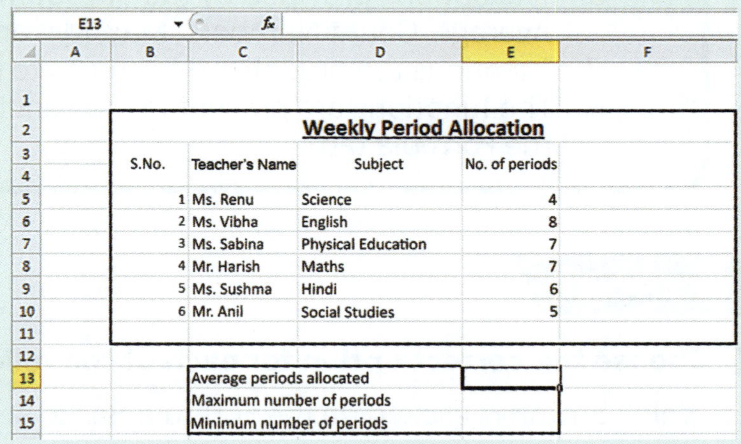

1. Type the data as shown in the worksheet.
2. Select cell E13. Click the arrow next to **AutoSum**.
3. From the drop-down menu, select Average.
4. The formula appears in the active cell. Check that the range in the formula is E5:E10. Press the Enter key. The average periods allocation appears in the active cell.
5. Select cell E14. Click the arrow next to **AutoSum** button and choose **Max** from the drop-down menu.
6. The formula appears in the active cell. Click cell E5. Drag the fill handle till E10. The range in the formula changes to E5:E10. Press the Enter key. The maximum number of periods appears in E14.
7. Select cell E15. Click the arrow next to **AutoSum** button and choose **Min** from the drop-down menu.
8. The formula appears in the active cell. Click cell E5. Drag the fill handle till E10. The range in the formula changes to E5:E10. Press the Enter key. The minimum number of periods appears in E15.

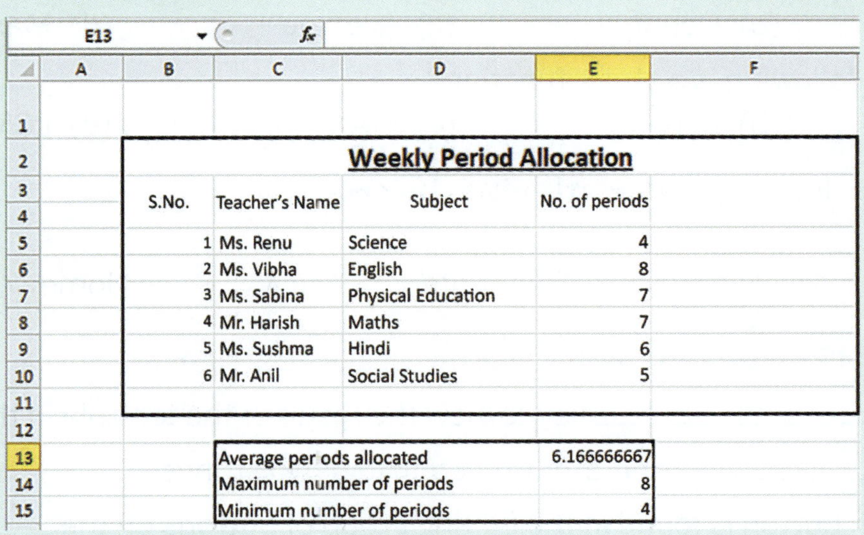

Quick Recap

1. Formula is a collection of cell references, constant values, operators and functions in a cell that results in a new value.
2. A formula in MS Excel always starts with an equal to (=) sign.
3. String is a set of characters on which you cannot do arithmetic operations such as subtraction, multiplication, etc.
4. Joining of strings is called concatenation. In Excel, concatenation is done by using '&' operator.
5. The AutoSum feature adds the numbers in the selected range of cells.
6. The options provided by the AutoSum drop-down menu are Sum, Average, Count Numbers, Max, Min and More Functions.
7. Functions are predefined formulas to perform certain operations.
8. The functions are present in the Function Library group of buttons on the Formula tab.

EXERCISE

A Choose the correct option for each of the following.

1. Which button is clicked on the Formula Bar to see the result of a formula?
   (a) ✓ (b) H (c) Both (a) and (b) (d) Neither (a) nor (b)
2. Which of the following can be performed on a string?
   (a) Addition (b) Concatenation (c) Subtraction (d) Division
3. What will be the result if you enter ="Best"&"Friend"?
   (a) Best Friend (b) BESTFRIEND (c) BestFriend (d) Bestfriend
4. Which of the following is not an option in the AutoSum drop-down menu?
   (a) Sum (b) Count (c) Average (d) Max
5. Which of the following is a string function?
   (a) TODAY (b) LEN (c) MAX (d) LCM

B Fill in the blanks using the words given below.

=	Functions	Enter	&	Home

1. A formula in MS Excel starts with ________________ sign.
2. Press the ________________ key to view the result of the formula in the active cell.
3. The ________________ operator is used to join two strings.
4. The AutoSum button is found in the Editing group of buttons on the __________ tab.
5. ________________ are predefined formulas in MS Excel.

C State whether the following statements are true (T) or false (F).

1. The data to be used within a formula should always be placed in a single cell. ☐
2. Providing cell ranges in the formula saves a lot of time. ☐
3. A formula can contain just one operator. ☐
4. You cannot join multiple strings. ☐
5. The evaluation of a formula is always from left to right. ☐

D Answer the following questions.

1. How can you enter formulas in MS Excel? Explain with an example.
2. 'Excel gives an advantage of auto editing the result.' Explain.
3. Define a string.
4. What will you infer if you see a couple of '#' in a cell?
5. Explain the AutoSum feature of MS Excel.

Lab Activity

FA

1. Nikhil's father is the president of Vidya Housing Society. He has to make a list of flat owners who have paid maintenance charges of the society.

   Also, he wants the count of the number of flat owners who have paid and the total collection made. Help him to complete the task using MS Excel.

	A	B	C	D
1				
2		**Vidya Housing Society**		
3				
4–5		**Flat No.**	**Owner**	**Maintenance Charges**
6		1	Mr. Manish	20000
7		2	Mr. Karan	Not Paid
8		3	Ms. Mallika	22000
9		4	Ms. Kiran	10000
10		5	Ms. Bharti	13000
11		6	Mr. Deepak	Not Paid
12				
13				
14		No. of flat owners who have paid		
15		Total Collection		
16				

2. The total salary of an employee in an organisation is the sum of basic, DA (40% of basic) and allowances (20% of basic). Make an Excel worksheet that displays the total salary of 10 employees. Thereafter, display the average salary of these 10 employees.

Research Project

FA

Try to understand the use of the various statistical and engineering functions available under the More Functions category in the Function Library of MS Excel 2010.
(Hint: Select More Functions from the AutoSum group and search for specific categories of functions to use.)

Teacher's Notes

(a) Discuss the benefits of using formulas and functions.
(b) Demonstrate with examples how formula errors can be rectified.

2 Organizing Data in MS Excel 2010

Learning Objectives

By the end of this chapter you should be able to
- understand sorting of data.
- learn filtering of data.
- understand conditional formatting.

Introduction

Data looks presentable when it is organized in a particular order. The process of arranging data in a particular order is called **sorting**. Data in MS Excel can be sorted in ascending or descending order.

MS Excel also gives you the option of viewing selective data. This feature is called **filtering of data**.

Both sorting and filtering of data helps in organizing it. You have learnt in earlier classes that data can be made presentable through the formatting features of MS Excel. **Formatting** is the process of making changes in a worksheet in order to enhance its appearance or lay focus on specific data in the worksheet. In this chapter, you will learn **conditional formatting** where cells are formatted according to some specific conditions.

TYPES OF CELL REFERENCING

You have studied that the address of a cell used in calculating formulas is called a **cell reference**. A formula can be copied from one part of the worksheet to another. It may even be copied from one worksheet to another. Based on how a cell reference in the formula is copied and used, there are three types of cell referencing techniques:

(a) **Relative Referencing**: This referencing is based on the relative position of the cell in which the formula is being written with respect to the cell address appearing in the formula. When we copy or move the formula to other cells, the reference automatically changes according to the relative position. For example in Fig. 2.1, the formula in the cell F6 is (=E6/50*100). If we copy the formula for the cells F7 to F17, the relative referencing would change the formula accordingly and replace the row 6 of Column E in the formula with corresponding row values of the column E.

(b) **Absolute Referencing**: This type of referencing is used when we do not want to change the address of the cell while copying the formula to another cell. To implement absolute referencing, make absolute reference of a formula, that is, add a dollar sign **($)** before the column and the row number. For example in Fig. 2.2, $E$4 can be used instead of the number 50 for calculating percentage in Column F. When a formula containing absolute reference of a cell is copied, the address of this cell will not change anywhere.

(c) **Mixed Referencing**: This type of cell referencing is the combination of absolute and relative referencing. While implementing mixed referencing, either the row or the column of the cell reference being used in the formula is fixed. The cell references such as $A5 or A$5 are examples of mixed referencing.

You Should Know

To refer to a cell in another worksheet, use the sheet number followed by an exclamation mark (!) and then the cell address. For example, if you want to refer to cell A1 in Sheet 2, the cell reference will be Sheet2!A1 or Sheet2!$A$1.

	A	B	C	D	E	F
1						
2			Class VII - Result			
3						
4			Maximum Marks :		50	
5		S. No	Name	Class	Marks	Percentage
6		8	Anirudh	VII C	49	=E6/50*100
7		3	Astha	VII A	48	
8		12	Dhruv	VII D	45.5	
9		6	Chandni	VII B	43.5	
10		5	Jia	VII B	42	
11		9	Tejasvi	VII C	42	
12		10	Soumya	VII D	42	
13		11	Allen	VII D	41	
14		4	Tanvi	VII B	39.5	
15		2	Aarav	VII A	36	
16		1	Pooja	VII A	35	
17		7	Supriya	VII C	30	

Fig. 2.1: Relative Referencing

F6 f_x =E6/$E$4*100

	A	B	C	D	E	F
1						
2			Class VII - Result			
3						
4			Maximum Marks :		50	
5		S. No	Name	Class	Marks	Percentage
6		8	Anirudh	VII C	49	98
7		3	Astha	VII A	48	96
8		12	Dhruv	VII D	45.5	91
9		6	Chandni	VII B	43.5	87
10		5	Jia	VII B	42	84
11		9	Tejasvi	VII C	42	84
12		10	Soumya	VII D	42	84
13		11	Allen	VII D	41	82
14		4	Tanvi	VII B	39.5	79
15		2	Aarav	VII A	36	72
16		1	Pooja	VII A	35	70
17		7	Supriya	VII C	30	60

Fig. 2.2: Absolute Referencing

SORTING DATA

Sorting of data is done to arrange data in ascending or descending order. The data in the cells being sorted may be numeric or textual or both. There are three buttons to sort data in the **Sort & Filter** group of buttons on the **Data** tab.

(a) **Sort** : This displays a Sort dialog box to sort data based on various criteria at one go.

(b) **Sort Smallest to Largest**: Sorts the data in ascending order.

(c) **Sort Largest to Smallest**: Sorts the data in descending order.

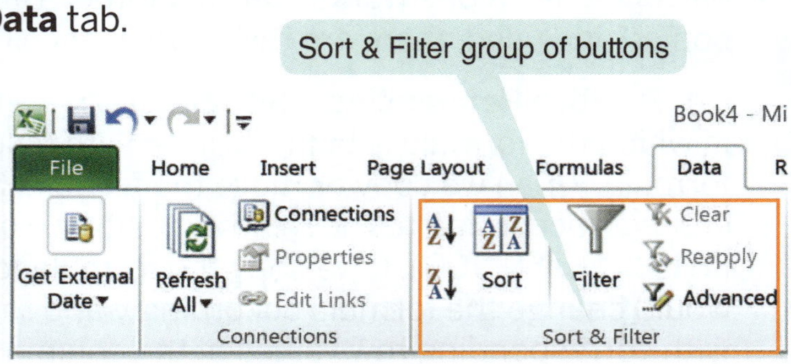

Fig. 2.3: Sort & Filter group of buttons

Sorting can be done in any of the following ways—single-column sorting and multiple-column sorting.

Single-column Sorting

In this type of sorting, the data is sorted according to the values in one column only. Consider the table given below containing average temperature and average rainfall of India in each month. In this example, we will be sorting the data in ascending order of temperature. To do so, follow the steps given below:

1. Select the cell in the column according to which you want to sort the data. Since data is to be sorted according to average temperature, so select any cell in column C, say C7.
2. Click **Select Smallest to Largest** button to sort data in ascending order of temperature. You will see that the entire data is arranged according to the data values in a single column (C) containing average temperature.

	A	B	C	D
1				
2		Average Temperature and Rainfall In India		
3				
4		Month	Average Temperature (°F)	Average Rainfall (in mm)
5				
6		January	65	0.7
7		February	68.4	0.8
8		March	75.1	1.1
9		April	81.3	2.1
10		May	84.7	3.9
11		June	83.8	9.8
12		July	80.9	13.9
13		August	80.1	11.5
14		September	79.7	7.8
15		October	77.2	4.1
16		November	71.3	2
17		December	66.2	1

Fig. 2.4: Unsorted Data

	A	B	C	D
1				
2		Average Temperature and Rainfall In India		
3				
4		Month	Average Temperature (°F)	Average Rainfall (in mm)
5				
6		January	65	0.7
7		December	66.2	1
8		February	68.4	0.8
9		November	71.3	2
10		March	75.1	1.1
11		October	77.2	4.1
12		September	79.7	7.8
13		August	80.1	11.5
14		July	80.9	13.9
15		April	81.3	2.1
16		June	83.8	9.8
17		May	84.7	3.9

Fig. 2.5: Data sorted in ascending order of temperature

Multiple-column Sorting

In this type of sorting technique, the data is sorted according to values in multiple columns. For example, in Fig 2.6, the data has to be sorted in ascending order of month and in descending order of average temperature.

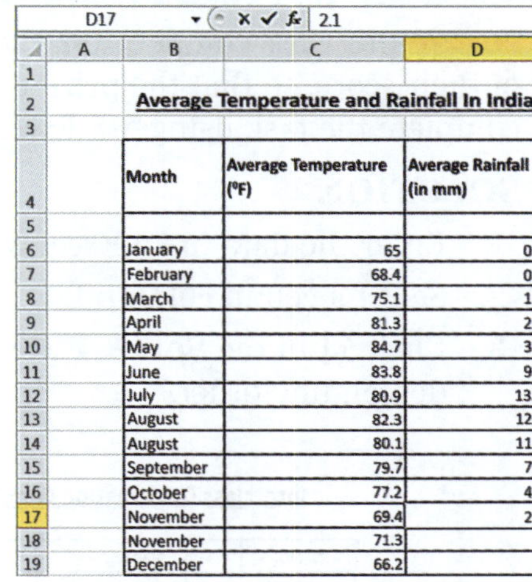

D17 | 2.1

	Month	Average Temperature (°F)	Average Rainfall (in mm)
2	Average Temperature and Rainfall In India		
6	January	65	0.7
7	February	68.4	0.8
8	March	75.1	1.1
9	April	81.3	2.1
10	May	84.7	3.9
11	June	83.8	9.8
12	July	80.9	13.9
13	August	82.3	12.6
14	August	80.1	11.5
15	September	79.7	7.8
16	October	77.2	4.1
17	November	69.4	2.1
18	November	71.3	2
19	December	66.2	1

Fig. 2.6: Unsorted data

To understand the concept of multiple-column sorting, first add two rows in the table containing data for any two months, say August and November.

The steps to sort data according to values in multiple columns are as follows:

1. Select the range of cells that need to be sorted. Alternatively, you can also select any cell in the range. For example, select B4:D19.
2. Click **Sort** button in the **Sort & Filter** group of buttons on the **Data** tab. The **Sort** dialog box appears.

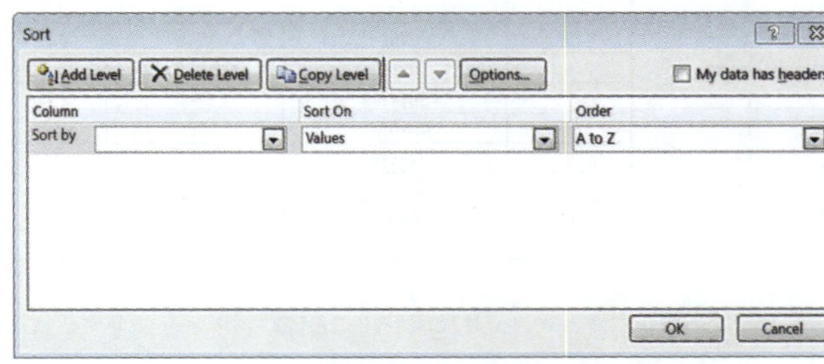

Fig. 2.7: Sort dialog box

3. On the top right corner of the dialog box there is an option—**My data has headers**. This option should be checked if your selected range consists of column headings in the top row of the selected range. Since our range consists of column headings, so check the option.
4. Under **Column** section, you have **Sort by** list box. Choose the column by which you want to sort data. You will have all the column headings in the list box to choose from. Select Month from the available list of options.

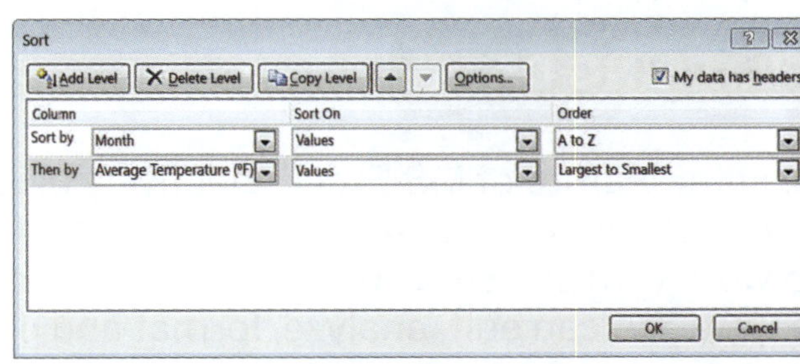

Fig. 2.8: Adding another column in Sort dialog box

5. Under **Order**, A to Z is already selected. If you have to sort in descending order, then choose Z to A.
6. Click **Add Level** button on the top left corner of the dialog box. A new row appears as shown in Fig. 2.8. Select Average Temperature for **Then by** list box in **Column** section. Under **Order**, select **Largest to Smallest**.
7. Click **OK**. The data is arranged in ascending order of month (alphabetically) and in descending order of average temperature as shown in Fig. 2.9.

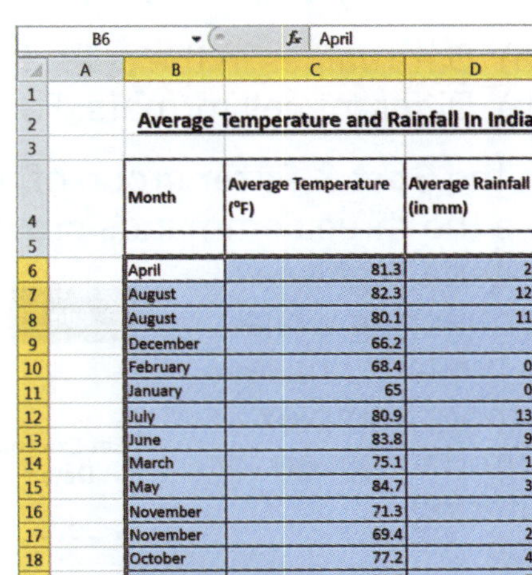

B6 | April

	Month	Average Temperature (°F)	Average Rainfall (in mm)
2	Average Temperature and Rainfall In India		
6	April	81.3	2.1
7	August	82.3	12.6
8	August	80.1	11.5
9	December	66.2	1
10	February	68.4	0.8
11	January	65	0.7
12	July	80.9	13.9
13	June	83.8	9.8
14	March	75.1	1.1
15	May	84.7	3.9
16	November	71.3	2
17	November	69.4	2.1
18	October	77.2	4.1
19	September	79.7	7.8

Fig. 2.9: Sorted data

Practice Time 1

For an interclass competition, the teacher wants the list of participants to be arranged in order of their score, so that the prize winners can be identified easily. The teacher has asked Geetika to complete the task using MS Excel. Help Geetika complete the task.

SOLUTION

1. Enter the data in an Excel worksheet.
2. Select a cell in column E.
3. Click ZA↓ in the **Sort & Filter** group under the **Data** tab. The data will be sorted in descending order.

Interclass Declamation Competition

S. No.	Name	Class	Score
1	Pooja	VII A	35
2	Aarav	VII A	36
3	Astha	VII A	48
4	Tanvi	VII B	39.5
5	Jia	VII B	42
6	Chandni	VII B	43.5
7	Supriya	VII C	30
8	Anirudh	VII C	49
9	Tejasvi	VII C	42
10	Soumya	VII D	42
11	Allen	VII D	41
12	Dhruv	VII D	45.5

Original data

Interclass Declamation Competition

S. No.	Name	Class	Score	
8	Anirudh	VII C	49	FIRST
3	Astha	VII A	48	SECOND
12	Dhruv	VII D	45.5	THIRD
6	Chandni	VII B	43.5	
5	Jia	VII B	42	
9	Tejasvi	VII C	42	
10	Soumya	VII D	42	
11	Allen	VII D	41	
4	Tanvi	VII B	39.5	
2	Aarav	VII A	36	
1	Pooja	VII A	36	
7	Supriya	VII C	30	

Sorted data

FILTERING DATA

The Filter feature of MS Excel selectively blocks or hides data. Only that part of data is displayed which meets the criteria specified for a column. This feature helps to retrieve and work with selected subset of data as the unwanted data is temporarily hidden from the view. You can edit, analyze, format and even print the filtered data. Remember filtering does not rearrange data as is done while sorting. The filtering of data can be done on the basis of any or both of the following:

(a) Data values in the cells: For example, cells with values greater than 50 to be filtered.
(b) Different cell formats: For example, red-coloured cells to be filtered.

In the **Sort & Filter** group of buttons, **AutoFilter**, **Advanced Filter** and **Custom Filtering** are the three commands provided by Excel for filtering ranges. In the former, a simple criteria is given for filtering while in the latter case, a more complex criteria is given for filtering.

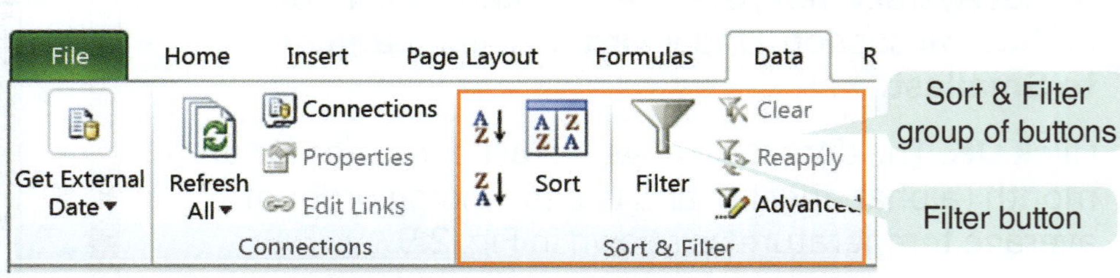

Fig. 2.10: Filter commands in Sort & Filter group of buttons

AutoFilter Command

You can filter a column or row to view the data that meets a specific criteria by using **AutoFilter** command. The steps to use it are as follows:

1. Form a table as shown containing marks of students in FA1, FA2, SA1 and SA2.
2. Select any cell in the range A3:F9, say C5.

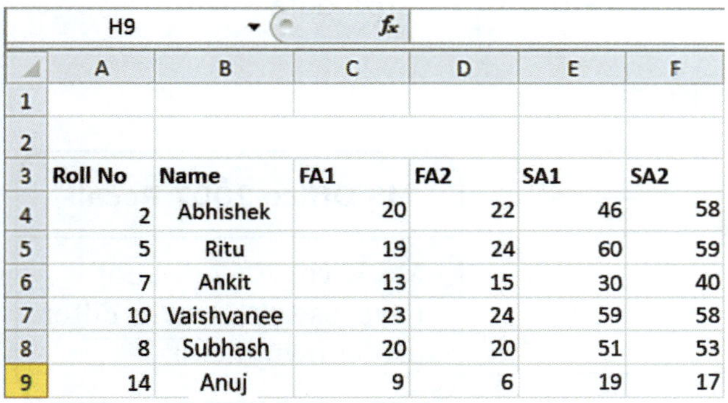

Fig. 2.11: Unfiltered data

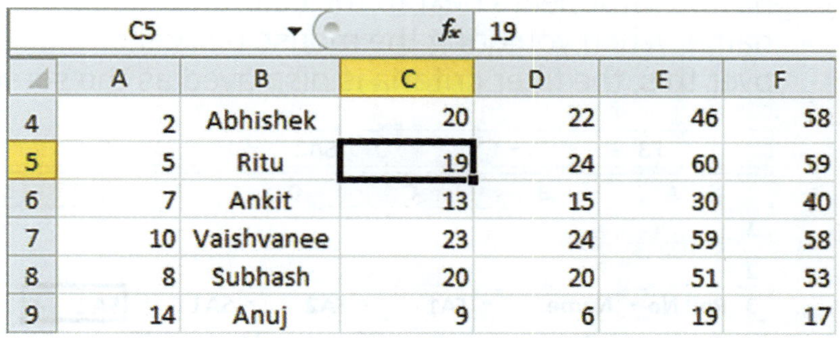

Fig. 2.12: Selecting a cell to apply filter criteria

3. Under the **Data** tab, click the **Filter** button in the **Sort & Filter** group of buttons. Small arrows will be seen next to each column heading with the filter icon. This indicates that the filtering has been turned on. Once filtering is turned on, click the arrow in the column header to choose the filter for the column, say SA2. A drop-down menu is displayed.
4. You will see that **Select All** option is checked. Deselect **Select All** and select 58 and 59 from the drop-down menu to retain only the numbers which are more than 55. You can even type the value in the **Search pane** given in the drop-down menu.

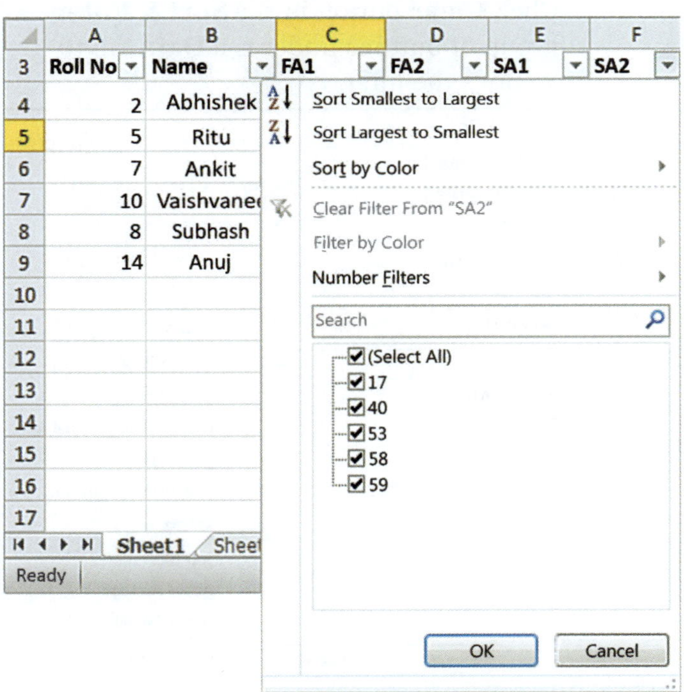

Fig. 2.13: Filter drop-down menu

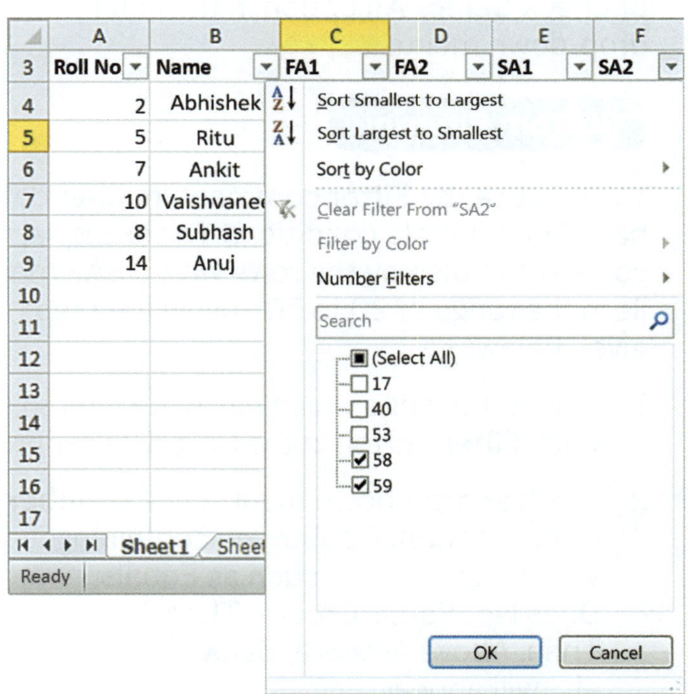

Fig. 2.14: Deselect Select All

5. Click **OK**. The rows with more than 55 marks in SA2 will be filtered from the original table and displayed.

When filtering is enabled but not applied, a drop-down menu arrow appears next to the column name. When a filter is applied on a particular column, a filter button appears next to the column name. When you bring the mouse pointer over this, the filter criteria is displayed as the screen tip.

A	B	C	D	E	F
Roll No	**Name**	**FA1**	**FA2**	**SA1**	**SA2**
2	Abhishek	20	22	46	58
5	Ritu	19	24	60	59
10	Vaishvanee	23	24	59	58

Fig. 2.15: Filtered data

F3 | f_x | SA2

	A	B	C	D	E	F	G	H
1								
2								
3	**Roll No**	**Name**	**FA1**	**FA2**	**SA1**	**SA2**		
4	2	Abhishek	20	22	46	SA2: Equals "58" or Equals "59"		
5	5	Ritu	19	24	60			
7	10	Vaishvanee	23	24	59	58		

Fig. 2.16: Filter criteria

MS Office 2007 Recall

MS Excel 2007 did not have a search bar in Filter drop-down menu.

If you edit the data within the selected range, click **Reapply** button in the **Sort & Filter** group. The filter criteria is reapplied to the new data.

Quick Way

Shortcut key to filter data is **Ctrl+Shift+L**.

To remove the filter, click the arrow next to the column heading where filter was placed (SA2 in our case) and select **Clear Filter** from SA2 or check **Select All** option in the Filter drop-down menu.

Quick Way

Click **Clear** button in the **Sort & Filter** group of buttons under the **Data** tab to remove the filter.

Custom Filtering

You can use the **Filter** command to filter data based on multiple conditions. For example, if you want to display the rows where SA2 marks lie in the range of 20 to 50, follow the steps given below:

1. Select the range which has to be filtered. Click **Filter** button in the **Sort & Filter** group.
2. In **Filter** drop-down menu, click **Number Filters** option. A submenu containing various operations such as Equals, Does Not Equal, Greater Than, Less Than, Above Average, Below Average, etc. will appear.

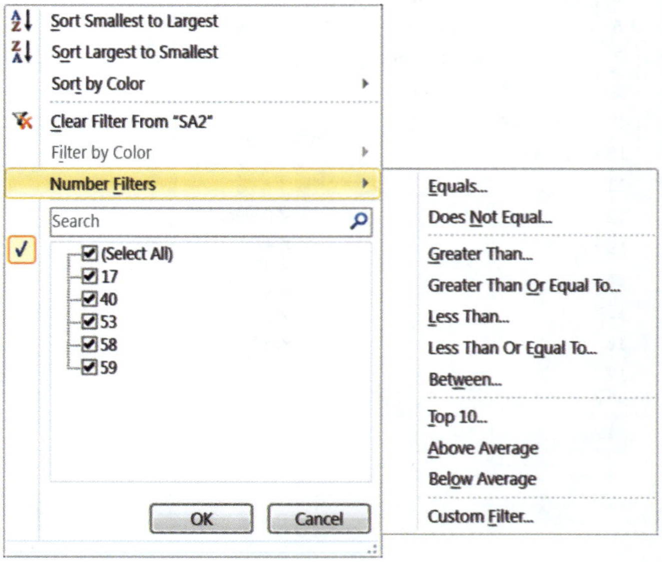

Fig. 2.17: Number Filters

3. Choose the desired filter, say **Between**. The **Custom AutoFilter** dialog box is displayed. Fill in less than 50 and greater than 20.
4. Click **OK**. The rows that have SA2 marks between 20 and 50 will be displayed.

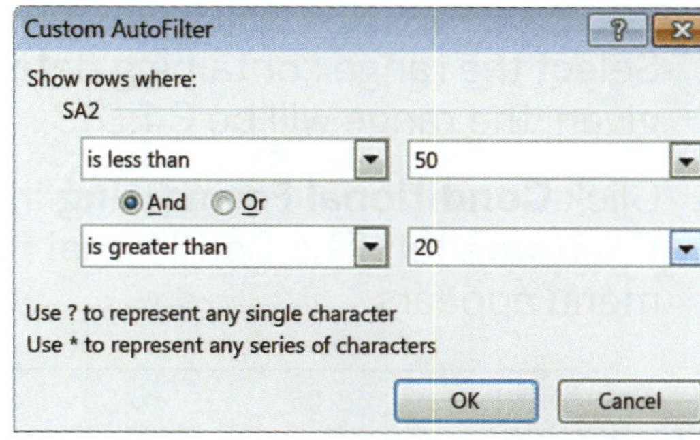

Fig. 2.18: Custom AutoFilter dialog box

You can even filter the top scorers or low scorers in SA2. Select **Top 10** option from the **Number Filters** submenu. In the **Top 10 AutoFilter** dialog box, you can customize the number of rows that you want to view by selecting Top/ Bottom option.

You can also select **Above Average** or **Below Average** from the submenu to display rows with total marks above or below the average.

	A	B	C	D	E	F
1						
2						
3	Roll No	Name	FA1	FA2	SA1	SA2
6	7	Ankit	13	15	30	40

Fig. 2.19: Custom AutoFilter dialog box

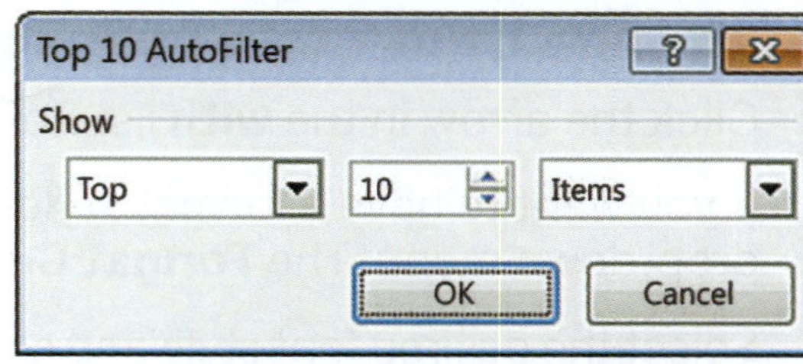

Fig. 2.20: Top 10 AutoFilter dialog box

CONDITIONAL FORMATTING

Conditional formatting in MS Excel highlights important information in a spreadsheet. It allows you to set the cell's format according to the given conditions so that you can easily identify the variations in the data. You can highlight selected cells or emphasize certain rows using this feature. The **Conditional formatting** command is in the **Styles** group of buttons under the **Home** tab.

	A	B	C	D
1	Class Test - Social Science			
2				
3	Roll No	Name	History	Geography
4	1	Geeta	45	43
5	2	Ratan	34	39
6	3	Siddarth	49	26
7	4	Aparna	45	17
8	5	Vishnu	12	8
9	6	Amrit	38	45
10	7	Aditi	19	28
11	8	Karishma	40	45
12	9	Sudershan	42	41
13	10	Ritwik	33	36

Fig. 2.21: Selecting the range

You can display data in a particular colour or style depending on a particular condition. For example, if you want to display the data of the students who have secured more than 50% marks in green colour, conditional formatting helps you to do so. You can highlight selected cells, rows or columns based on specific condition(s). Consider the table shown in Fig. 2.21 in which we want the marks which are less than 20, to be displayed in orange colour.

1. Select the range containing data. In the example given, the range will be C4:D13.
2. Click **Conditional Formatting** in the **Styles** group of the **Home** tab. The Conditional Formatting drop-down menu appears.

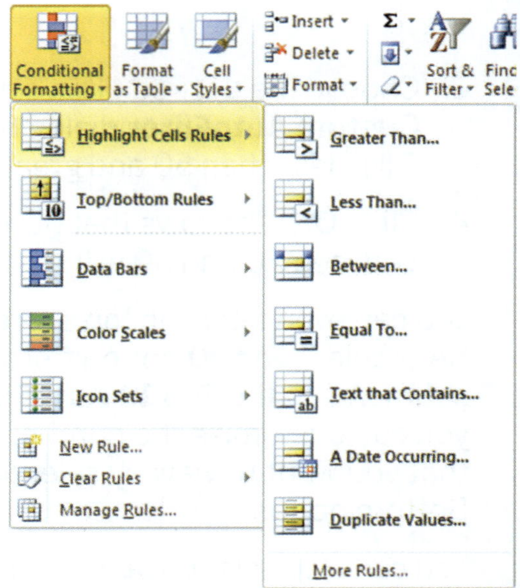

Fig. 2.22: Conditional Formatting

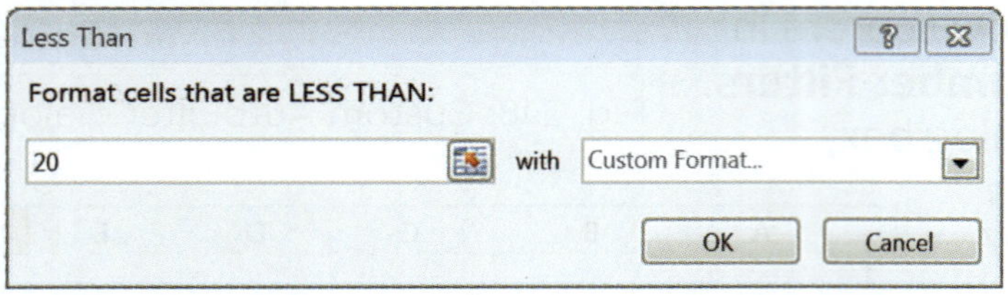

Fig. 2.23: Setting criteria in Conditional Formatting

3. Select **Highlight Cells Rules** and choose **Less Than** from the submenu.
4. The **Less Than** dialog box appears. Type 20 in the text box labelled **Format cells that are LESS THAN**.
5. Click the arrow in the **with** list box. Select the desired format option.
6. If you want to have a format style of your own, click **Custom Format** option from the drop-down menu. The **Format Cells** dialog box is displayed.
7. Select the desired font style and colour. Click **OK**. The **Less Than** dialog box appears again.
8. Click **OK**. You will see that all cell values with marks less than 20 are displayed in orange colour.

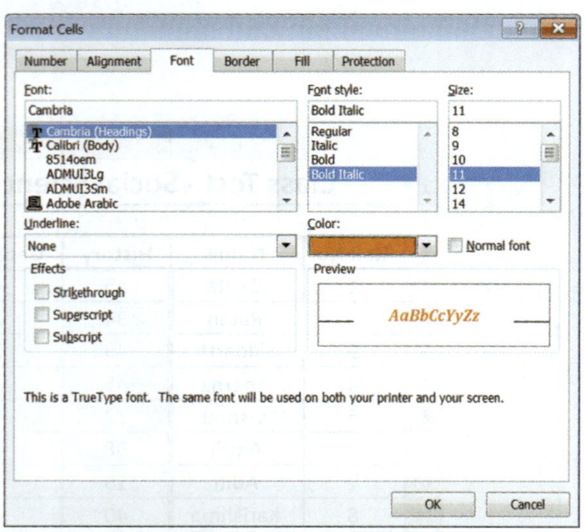

Fig. 2.24: Format Cells dialog box

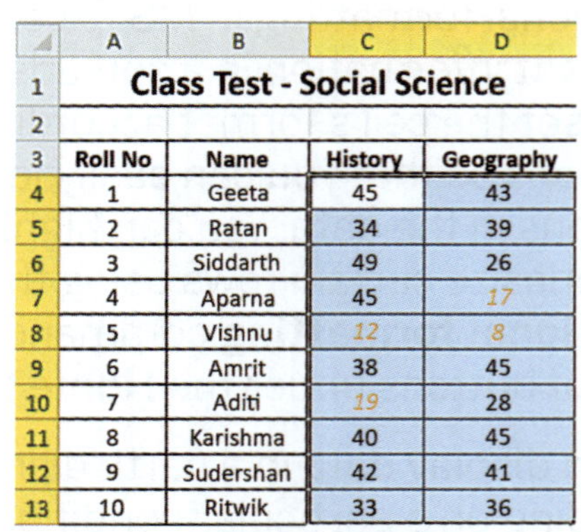

	A	B	C	D
1	Class Test - Social Science			
2				
3	Roll No	Name	History	Geography
4	1	Geeta	45	43
5	2	Ratan	34	39
6	3	Siddarth	49	26
7	4	Aparna	45	17
8	5	Vishnu	12	8
9	6	Amrit	38	45
10	7	Aditi	19	28
11	8	Karishma	40	45
12	9	Sudershan	42	41
13	10	Ritwik	33	36

Fig. 2.25: Result of the criteria using Conditional Formatting

To clear Conditional Formatting, click the arrow next to the **Clear Rules** option in the **Conditional Formatting** drop-down menu. Choose any of the two options—**Clear Rules from Selected Cells** or **Clear Rules from Entire Sheet**.

If you want to apply conditional formatting to selected rows, then follow the steps given below:

1. Select the entire table.
2. In the **Conditional Formatting** drop-down menu, click **New Rule**. The **New Formatting Rule** dialog box appears.
3. In the **Select a Rule Type** section, click **Use a formula to determine which cells to format**. You also have options to format rows having values above or below average or a particular value or having unique or duplicate values.

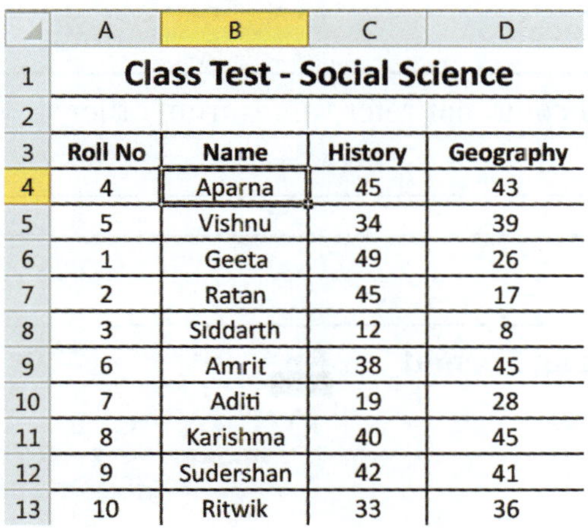

	A	B	C	D
1	Class Test - Social Science			
2				
3	Roll No	Name	History	Geography
4	4	Aparna	45	43
5	5	Vishnu	34	39
6	1	Geeta	49	26
7	2	Ratan	45	17
8	3	Siddarth	12	8
9	6	Amrit	38	45
10	7	Aditi	19	28
11	8	Karishma	40	45
12	9	Sudershan	42	41
13	10	Ritwik	33	36

Fig. 2.26: Conditional Formatting for selected rows

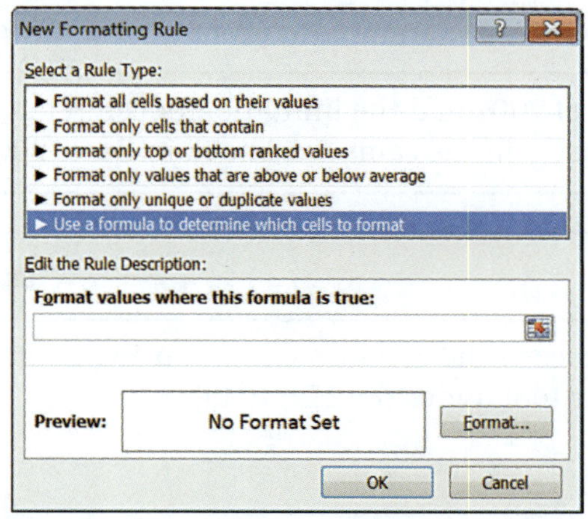

Fig. 2.27: Setting rules for selected rows

4. In the **New Formatting Rule** dialog box, type = and then click any cell in the Geography column.
5. Delete the dollar sign before the row number and type <20 so that the final expression becomes =$D4<20.
6. Click **Format**. The **Format Cells** dialog box appears.
7. Click the **Fill** tab and choose orange as the background colour. Click **OK**.
8. Click **OK** in the **New Formatting Rule** dialog box. The rows with less than 20 marks in Geography will be filled with orange colour.

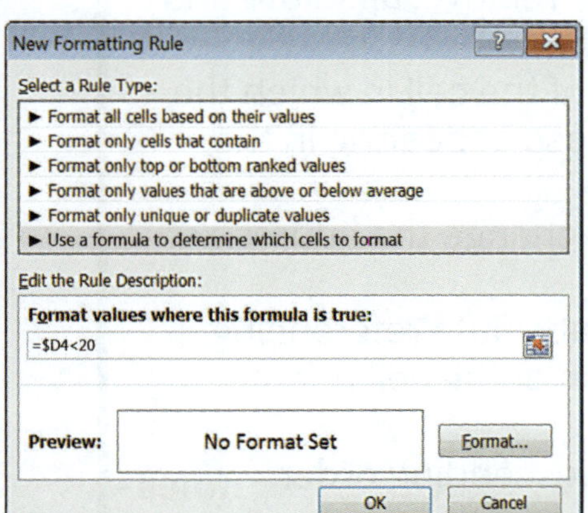

Fig. 2.28: Setting new formatting rules

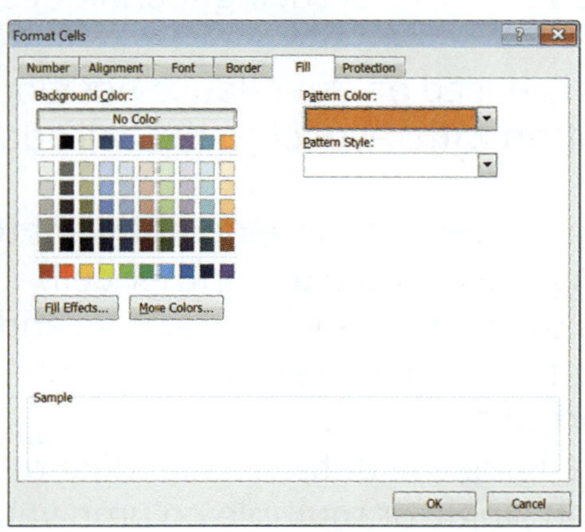

Fig. 2.29: Setting Fill criteria

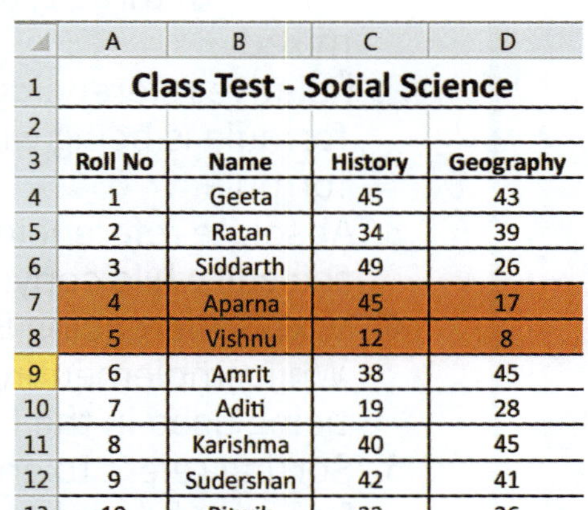

	A	B	C	D
1	Class Test - Social Science			
2				
3	Roll No	Name	History	Geography
4	1	Geeta	45	43
5	2	Ratan	34	39
6	3	Siddarth	49	26
7	4	Aparna	45	17
8	5	Vishnu	12	8
9	6	Amrit	38	45
10	7	Aditi	19	28
11	8	Karishma	40	45
12	9	Sudershan	42	41
13	10	Ritwik	33	36

Fig. 2.30: Final Result of Conditional Formatting for selected rows

You Should Know

MS Excel allows you to sort and filter data by cell colour also. For sorting, select **Cell Color** under **Sort On** in the **Sort** dialog box.

For filtering by cell colour, select **Filter By Color** in the **Filter** drop-down menu. Thereafter, specify the colour and the data will be sorted/filtered.

MS Office 2007 Recall

MS Excel 2007 had the limitation of cell referencing. You could not refer values from other worksheets in the same workbook in Excel 2007.

Quick Way

You can copy the conditional formatting to other cells using **Format Painter** tool under the **Home** tab.

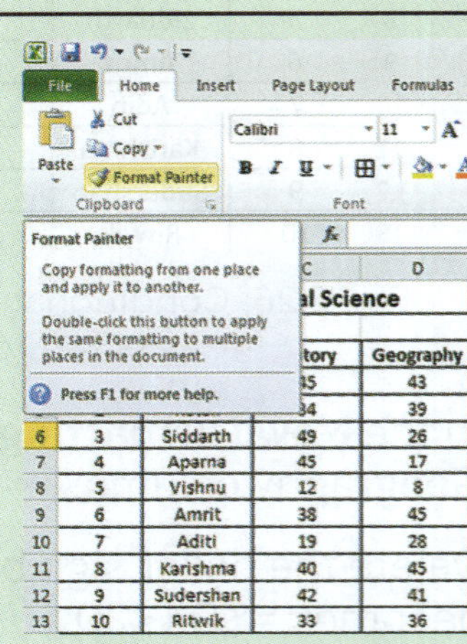

Quick Recap

1. The address of a cell used in calculating the formula is called a cell reference. There are three types of cell referencing techniques – relative, absolute and mixed.
2. Relative referencing is based on the relative position of the cell in which the formula is being written with respect to the cell address appearing in the formula.
3. Absolute referencing is used when we do not want to change the address of the cell while copying the formula to another cell.
4. Mixed referencing is the combination of relative and absolute referencing. While implementing this, either the row or the column of the cell reference being used in the formula is fixed.
5. Sorting refers to arranging the data in ascending or descending order.
6. Data can be sorted on single or multiple column values.
7. Filtering displays selective data that meets the criteria specified for a column.
8. Conditional Formatting sets the cell's format according to the given conditions.

EXERCISE

A Choose the correct option for each of the following.

1. In ______________ referencing, the cell reference in a formula changes.

   (a) Mixed (b) Absolute (c) Formula (d) Relative

2. = $A$1 * B14 is an example of which type of referencing?

   (a) Relative (b) Absolute (c) Mixed (d) None of these

3. Sorting can be based on cell values of

   (a) Single column only
   (b) Multiple columns only
   (c) Both single and multiple columns
   (d) None of these

4. Which of the following is the button to sort data in descending order?

   (a)  – Sorting Data
   (b)  – Sorting Data
   (c)  – Sorting Data
   (d) None of these

5. In the Sort dialog box, ______________ option is selected if the selected range consists of column headings in the top row of the selected range.

   (a) My headers
   (b) My Data
   (c) My data has headers
   (d) My headers have data

B Fill in the blanks using the words given below.

Sorting Mixed Conditional Formatting Sort & Filter Sorting Filtering

1. The process of arranging data in a particular order is called ______________.
2. ______________ and ______________ of data helps to organize data.
3. When data is formatted according to the specific conditions, it is called ______________.
4. ______________ referencing is the combination of absolute and relative referencing.
5. The buttons to sort data are in ______________ group of buttons on Data tab.

C State whether the following statements are true (T) or false (F).

1. Data can only be sorted from smallest to largest value. ☐
2. A formula cannot be copied from one cell to another. ☐
3. H$3 is an example of mixed referencing. ☐
4. Data is not rearranged while filtering. ☐
5. You cannot copy filtered records. ☐

D Answer the following questions.

1. Name different types of cell referencing techniques.

2. How can data be sorted on multiple columns?
3. On what basis can filtering of data be done?
4. How do we get to know when filtering is turned on?
5. Define conditional formatting. How can it be copied from one cell to another?

FA

Lab Activity

1. Your father has asked you to make a list of any eight families in the neighbourhood and create the following Excel sheet containing their details:

RSG Residential Society

S No.	Name	Female Members	Male Members	Income	Occupation
1	Gaba	3	4	95000	Business
2	Sachdeva	3	3	109000	Service
3	Pandit	2	5	98000	Mixed
4	Khan	4	2	145000	Farming
5	Batra	5	1	99000	Mixed
6	Zarin	3	2	134000	Service
7	Anand	1	1	155000	Farming
8	Sharma	2	3	140000	Service

   After creating the table, you have been asked to perform the following tasks:
   a. Display the details of families in alphabetical order of their names.
   b. Display the details of families in descending order of income.
   c. Display the data in descending order of male members.
   d. Display the income that is more than 50000 in yellow colour.
   e. Highlight the rows of Business families with green colour.
   f. Display the rows where the income is more than average income.

2. Sushma is working in a Health Care Clinic. She has been asked to create an Excel worksheet containing details of the patients visiting the hospital. Help her to perform the following tasks:

Health Care Clinic

No.	Name	Age	Department	OPD_Date	Charges	Sex
1	Navin	44	Neuro	13-05-2014	500	M
2	Rakesh	55	Orthopaedic	20-10-2014	1000	M
3	Nimmi	4	Eye	10-07-2014	550	F
4	Jeet	19	Surgery	21-01-2014	200	M
5	June	61	ENT	17-02-2014	650	F
6	Penny	14	ENT	27-07-2014	550	F
7	Kunal	36	Cardiology	20-11-2014	500	M
8	Phoola	66	Gardiology	22-05-2014	300	F
9	Shipra	19	Cardiology	14-03-2014	900	F
10	Anuj	21	Paediatrics	19-10-2014	1400	M

   a. Display the data in descending order of age.
   b. Highlight the data of the patients visiting the ENT department in green colour.
   c. Display the charges which are less than 300 in blue colour.
   d. Display the patients paying the maximum consultation charges in yellow colour.

FA

Research Project

Explore the option of 'Format only top or bottom ranked values' that appears in New Formatting Rule while setting the rules for selected rows in Conditional Formatting.

Teacher's Notes

(a) Discuss why data should be organized.
(b) Discuss why and in which situations should the data be sorted and/or filtered.
(c) Discuss how conditional formatting helps to deliver a better worksheet.

3 Charts in MS Excel 2010

Learning Objectives

By the end of this chapter you should be able to

- know various types of charts.
- understand the components of a chart.
- know how to create a chart.
- know how to format a chart using chart tools.
- know Sparklines.

Introduction

A chart is an effective way to represent data in pictorial form. A good graph or chart displays information quickly and easily to the user. MS Excel provides various types of charts. The data from the table is taken as input for making the chart. As the data in the table changes, the chart also changes automatically. It is easier to analyse and compare data using charts. They can show relationships that are not easily understood by studying a list of numbers. Charts can also provide a convenient way to compare different sets of data.

TYPES OF CHARTS

Excel provides different types of charts. To understand them, consider the table shown in Fig. 3.1 that shows different hobbies of people in two residential societies.

Hobbies

	Reading	Travelling	Sports	Painting	Dancing
Society A	25	32	23	11	9
Society B	30	27	19	11	13

Fig. 3.1: Data table

Bar Chart

It displays data in the form of long, rectangular rods called bars of different heights, displayed either vertically or horizontally. So, comparisons between various data items can be done easily. In a bar chart, the categories are organized vertically and the values horizontally. The data displayed on the bar chart may include various types of information such as sales of a particular item over a period of time or comparing salaries of private and public school teachers and so on. The information displayed through the bar chart helps us to analyse data and reach to conclusions quickly and easily. The bar chart here compares the hobbies of people in Society A (in blue) and Society B (in red).

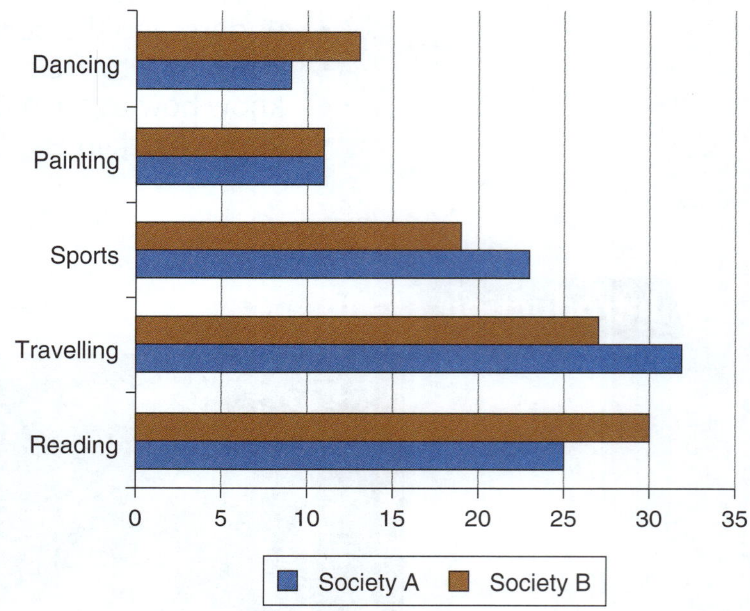

Fig. 3.2: Bar chart

Line Chart

It is the most basic type of chart and is used to depict information that is related in some manner. It is created by connecting a series of data points together with a line. These are often used to plot changes in data over a period of time such as change in fuel prices over a period of year, production or sales trends over a period of time, monthly temperature changes, effects of scientific experiments, etc. Usually, in a line chart, category is plotted along the horizontal or X-axis and data is plotted as individual points along the vertical or Y-axis. Line chart is preferred when there are many data points or when data trends are important. Figure 3.3 shows a line chart for the table given above.

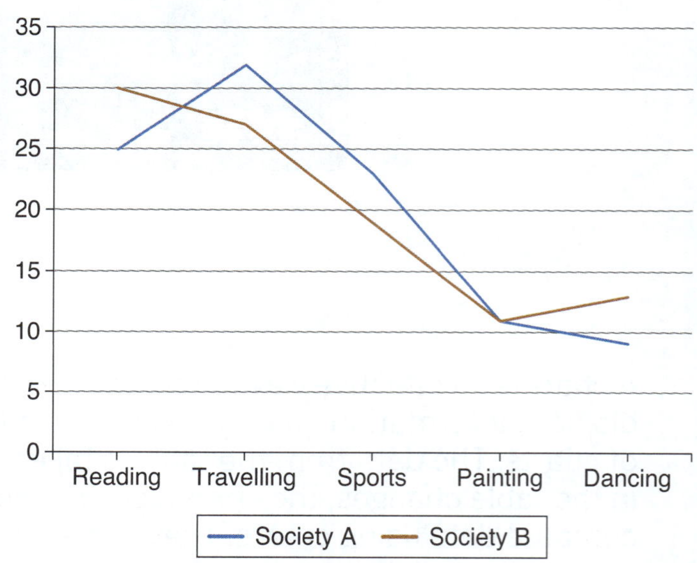

Fig. 3.3: Line chart

Column Chart

This is one of the most commonly used charts in which the data is represented in the form of vertical bars. It is similar to a bar chart but in this type of chart, the bars are placed vertically. The lengths of the rectangular bars are proportionate to the magnitude of data.

Generally, the categories are organized along the horizontal axis and the values along the vertical axis. Each data point in a series is represented by a column that rises from the X-axis. The column chart is used to show changes in data over a period of time or to illustrate comparisons between different data items. A column chart is preferred when height of individual points is more important than the trend in series.

The various subtypes of column chart available in Excel 2010 are—cylinder, cone and pyramid.

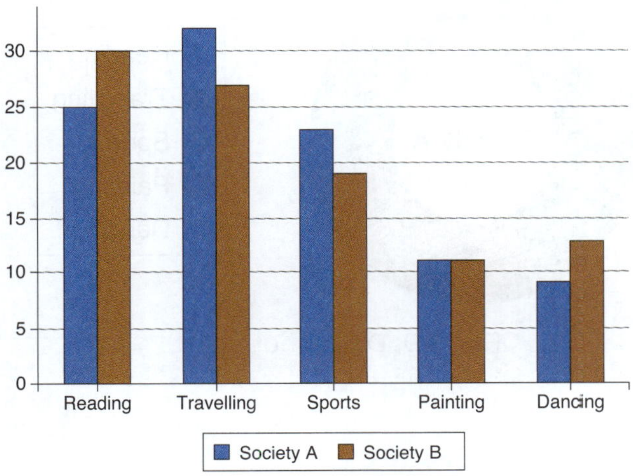

Fig. 3.4: Column chart

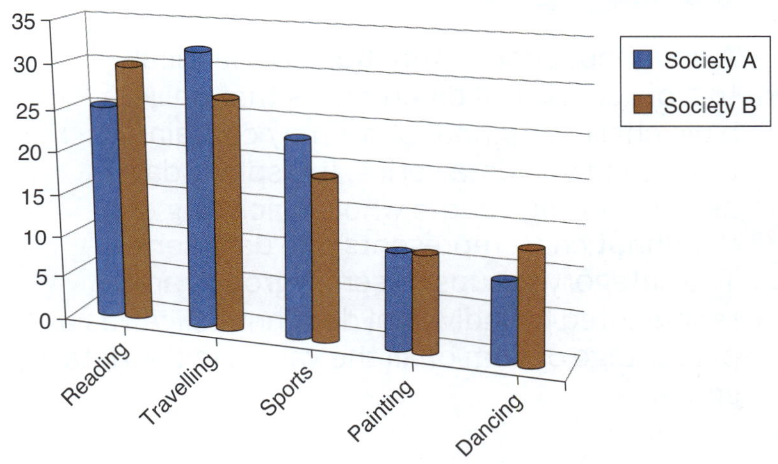

Fig. 3.5: Cylinder subtype of column chart

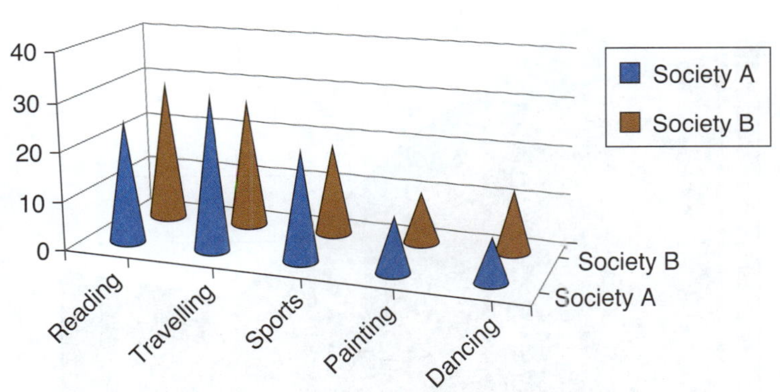

Fig. 3.6: Cone subtype of column chart

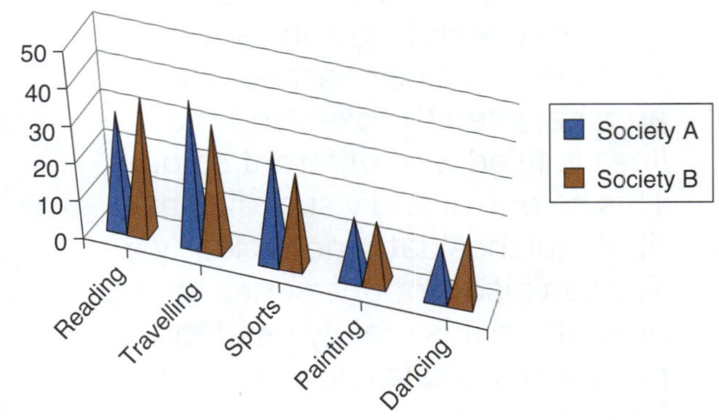

Fig. 3.7: Pyramid subtype of column chart

Pie Chart

The data in this type of chart is displayed in the form of a circle which is divided into sectors. Each data value represents one sector and the size of each sector is proportional to the value it represents. Hence, all the sectors summed up together make the full circle. In a pie chart, data is plotted for a single-data series. The pie charts are used in business world and mass media.

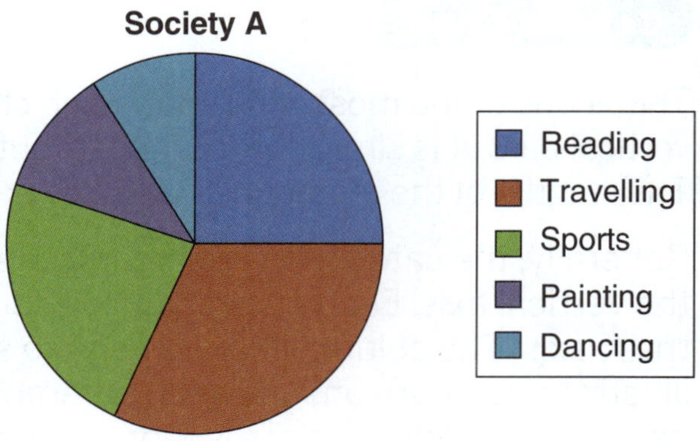

Fig. 3.8: Pie chart

Doughnut Chart

A doughnut chart is functionally identical to a pie chart. The difference is that unlike a pie chart, doughnut chart may contain more than one data series. It displays data as a percentage of the whole. Each ring of a doughnut chart represents one data series. The category groups or series groups are represented by individual doughnut slices as a percentage of sum of all the values in the data series.

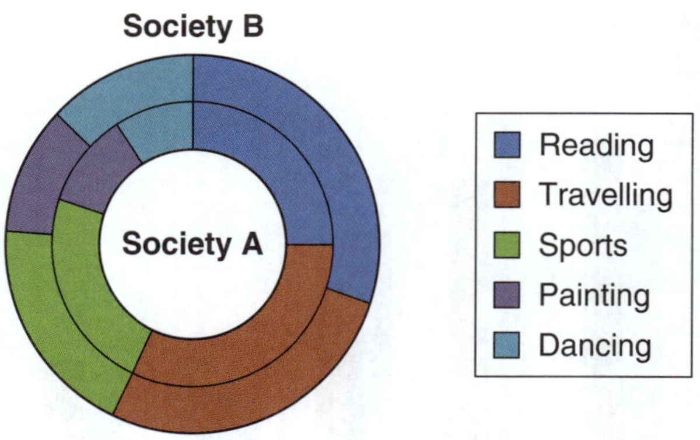

Fig. 3.9: Doughnut chart

Area Chart

An area chart is used to display quantitative data graphically. It is based on a line chart but the area between the axes and the lines is filled with different colours. This colourful and visual display distinguishes data more clearly. You can also plot one series on top of another. It is mainly used for representing sales and production figures.

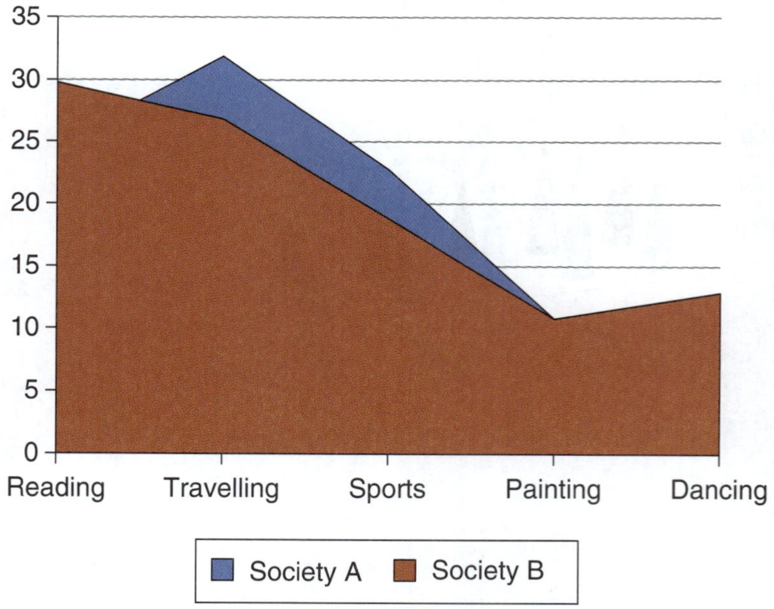

Fig. 3.10: Area chart

3D Surface Chart

It creates a three-dimensional view of data. It shows a three-dimensional surface that connects a set of data points. Unlike other charts, colours in surface chart are used to distinguish values and not each data series. A topographic map is an example of a 3D surface chart in which the same colour represents the same range of values.

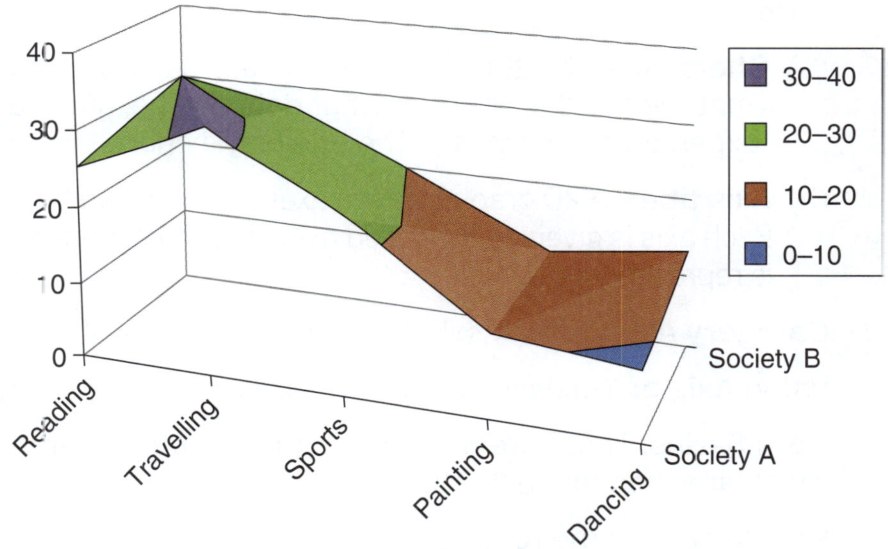

Fig. 3.11: 3D Surface Chart

COMPONENTS OF A CHART

The various components of a chart are shown in Fig. 3.12. When you move the mouse pointer over a chart object, a screen tip giving the component name is displayed.

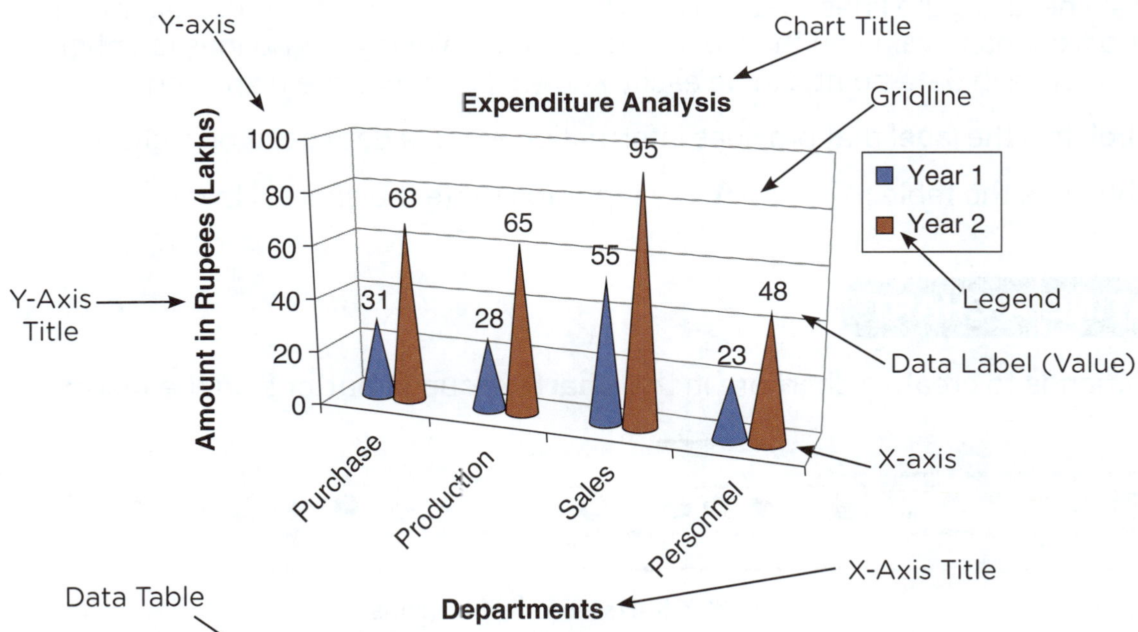

	Purchase	Production	Sales	Personnel
Year 1	31	28	55	23
Year 2	68	65	95	48

Fig. 3.12: Components of chart

Chart Area: It refers to the area in which all the components or objects of the chart are placed.

Titles

(a) **Chart Title**: It is the topic of the chart, usually given at the top, and it lets us know what the chart is about or what data can be inferred from the chart. In Fig. 3.12, 'Expenditure Analysis' is the title of the chart.

(b) **Axis titles**: A 2D graph has two axes (X and Y) while a 3D chart has three axes (X, Y and Z). Each axis is given a title, called axis title, which depicts what data series the respective axis is representing.

Category Axis or X-axis: It is the horizontal axis of the chart.

Value Axis or Y-axis: It is the vertical axis used to plot the value of each data point.

Data Series: These are the bars, sectors or other elements that represent data values which are used to create the chart.

Plot Area: It is the rectangular area or a window within the chart area bound by two axes for a 2D chart. 3D charts, on the other hand, have a base area constituted by the XY plane. This is known as the floor. The vertical areas, that is, the YZ and XZ planes are known as the walls. The two walls and the floor constitute the plot area in a 3D chart. It contains the actual chart and includes the plotted data, data series and value axis.

Legend: It identifies the data series being represented by the chart. A unique colour, pattern or symbol is assigned to each data series so that it can be easily distinguished.

Gridlines: These are the lines that run across the plot area from each category on the X-axis and from each value on the Y-axis. Although displaying of gridlines is optional, the exact value of each data point can be easily known if gridlines are displayed.

Data Label: It is the label that provides information about a data point on a chart.

Data Table: It is the table from where the input to create the chart is taken.

CREATING A CHART

The commands to create a chart are in the **Charts** group of buttons on the **Insert** tab.

Fig. 3.13: **Charts** group of buttons

To create a chart in MS Excel 2010, follow the steps given below:

1. Enter the data in a worksheet. Refer to the table shown in Fig. 3.14 that shows the salary and donations of five employees of an organization. The range of the data is A1:C7.
2. Select the data range (A1:C7) and click on the **Insert** tab.
3. From the **Charts** group of buttons, choose any chart type, say **Bar Chart**.

	A	B	C	D
1	Name	Salary	Donation	
2				
3	Arvind	14000	200	
4	Sumita	25000	380	
5	Pushp	17000	400	
6	Vandana	29000	550	
7	Abhishek	33000	500	
8				

Fig. 3.14: Data in Excel

4. Click the arrow below the **Bar Chart** button and choose the desired subtype from the submenu. The chosen chart subtype will be displayed in the centre of the worksheet. You can move it to any other location on the worksheet by clicking and dragging its white background. The size of the chart can be changed by dragging its corners.

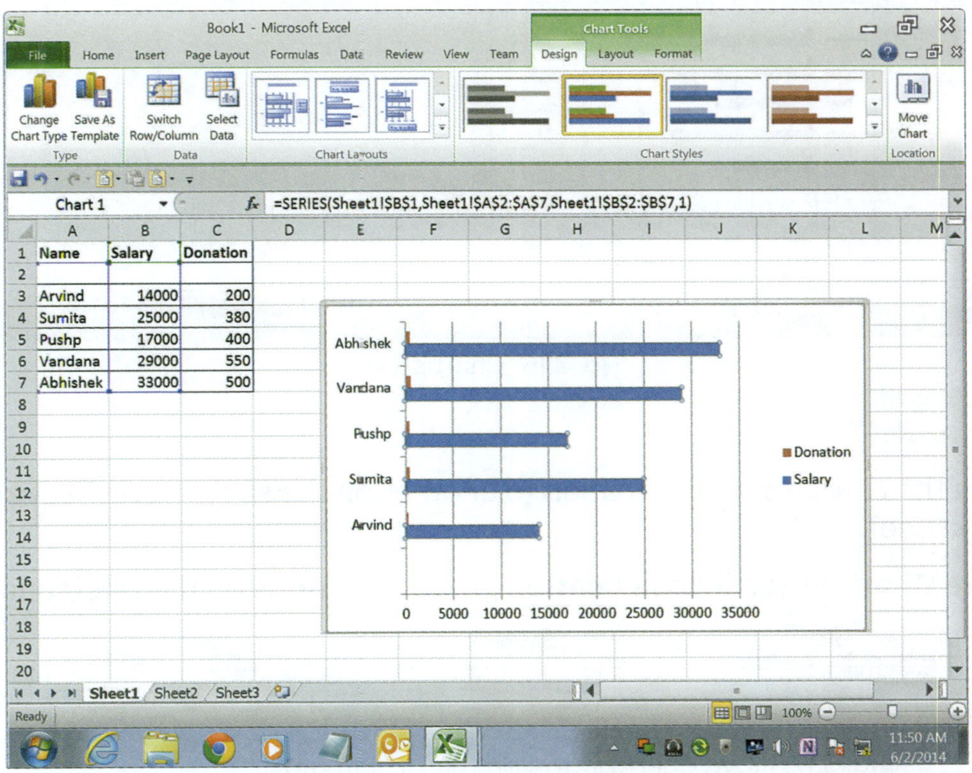

Fig. 3.15: Bar chart inserted on a worksheet

Chart Tools

MS Excel allows you to format the chart by changing its layout, design, style, location, etc. in order to improve the appearance of the chart. As the chart is inserted in the worksheet, three new chart tools tabs appear on the ribbon. These are **Design**, **Layout** and **Format**.

> **Quick Way**
>
> Select the data range that you want to represent on a chart and press **F11** function key to create the chart instantly.

Applying Chart Styles

The **Design** tab on the ribbon provides various chart style options in the **Styles** group of buttons. Click the arrow in the **Styles** group of buttons. All chart styles will be displayed as shown in Fig. 3.16. Click on any of the styles to give your chart the desired look.

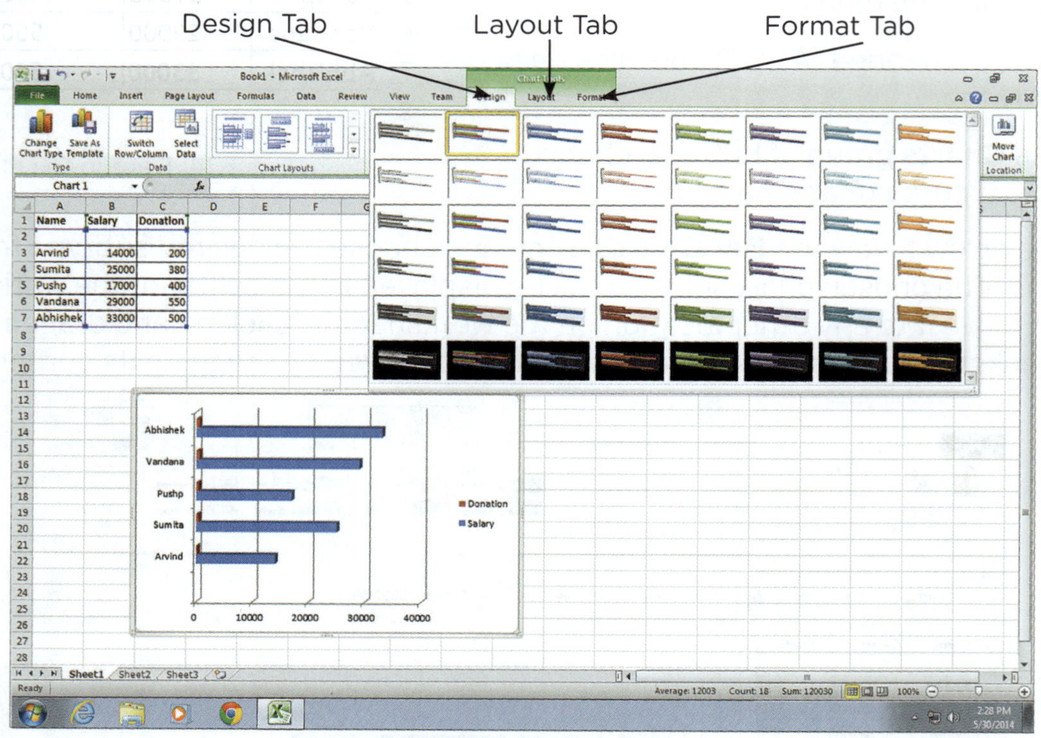

Fig. 3.16: Chart styles

Moving the Chart

You can move the chart from one location to another on the same worksheet or on a different worksheet.

1. Click **Move Chart** button in the **Location** group of buttons on the **Design** tab.

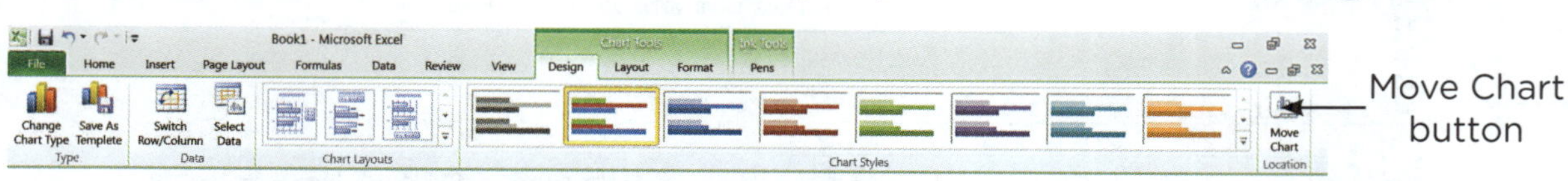

Fig. 3.17: Move Chart button on the Design tab

2. The **Move Chart** dialog box appears.

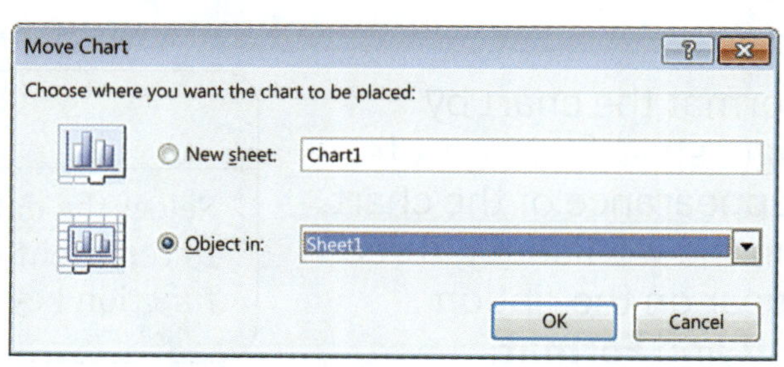

Fig. 3.18: Move Chart dialog box

3. The **Object in** radio button is already selected and you can choose any of the existing worksheets for the destination location of your chart. If you want to move the chart to a new worksheet, click **New sheet** radio button and type the name of the new worksheet, say Chart1.
4. Click **OK**. A new worksheet named Chart1, containing the chart is created. The chart inserted is also automatically scaled to fill the entire page in landscape orientation.

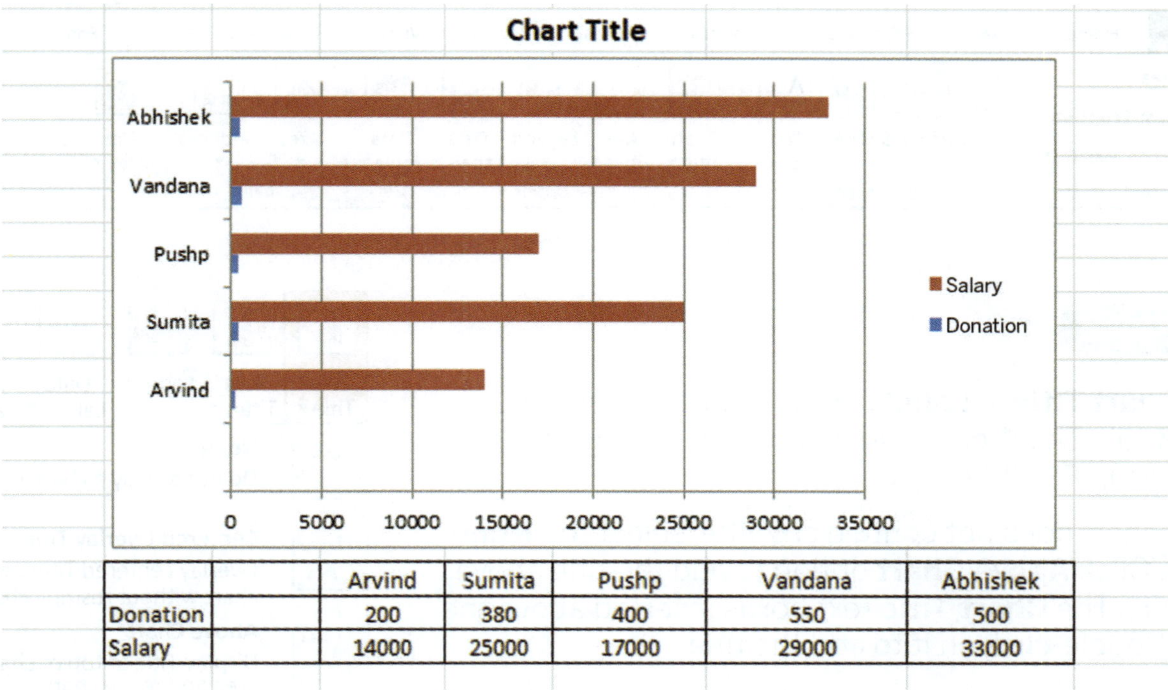

Fig. 3.19: Chart inserted in a new worksheet

5. You can double-click on the **Chart Title** in the new sheet to give a title to your bar chart.
6. In the **Layout** group of buttons on the **Design** tab, you can choose a desired layout of your bar chart. For example, you might want to have gridlines or display the data values or move the legends to the bottom and so on. You also get more layout options on the **Layout** tab which is covered in the next section.

You Should Know

You can swap the data over the axis using **Switch Row/Column** button in the **Data** group of buttons on the **Design** tab. By clicking this button, data being charted on the X-axis will move to Y-axis and vice versa.

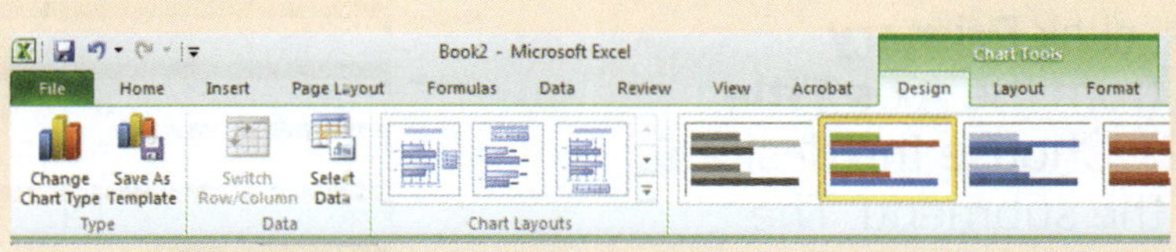

Changing the Layout

The **Layout** tab allows you to edit, that is, add or change the components of the chart. You can change the titles, legends, data labels, background and other properties of the chart.

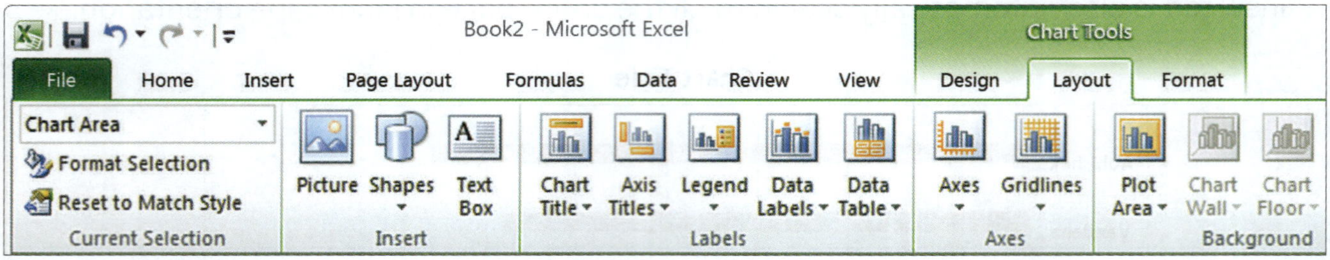

Fig. 3.20: **Layout** Tab

Chart Title

Click **Chart Title** in **Labels** group of buttons on the **Layout** tab. The drop-down menu gives you the options as shown in Fig. 3.21.

If your chart does not contain any title, select the **None** option. Click **Above Chart** option to add the title above the chart. The **Chart Title** text box is inserted above the chart. Double-click on it to add the title.

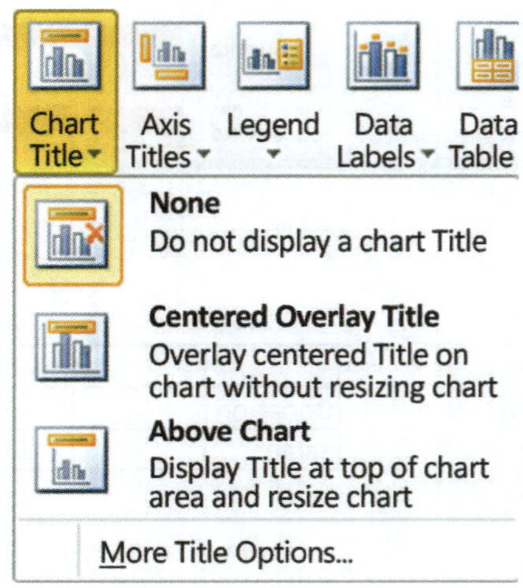

Fig. 3.21: Chart Title options

Axis Titles

This command allows you to add/edit titles along the X-axis and Y-axis.

To add an X-axis title, click **Axis Titles**. Click **Primary Horizontal Axis Title** and from the submenu, choose the option **Title Below Axis**. The X-axis title text box appears below the axis. Double-click on it and type the new title.

To add a Y-axis title, click **Primary Vertical Axis Title** from the **Axis Title** submenu (Fig. 3.22). Choose the desired layout of title from the submenu. The Y-axis title text box is inserted. Double-click to type the new title.

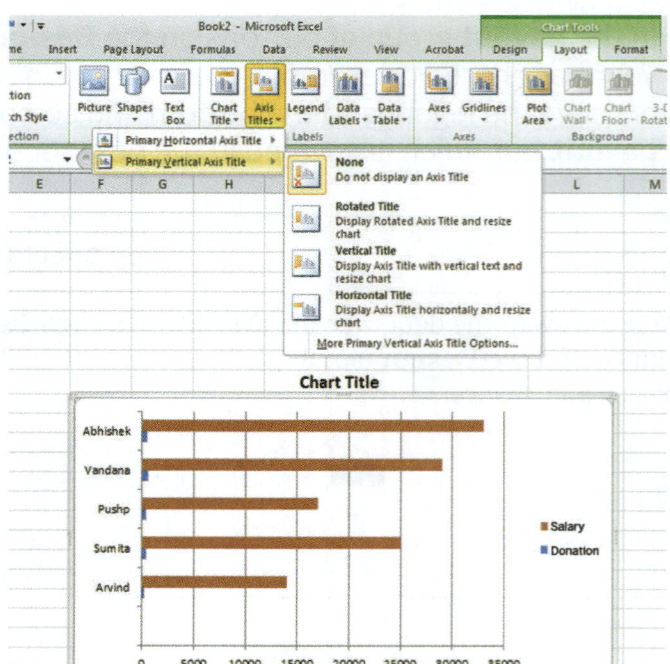

Fig. 3.22: Axis submenu

Legend

Click on **Legend** button and a drop-down menu containing various options for inserting the legends with respect to the chart is displayed.

The legends can be inserted on the top, bottom, left or right of the chart.

Choose the desired option and the legends will be displayed accordingly. If you do not want to display any legend, click **None** from the drop-down menu.

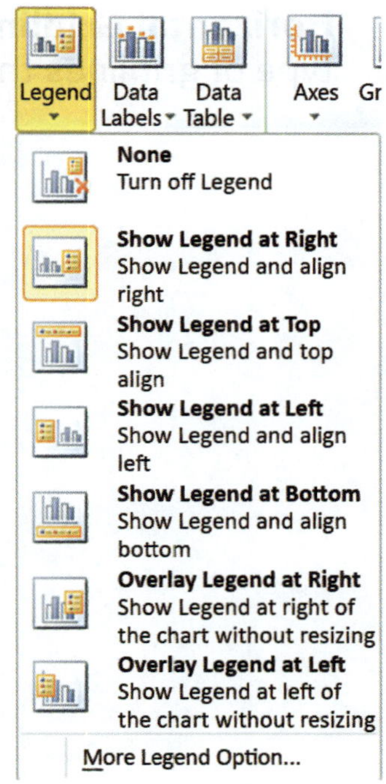

Fig. 3.23: Legend options

Data Labels

If you want to display the value of each data point or column on the chart, click **Data Labels** button.

Choose the location where you want to place the labels.

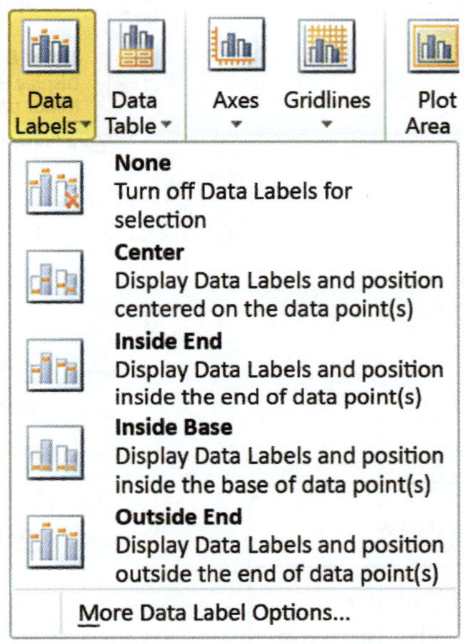

Fig. 3.24: Data Labels menu

Data Table

This command adds the table on which the chart is based below the chart. Click **Data Table** button and then select **Show Data Table** option from the drop-down menu.

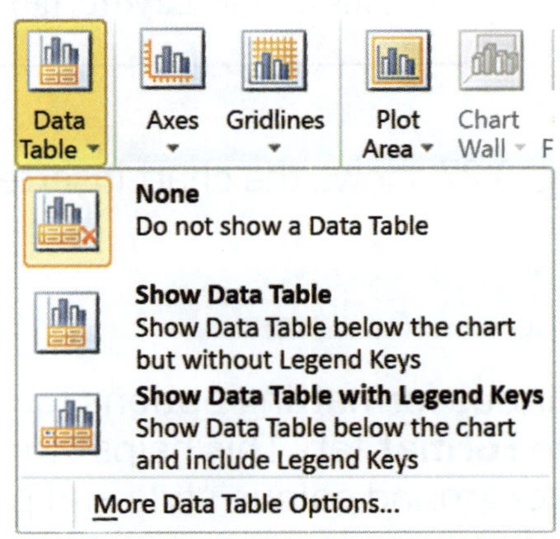

Fig. 3.25: Data Table submenu

Gridlines

This command in the **Axes** group of buttons turns gridlines on or off. Gridlines are of two types—major gridlines and minor gridlines. Major gridlines are darker gridlines and placed at a distance while minor gridlines are lighter and are closer. You can choose the gridlines that you would like to display for different axes by using the **Primary**

Horizontal Gridlines or **Primary Vertical Gridlines** option. Thereafter, choose the type of gridlines that you want to insert from the submenu.

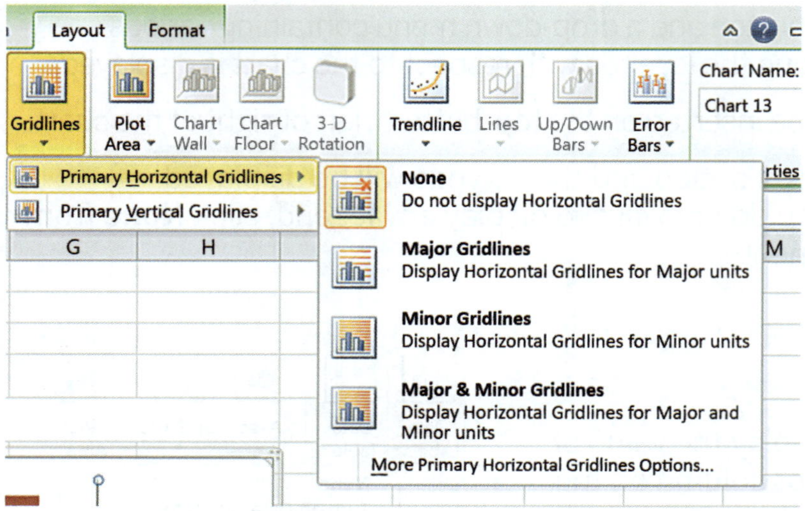

Fig. 3.26: Gridlines menu

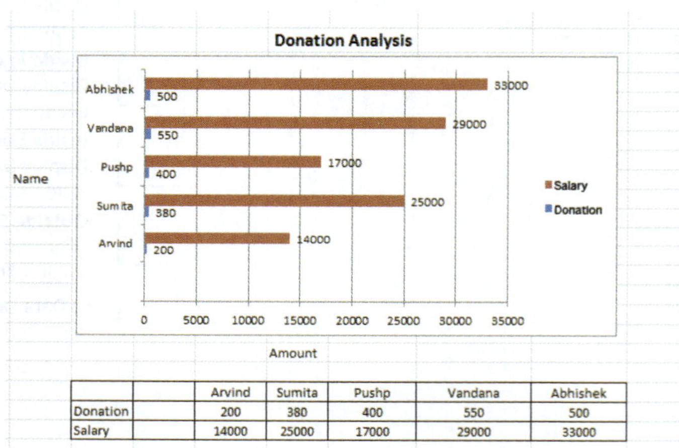

Fig. 3.27: Chart with all the components

> **You Should Know**
>
> You can even insert pictures and text to a chart. The buttons to insert pictures, shapes and text are in the **Insert** group of buttons on the **Layout** tab.

Fig. 3.27 shows the chart inserted on the new sheet with all the components discussed above.

Chart Formatting

Various formatting options for formatting text and numbers in a chart are available on the **Format** tab. This helps to improve the appearance of the chart. You can change the background colour, style and pattern, format the titles and legends, edit the border style and colour, etc. using the commands on the **Format** tab.

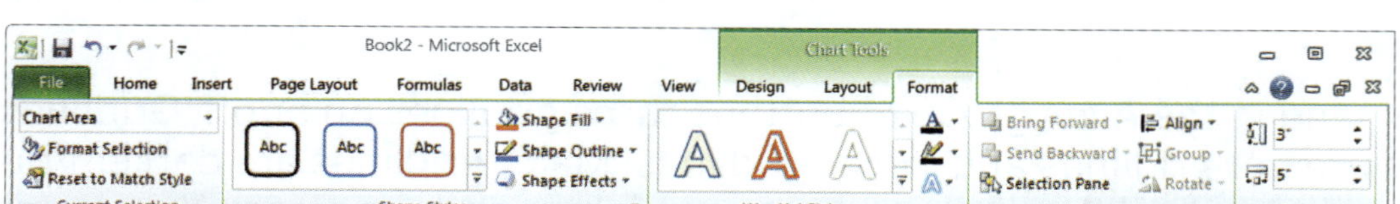

Fig. 3.28: **Format** tab

From the **Shape Styles** group of buttons on the **Format** tab, choose the desired style that you want to apply to your chart. You can select the desired background colour by clicking the **Shape Fill** command and then selecting the desired colour from the colour palette. Similarly, desired **Shape Outline** and **Shape Effects** can be applied to the chart.

Every chart has text in the forms of titles, data or legends. The **WordArt Styles** group of buttons has commands to change the font style, colour and other effects.

> **Quick Way**
>
> You can access formatting options instantly by double-clicking any particular chart component.

SPARKLINES

This feature has been introduced in MS Excel 2010 and it is very helpful to show and analyse the data trends. A sparkline is a miniature chart embedded in a single spreadsheet cell that provides visual representation of the data. Consider the table shown in Fig. 3.30.

1. Select the data range. In the example given, it will be B2:C8.
2. From the **Sparklines** group of buttons on the **Insert** tab, choose the desired option from **Line**, **Column** or **Win/Loss**. The **Create Sparklines** dialog box is displayed.

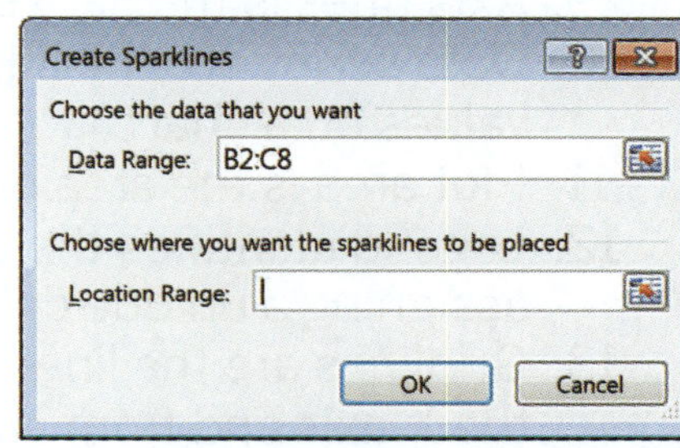

Fig. 3.29: Create Sparklines dialog box

3. The **data range** is already entered. Specify the **Location Range** which specifies the destination cells where you want the sparklines to be displayed. The location range must be either rows or columns in a single line. Also, the number of rows/columns should be two more than the number of rows/columns in the data range. For example, the data in the selected range is in five rows, so seven cells in a single column or single row should be selected for the data range.

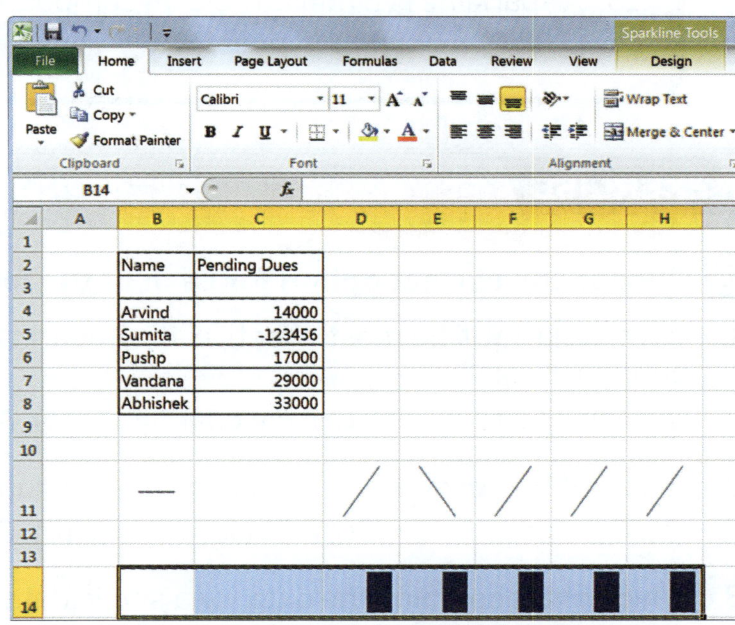

Fig. 3.30: Sparklines inserted on the worksheet

4. Click **OK**. The sparklines will be displayed. Increase the row width to have a clear look at them. Figure 3.30 contains two options of sparklines—**Line** (row 11) and **Column** (row 14). Notice that the sparklines show change in data trends by displaying the complete chart in a single cell for entire data range. So, you can have comparative analysis of the data by using this feature.

Quick Recap

1. Chart is a pictorial representation of data.
2. Some of the charts provided by MS Excel are bar, line, column, pie, doughnut, area and 3D surface.
3. Column and bar chart compare values across categories.
4. Pie chart and doughnut chart show the relationships of parts to the whole.
5. Line chart shows changes in data over a period of time.
6. The various components of the chart are—chart area, chart title, axis titles, X-axis, Y-axis, data series, plot area, legends, gridlines, data labels and data table.
7. Chart area includes the area in which all the components or objects of the chart are placed.
8. Chart title refers to the topic of the chart, usually given at the top.
9. Axis titles is the data series that the respective axis is representing.
10. Data series are the bars, slices or other data points that represent data values on a chart.
11. Plot area is the area or a window within the chart area, bounded by the axes.
12. Legend identifies the data series being represented in the chart, by assigning a unique colour, pattern or symbol to each data series.
13. Gridlines are the lines that run across the plot area from each category on the X-axis and from each value on the Y-axis.
14. Data label is the label that provides information about a data point on a chart.
15. A sparkline is a miniature chart embedded in a single spreadsheet cell and is helpful to analyse data trends.

EXERCISE

A Choose the correct option for each of the following.

1. Which chart will be most effective in comparing the tuition fee of private and public schools?
   (a) Bar chart (b) Pie chart (c) Area chart (d) Doughnut chart
2. Which of the following is not a subtype of column chart?
   (a) Cylinder (b) Circle (c) Cone (d) Pyramid
3. Which chart contains the data for a single data series?
   (a) Column (b) Bar (c) Line (d) Pie
4. Which of the following is used to identify the data series being represented in the chart?
   (a) Data Label (b) Plot area (c) Chart (d) Legends

5. As the chart is inserted in the worksheet, which of the following tabs do not appear on the ribbon?
   (a) Design (b) View (c) Layout (d) Format

B Fill in the blanks using the words given below.

bar	line	F11	area	sparklines

1. In a ________________ chart, the categories are organized vertically and the values horizontally.
2. The ________________ chart is created by connecting a series of data points.
3. A ________________ chart is used to display quantitative data graphically.
4. The ____________ feature introduced in MS Excel 2010 is used to analyse data trends.
5. The shortcut key to create the chart instantly is ________________.

C State whether the following statements are true (T) or false (F).

1. All the sectors summed up together in a pie chart make up the full circle. ☐
2. A chart can never be inserted in a separate sheet. ☐
3. A data table can be inserted with the chart. ☐
4. You cannot change the title of the chart once it is inserted. ☐
5. In a bar chart, X-axis is the category axis. ☐

D Match the following.

Column A	**Column B**
(a) Sparkline	(i) Contains all the chart components
(b) Layout tab	(ii) Information on a data point
(c) Chart area	(iii) Chart in a single cell
(d) Legend	(iv) Edit chart components
(e) Data label	(v) Identification of a data series

E Answer the following questions.

1. Define a chart. Name any five components of a chart.
2. Distinguish between a bar chart and a column chart.
3. What is sparkline feature of MS Excel 2010? Write steps to create a sparkline with the line option.
4. Write the steps to move a chart to a different worksheet.
5. Give one point of difference between the chart area and the plot area.

Lab Activity

1. Your class teacher has to show the class performance through a pie chart. The adjacent table shows the names of the students and marks scored by them. Help her to complete the chart.

Roll No.	Name	Marks
1	Ashwant	69
2	Ashmia	98
3	Dolma	34
4	Geeta	78
5	Jatin	90
6	Lokesh	35
7	Manju	67
8	Nitin	78
9	Savita	82
10	Yaseen	75

2. Arun and Manjeet are working in the Sales department of a garment company. The adjacent table gives the sales figures of both for the past six months. Compare their performances through an appropriate chart.

	Amit	Manjeet
Jan	12000	10000
Feb	9870	9980
Mar	12000	16000
Apr	6790	5647
May	2094	3481
Jun	10710	11999

3. The adjacent table shows the average rainfall in a city during the monsoons over last 10 years. Show the variations by inserting a line chart on a separate worksheet.

Year	Rainfall (in mm)
2004	564
2005	590
2006	678
2007	450
2008	589
2009	710
2010	679
2011	599
2012	648
2013	744
2014	654

4. The following table gives the percentage of number of students, male and female, dropping out of school. Insert an appropriate chart to illustrate the given data.

	2000	2001	2002	2003	2004	2005	2006	2007	2008	2009	2010	2011	2012
Total	10.9	10.7	10.5	9.9	10.3	9.4	9.3	8.7	8.0	8.1	7.4	7.1	6.6
Male	12.0	12.9	11.8	11.3	11.6	10.8	10.3	9.8	8.5	9.1	8.5	7.7	7.3
Female	9.9	9.5	9.2	8.4	9.0	8.0	8.3	7.6	7.5	7.0	6.3	6.5	5.9

Research Project

Collect data of the fee structure from 10 different students of your locality studying in different schools (government, aided and private schools). Form a table in MS Excel and then have a detailed analysis on the fee structure of all these schools using appropriate charts for illustration. Also, collect data for two consecutive academic sessions and show the data trends.

Teacher's Notes

(a) Discuss the importance of charts in data analysis.

(b) Discuss all types of charts and the situations in which a particular chart should be preferred.

WORKSHEET

A Choose the correct option for each of the following.

1. Which of the following can be the constituents of a formula in MS Excel?
   (a) Cell addresses
   (b) Constant values
   (c) Mathematical operators
   (d) All of the above
2. What will be the output if you type = "Black"&"and"&"White" in the formula bar?
   (a) Black&White
   (b) Black and White
   (c) Black & and & White
   (d) BlackandWhite
3. Which of the following arithmetic operators have got the highest precedence in MS Excel 2010?
   (a) + (b) ^ (c) * (d) /
4. Conditional formatting command is in the Styles group of buttons under the ________ tab.
   (a) File (b) Insert (c) Home (d) Data
5. Which of the following is a type of filter?
   (a) By list values (b) By criteria (c) By format (d) All of the above
6. Which of the following cell references can be included in relative reference?
   (a) $F6 (b) A5 (c) $B$6 (d) None of the above
7. Name the function key that is pressed to create the chart instantly?
   (a) F11 (b) F5 (c) F10 (d) F15
8. A topographic map is an example of a ________ chart.
   (a) Line chart (b) Pie chart (c) Area chart (d) Surface chart
9. Which of the following is an optional feature of a chart?
   (a) Gridlines (b) Category axis (c) Data Table (d) Both (a) and (c)
10. Which chart should be preferred to view monthly temperature variations?
    (a) Pie chart (b) Line chart (c) Bar chart (d) Surface chart

B Unscramble the words to fill in the blanks.

1. The ______________ cell shows the result of the formula that you have entered but the actual formula is seen in ______________. (EITVAC/RAB UMALRFO)
2. This process of placing one string after another is called ______________ . (NIOANTTAECCON)
3. In ______________ referencing, the relative position of rows and columns changes when you copy a formula. (ELTIRAEV)
4. Using ______________ feature, you can display data in a particular colour or style depending on a particular condition. (TIONCONIDLA GFNORTMTAI)
5. ______________ is an effective way to represent data in pictorial form. (STCHRA)
6. Category axis is the ______________ axis of the chart. (X)
7. A ______________ chart is used to display quantitative data graphically. (AAER)
8. Two walls and the floor constitute the ______________ of a 3D chart. (TPLO AAER)
9. Sparklines group of buttons is under the ______________ tab. (TINSRE)
10. The value of each data point on the chart is represented by ______________. (AADT RIESSE)

C State whether the following statements are true (T) or false (F).

1. A formula in MS Excel always starts with a $ sign. ☐
2. Auto editing of result is possible in MS Excel 2010. ☐
3. In MS Excel 2010, the evaluation of a formula is always carried out from left to right. ☐
4. Only numeric data can be sorted. ☐
5. You can access formatting options instantly by double-clicking the particular chart component. ☐

D Label all the sorting and filtering commands in the toolbar given below.

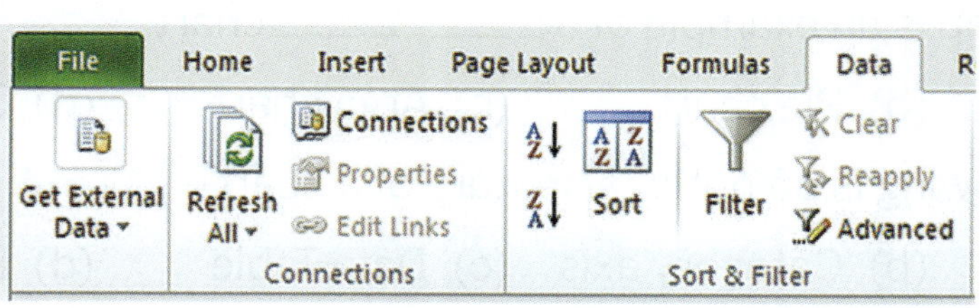

E Label the category axis, value axis, data labels and legends in the following chart.

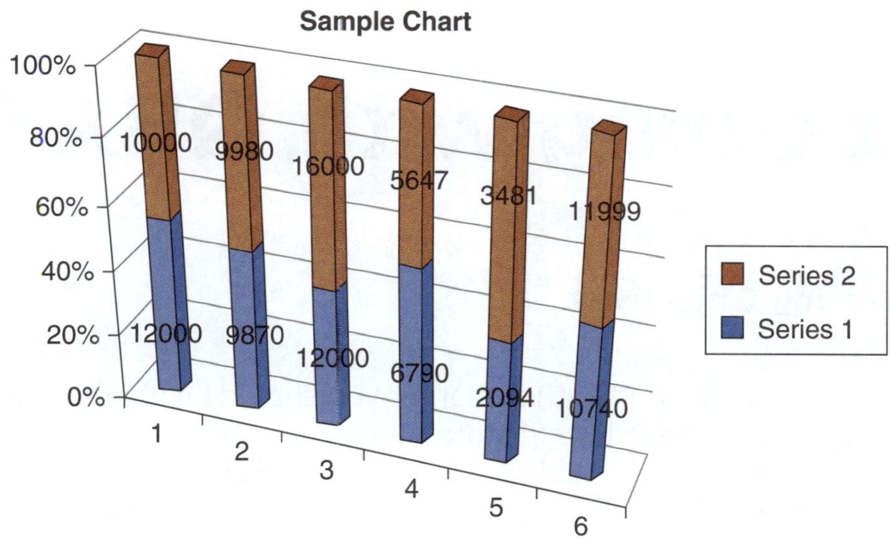

F Answer the following questions.

1. Name any three constituents of formula available in MS Excel.
2. Explain any two ways by which you can remove the filter.
3. What will be the output if you apply filter criteria "beginning with M" to a field containing data values Sunita, Babita, Mamata?
4. Explain absolute referencing with an example. Which character is used to convert the absolute referencing into relative referencing?
5. Differentiate between a pie chart and a doughnut chart.
6. What is the use of sparkline feature of MS Excel 2010?

Projects

1. Go to your school library and collect information on the number of books in each category—Thrillers, Poetry, Love stories, Historic novels, Science fiction and Autobiographies. The information should contain the number of books, average cost, popularity status (on a grade point of 1-10) and average number of books issued in each category. Thereafter, sort the data in descending order of their popularity status. Also, filter data for each category. Insert an appropriate chart to depict the collected information.

4 Looping with QBASIC

Learning Objectives

By the end of this chapter you should be able to learn and use the following statements

- WHILE...WEND
- DO WHILE...LOOP
- DO UNTIL...LOOP
- FOR...NEXT
- EXIT command

Introduction

Looping means repeated execution of a statement or a set of statements. What will you do to print the word 'WELCOME' 20 times? One option is to give the command PRINT "WELCOME" 20 times. This is obviously not a practical solution. Instead, you can use looping statements. These statements are much better to use as they make the program flexible, reduce the number of instructions and save memory space.

The statements used for looping in QBASIC are WHILE...WEND, DO WHILE...LOOP, DO UNTIL...LOOP and FOR...NEXT LOOP.

Any of the looping statements mentioned above must have the following four components:

(a) **Initialization**—the value from where the loop starts
(b) **Termination**—the value at which the loop ends
(c) **Step up/down**—specifies how the loop moves forward or backward
(d) **Body of the loop**—the statements inside the loop that are to be executed repeatedly.

To print the word 'WELCOME' 20 times, let us have a control variable, ctr, which starts from a starting value, say 1. This is the *initialization* of the loop. When 'WELCOME' is printed once, the value of ctr is increased by the step value (default value is 1). After printing 'WELCOME' for the second time, the value of ctr becomes 2 and so on. Hence, the value of ctr is increased every time the statement PRINT "WELCOME" is executed. As the value of ctr reaches 20, the termination point reaches and further execution of the body of the loop stops.

Always remember that the loop must move either forward or backward. That is, the value of the control variable should change every time the body of the loop is executed so that the termination condition is reached. If the loop does not terminate, it is called an *endless loop*. If such a condition arises, you can end this type of loop by pressing **Ctrl+Break**. This stops the current execution of the loop and QBASIC starts executing the next statement in the program.

> **You Should Know**
>
> A control variable is used to keep a track of the number of times the loop is executed.

WHILE...WEND

Syntax:

```
WHILE condition
        Statement(s)
WEND
```

The block of statements between WHILE and WEND constitutes the body of the loop. This body of the loop is executed only if the condition given after the WHILE keyword evaluates to True. When the condition becomes False, the execution of the loop stops.

Consider the following example to print all even numbers from 10 to 20.

```
CLS
NUM = 10
WHILE NUM <= 20
        PRINT NUM
        NUM = NUM + 2
WEND
```

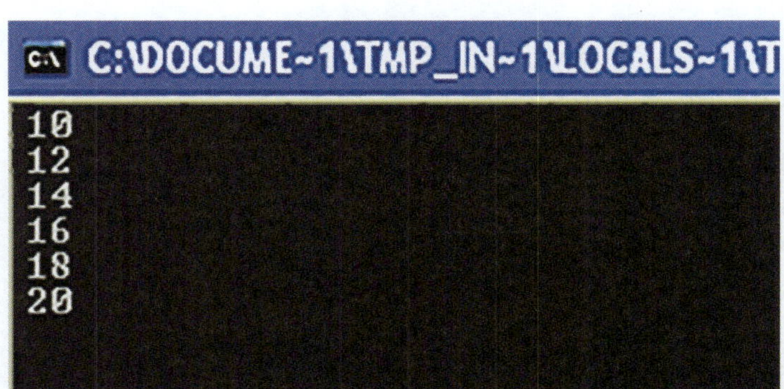

In the above program, the statements PRINT NUM and NUM = NUM + 2 constitute the body of the loop. The value of the control variable, NUM is initialized to 10. Since the value of NUM is less than 20, the condition becomes True and hence the body of the loop is executed, thereby printing 10. Thereafter, NUM is incremented by 2 and so the value of NUM is now 12. This new value of NUM is again compared with 20. The process continues till the value of NUM becomes more than 20 and the condition evaluates to False. This stops further execution of the loop.

Hence, the output of the above program will be as shown in the adjacent figure.

Practice Time 1

Harsh wants to print all odd numbers between 50 and 100 using WHILE...WEND statement. Help him to complete the task.

SOLUTION

```
CLS
VAR = 51
WHILE VAR < 100
    PRINT VAR
    VAR = VAR + 2
WEND
```

DO WHILE...LOOP

***Syntax*:**

```
DO WHILE condition
    Statement(s)
LOOP
```

In the above syntax, the condition either evaluates to True or False. The statement(s) between the keywords DO WHILE and LOOP form the body of the loop which is executed repeatedly as long as the condition evaluates to True.

Consider the example which prints multiples of 5 between 50 and 20 in the reverse order.

```
MULTIPLE = 50
DO WHILE MULTIPLE >= 20
    PRINT MULTIPLE
    MULTIPLE = MULTIPLE – 5
LOOP
```

In the above program the variable MULTIPLE is initialized with the value 50. For the loop to be executed, the condition MULTIPLE >= 20 has to be True. To begin with, the value of MULTIPLE is 50, the condition evaluates to True and so the statement PRINT MULTIPLE is executed. After

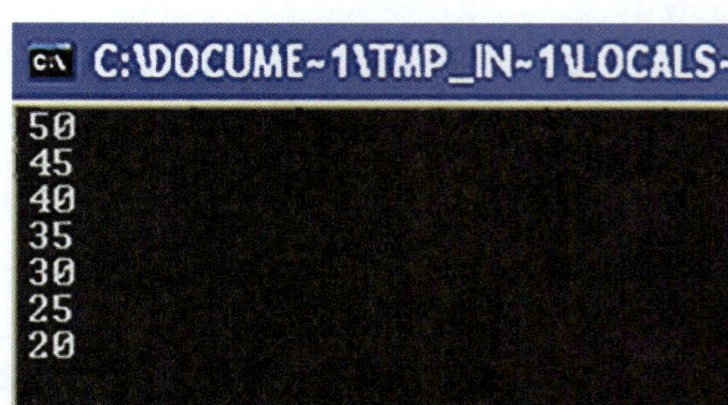

printing the value of MULTIPLE, its value is decreased by 5 and it becomes 45. The condition is again tested and the entire execution process is repeated again and again till the condition becomes False. The output of the above program is as shown in the adjacent figure.

DO UNTIL...LOOP

Syntax:

```
DO UNTIL condition
    Statement(s)
LOOP
```

This looping statement is similar to DO WHILE...LOOP. The only difference is that unlike DO WHILE... LOOP, this loop executes till the time the condition is False.

Let us display numbers from 20 to 10 using DO UNTIL...LOOP.

```
Number = 20
DO UNTIL Number < 10
    PRINT Number
    Number = Number – 1
LOOP
```

In the program given above, the body of the loop will be executed till the time the condition, Number < 10 is False. The variable Number is initialized with 20 and so the program will print numbers from 20 to 10. As the value of Number becomes less than 10, the condition becomes False and the loop terminates.

You Should Know

You can write the WHILE and UNTIL statements at the end of the loop also. The syntax then becomes

DO
    Statement(s)
LOOP WHILE condition
	DO
	    Statement(s)
	LOOP UNTIL condition

Since the condition is given at the end of the loop, the loop will be executed at least once in all circumstances, whether the condition is True or False. This is because the condition is evaluated after the body of the loop is executed at least once.

FOR...NEXT LOOP

In all the loops that you have done till now, the initialization, termination and step up/down statements are given separately. The FOR...NEXT looping statement provides a simpler way to create a loop. In this statement the initialization, termination and step up/down statements are given together.

Syntax:

FOR *control variable=initial value* to *termination value* STEP *index value*

Statement(s)

NEXT *control variable*

The FOR...NEXT statement works in the following manner:

(a) The control variable is first assigned an initial value and a final termination value. The set of statements between the FOR and NEXT statements constitute the body of the loop and are executed if the value of the control variable lies between the initial value and the termination value. The NEXT statement increases the value of the control variable by the index value specified after the keyword STEP. The index value or the step value is optional and can be positive or negative. The default index value is 1. Thereafter, the control shifts back to the FOR statement.

(b) The new value of control variable is compared against the final value specified in the FOR statement. If the value lies between the initial value and the final value, the whole process is repeated otherwise the statement after the NEXT statement is executed.

Consider the following example to display the word 'WELCOME' 5 times.

```
FOR A = 1 to 5
PRINT "WELCOME"
NEXT A
```

In the above example, A is the counter-looping variable which has been initialized to 1. The last value of the counter variable is set to 5. Since the index value is not specified, the default index value 1 will be taken as step value. With each execution of the loop, the counter variable will be increased by 1. Hence, the loop will run 5 times printing the word 'WELCOME' each time as shown in the adjacent output screen.

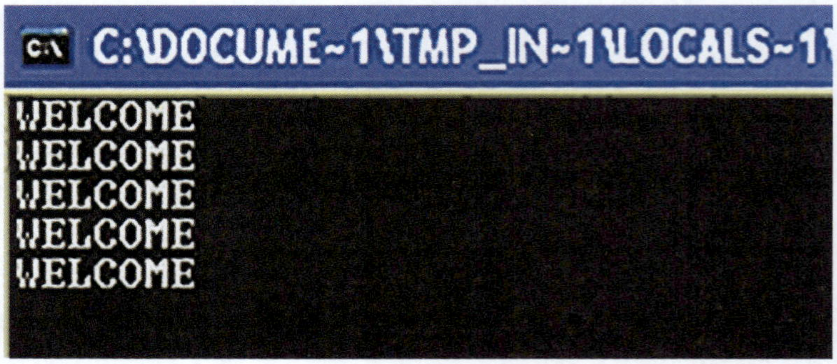

Now, alter the above program in the following manner:

```
FOR A = 1 to 5 STEP 2
    PRINT "WELCOME"
NEXT A
```

In the above example, the index value is set to 2. So, the counter variable A will be increased by 2 with each execution of the loop. Hence, the loop will now execute 3 times.

Practice Time 2

Anju is making her son learn the table of 7. Help her print the table of 7 using FOR...NEXT loop.

SOLUTION

```
REM To print table of 7
CLS
NUM = 7
FOR VAR = 1 TO 10
        PRINT NUM;  "*"; VAR; "="; NUM*VAR
NEXT VAR
END
```

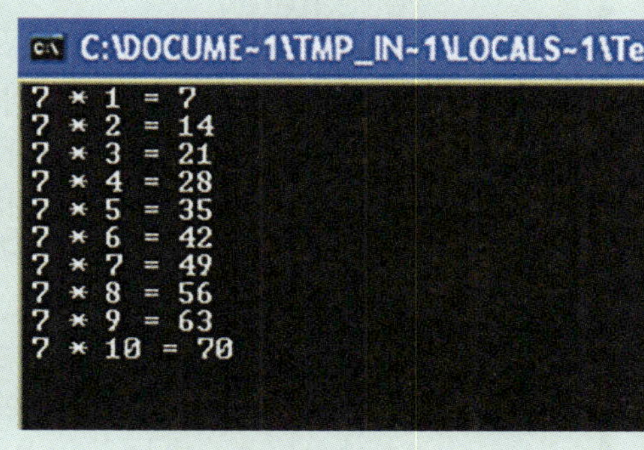

EXIT COMMAND

You have learnt that the loop terminates when the terminating condition is reached. The EXIT command or the EXIT statement in QBASIC is used to stop the execution of the loop before the termination condition is reached.

Syntax:

EXIT FOR — In case of FOR...NEXT loop

or

EXIT DO — In case of DO WHILE...LOOP and DO UNTIL...LOOP

For example,

```
FOR P = 150 to 100 STEP – 5
        PRINT P
        IF (P + 10 = 130) THEN EXIT FOR
NEXT P
```

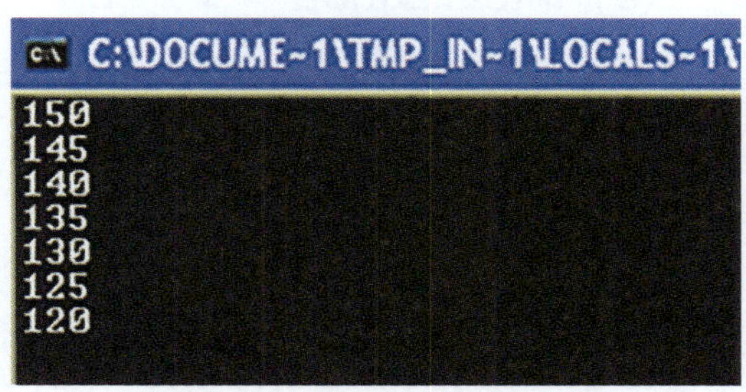

In the above program, the execution of the loop will stop as soon as the IF condition evaluates to True. Hence, the output of the above program will be as shown in the figure here.

You Should Know

The EXIT command does not work with WHILE...WEND loop.

Quick Recap

1. Looping means repeated execution of a statement or a set of statements.
2. Four components of a loop are initialization, termination, step up/down and body of the loop.
3. Initialization is the value from where the loop starts.
4. Termination is the value at which the loop ends.

5. Step up/down specifies how the loop execution moves forward or backward.
6. Body of the loop refers to the statements that are to be executed repeatedly.
7. The looping statements in QBASIC are WHILE...WEND, DO WHILE...LOOP, DO UNTIL...LOOP and FOR...NEXT.
8. The WHILE...WEND and DO WHILE...LOOP looping statements are executed till the condition is True.
9. The DO UNTIL...LOOP is executed till the condition is False.
10. While using the FOR...NEXT loop, the initialization, termination and step up/down are given in one single statement.
11. The FOR...NEXT statement is executed till the time the value of the control variable lies between the initial value and the final value.
12. The EXIT command is used to stop the execution of FOR...NEXT, DO WHILE...LOOP or DO UNTIL...LOOP statements.

EXERCISE

A Choose the correct option for each of the following.

1. The statements that are executed repeatedly till the condition is True, form the ________ of the loop.
   (a) Initialization (b) Termination (c) Body (d) None of these
2. The DO UNTIL...LOOP is executed till the condition is ________.
   (a) True (b) False (c) Either True or False (d) Neither True nor False
3. The FOR...NEXT loop will be executed till the control variable is ________ the initial value and the final value.
   (a) Less than (b) Greater than (c) In between (d) None of these
4. The execution of which of the following looping statements can be stopped by using the EXIT command?
   (a) DO WHILE...LOOP (b) FOR....NEXT (c) DO UNTIL...LOOP (d) All of these
5. You can stop the execution of an endless loop by pressing ________.
   (a) Ctrl+Alt (b) Ctrl+Break (c) Alt+Break (d) Shift+Break

B Fill in the blanks using the words given below.

Initialization	control	step	endless	Ctrl+Break	termination

1. ______________ is the point from where the loop starts and ______________ is the point where the loop ends.
2. In a FOR...NEXT loop, you may not specify the _________ value.
3. ______________ is the shortcut used to stop further execution of the loop.
4. If the loop does not terminate, it is called an _________ loop.
5. The ______________ variable keeps track of the number of times the loop is executed.

C State whether the following statements are true (T) or false (F).

1. The step value can only have a positive number. ☐
2. The FOR...NEXT statement cannot be stopped with the EXIT command. ☐
3. Every loop must have a terminating condition. ☐
4. In a FOR...NEXT loop, the default step value is 0. ☐
5. The statements between WHILE and WEND constitute the body of the loop. ☐

D Identify the errors in the following programs.

1.
```
DO WHILE
        PRINT A
        A = A*4
LOOP
```

2.
```
FOR MEMBER = 75 TO 20 STEP 15
      PRINT MEMBER
NEXT MEMBER
```

3.
```
X = 5
DO UNTIL X < 9
  X = X + 1
WEND
PRINT X
```

E Answer the following questions.

1. Name the looping statements used in QBASIC.
2. What are the components of a looping statement?
3. Differentiate between a DO WHILE...LOOP and DO UNTIL...LOOP.
4. What is the use of STEP in a FOR...NEXT statement? Is it necessary to give STEP in every FOR...NEXT statement?
5. What is the default STEP value in a FOR...NEXT loop? Is it possible to have a negative value in STEP?

FA

Lab Activity

1. Lata's mathematics teacher asks her to write a program in QBASIC that displays the factorial of a number. Help her to complete the task.
2. Sameer works as a manager in a sales firm. He wants to display the weekly sales of his salesmen. Develop a program in QBASIC that accepts sales figures for all six working days of the week and finally displays the total weekly sales made by each salesman.
3. The teacher asked Ashu to make a program in QBASIC that accepts a number and prints the following series till that particular number.
   1, 4, 9, 16, 25...n

   Help Ashu to complete the task.
4. Dhruv wants a program that accepts a number and prints its square and cube. He wants the program to continue till the time the user enters 0. Create a program for him.
5. Sushant wants a program that accepts a number and checks whether the number entered is a prime number or not. Create a program for him.

FA

Research Project

Write a program to print the Fibonacci series.

1, 1, 2, 3, 5, 8, 13, ...

(Hint: You can research on the Internet to understand what is 'Fibonacci Series'.)

Teacher's Notes

(a) Discuss the importance of using looping statements.
(b) Demonstrate the use of all the looping statements covered in the chapter giving different examples.

5

Information and Communication Technology

Learning Objectives

By the end of this chapter you should be able to
- understand Information and Communication Technology.
- know about e-commerce.
- know about e-governance.
- know about e-learning.

Introduction

Information and Communication Technology (ICT) refers to technologies that provide access to information through telecommunications. Modern information and communication technologies have connected people all over the world at all times through various means. In this chapter, you will study various applications of ICT and how they have affected the society.

You Should Know

The term Information and Communication Technology was first coined by Dennis Stevenson in 1997.

INFORMATION AND COMMUNICATION TECHNOLOGY (ICT)

ICT is an umbrella term that includes any communication device or application, such as, radio, television, mobile phones, smart phones, satellite systems, networks and network devices. The term even includes various services and applications such as broadband services, videoconferencing, e-commerce, e-learning, etc. Also, any form of information from all over the world is gathered, stored, shared and distributed with the help of ICT.

> **Word Web**
>
> **Umbrella term**: term that covers wide range of things

In the past few decades, ICT has made communication a very fast and simple process. People can communicate with anyone across the world and at any time using technologies such as instant messaging, chat rooms, videoconferencing, etc. Social networking sites such as Facebook and Twitter allow users from all over the world to be in touch with each other all the time. You will find applications of ICT in almost all spheres of life such as education, business, health care, agriculture, governance, art, employment, transport, space and environment study, etc.

Advantages of ICT

1. People from all over the world stay connected to each other through emails, SMSs, mobile applications such as WhatsApp and social networking sites such as Facebook and Twitter. Like-minded people form groups and can collectively work for a cause.
2. ICT has made distance learning possible. Various e-learning sites provide study materials and tutorials. Also, many universities are now conducting online courses and examinations. This is very helpful for students who cannot attend a regular course in schools and colleges.
3. Through ICT, payment of bills, making reservations, paying taxes, applying for driving license or passport can be done conveniently from home. Even online complaint cells and helpline services have been set up by the government to redress public grievances providing transparency in the system.
4. ICT has lowered expenses and improved cash flow in the market. Online money transactions are very convenient and a fast method for payments or transfer of money. Online trading enables smaller investors to coordinate their own trading plans. E-banking services allow access to one's bank accounts at a mouse's click. Online shopping enables consumers to search for low-priced goods and get them delivered at their homes.

Disadvantages of ICT

1. More and more people are becoming victims of online frauds. Criminals steal the identity and bank account details of people and then execute unauthorized money transfers and purchases.
2. Personal profiles of people posted on various social networking sites are being misused.
3. A lot of time gets wasted on messaging, mobile applications and social networking sites. In many cases, these are being overused to the level of addiction causing reduced concentration levels.

ELECTRONIC COMMERCE (E-commerce)

Electronic commerce or e-commerce is the buying, selling and exchange of goods and services over computer networks, predominantly on the Internet. The transactions, exchange of data for such business transactions and terms of sale are all performed electronically.

This is one of the most effective and efficient ways of conducting business nowadays. The web is rapidly becoming a multibillion-dollar source of revenue for the world's businesses.

Fig. 5.1: Shopping on the Internet

Companies set up websites that provide details of their products and services. Consumers then buy the desired products using credit cards, debit cards, net banking, cash-on-delivery, etc. But e-commerce sites need to implement extra security features to prevent online frauds.

Word Web

Encrypting: putting the information for communication in a code that is not understood by all

Some of the security measures adopted by e-commerce sites are as follows:

1. Authenticating people to carry on the transactions
2. Controlling access to resources for registered or selected users
3. Encrypting communication
4. Ensuring the privacy and effectiveness of transactions

You Should Know

Secure Sockets Layer (SSL) is the most widely used security technology used by the web browsers.

Categories of e-commerce

E-commerce can be divided into four main categories. These are as follows:

Business-to-Business (B2B): In this category of e-commerce, companies do business with each other. For example, manufacturers selling to distributors or wholesalers selling to retailers fall into this category. Thousands of companies who sell their products to other companies in this manner have discovered that web is a quick way to reach the consumers at any point of time.

Business-to-Consumer (B2C): This category of e-commerce refers to businesses selling their products to the general public, typically through catalogues and utilizing the shopping-cart software. There are several websites such as *myntra.com*, *flipkart.com* where companies provide information directly to actual consumers who can order products and services directly from the site. Be it buying clothes, footwear, accessories, household items or even booking a holiday, with e-commerce all these purchases can be done round the clock and just at a click of the mouse.

Consumer-to-Business (C2B): In this category of e-commerce, a consumer posts his project online with a detailed business proposal containing a set budget. The interested companies review the consumer's proposal and bid on the project.

The consumer then reviews the bids and selects the best option. This category is often referred to as *Digital Middlemen*.

Consumer-to-Consumer (C2C): In this category of e-commerce, individual consumers put up items for sale through auctions, free classifieds and forums on certain websites. The interested consumers can bid on such sites to purchase any item. eBay's auction service is a very good example of this category, where person-to-person transactions take place every day since 1995.

Other than the categories of e-commerce discussed above, G2G (Government-to-Government), G2E (Government-to-Employee), G2B (Government-to-Business), B2G (Business-to-Government), G2C (Government-to-Citizen), C2G (Citizen-to-Government) are other forms of e-commerce that involve transactions with the government. These deliver services that include procurement of items, filing of taxes, business registrations, renewal of licenses, etc.

Advantages of e-commerce

1. It is available round the clock and 365 days a year.
2. The buying and selling can be done from any place where Internet connection is available.
3. Customers can select the desired product from the choices given by different providers. Also, the products and services can be delivered at home.
4. The process of buying and selling is fast and convenient.
5. E-commerce is cost-efficient for businesses as it helps in reducing costs.

Disadvantage of e-commerce

1. Extra security measures have to be taken to avoid online fraud and misallocation of funds.

E-GOVERNANCE

E-governance or electronic-governance is an emerging trend to re-invent the manner in which the government functions. In the term electronic-governance, the word 'electronic' implies technology-driven governance. It is the use of modern information and communication technologies such as Internet, smart phones, mobiles, local networks, etc. by the government to improve its effectiveness, transparency, efficiency and service delivery. Through e-governance, government services are made available to the citizens in a convenient, efficient and transparent manner, thereby promoting democracy. It also enables participation of citizens in government affairs and matters, and enhances their economic and social opportunities, so that they can make better lives for themselves and for the coming generations. With the ongoing era of digital economy, governments all over the world have recognized information technology as an effective tool in promoting the economic activities and developing human resources of their countries.

Advantages of e-governance

1. It improves transparency.

2. It provides information speedily to all citizens and allows direct interaction with them.
3. It improves administration's efficiency.
4. It improves delivery of public services such as transportation, power, health, water, security and municipal services.

Disadvantages of e-governance

1. Despite government's efforts to ensure safety of data, e-governance websites may get attacked by hackers. This leads to online frauds.
2. Internet-enabled devices, hardware such as routers, advanced servers and security systems constitute a costly infrastructure. Many developing countries may not be able to afford this technology.

E-governance in India

In India, the aim is to redefine governance in the ICT age so as to provide smart governance to the citizens. Several significant initiatives have been taken at the Centre and the State level in this direction. The website shown in Fig. 5.2 is the home page of National Portal of India.

Fig. 5.2: E-governance page of the National Portal of India (*http://india.gov.in/*)

Some of the initiatives taken by the Central and State governments are listed below:

1. Both the Central and State governments have taken steps to extensively promote the use of Information Technology (IT) in managing its internal processes. Various online services are being provided to the citizens of India. The applications that have been implemented are targeted towards providing G2B, G2C and B2G services with emphasis on the use of local language.
2. The ministries/departments have kept a provision of about 3 to 5 per cent of their annual budgets to be spent on IT-related services.
3. The government has enacted IT Act 2000 which provides legal status to the information and transactions carried on the Internet.
4. The Ministry of Information and Communications Technology has set up a Centre for E-Governance (CEG) at Electronics Niketan, New Delhi. It showcases several e-governance applications deployed in various states and also provides technical consultation to people.

5. Some of the e-governance projects operational across India are:
   (a) Bhoomi
   (b) Stamps Registration and Archiving (SARITA)
   (c) Versatile Online Information for Citizen Empowerment (VOICE)
   (d) e-Seva
   (e) VidyaVahini

E-LEARNING

E-learning is the use of electronic media and ICT to enable people to learn anytime and anywhere. It includes providing course material, trainings, guidance from experts and conducting examinations. It is being accepted as the next evolution of the training and education industry.

E-learning includes numerous types of media to deliver text, audio, video, images, animations, etc. It facilitates the learning and delivery process for both teachers and students.

Fig. 5.3: Learning using the Internet

Advantages of e-learning

1. E-learning can occur in and out of classrooms with or without instructors.
2. E-learning can be done as per the student's convenience, at any time making it flexible learning.
3. It can be self-paced and is best suited to distance learning. Students can study wherever they have an access to the Internet.
4. The ICT tools can be effectively used to enrich the courseware content with multimedia features such as audio, video, graphics, 3D animation, etc. This results in better visualization and better understanding of the subject.
5. It reduces travel cost and time.
6. Learners have the option of selecting study material that meets their level of understanding and interest.

Disadvantages of e-learning

1. Students may lack competitive spirit as they do not have social interaction with fellow students and peers.
2. Slow or unreliable Internet connections may be a hindrance.
3. Certain vocational or traditional hands-on courses can be difficult to simulate with e-learning.
4. Instructor may not always be available on demand.

Quick Recap

1. Information and Communication Technology (ICT) is the technology that provides access to information through telecommunications.
2. ICT provides access to information through any communication device or application such as, radio, television, mobile phones, smart phones, satellite systems, networks and network devices.
3. Electronic commerce or e-commerce is buying, selling and exchange of goods and services over computer networks, predominantly on the Internet.
4. Categories of e-commerce are Business-to-Business (B2B), Business-to-Consumer (B2C), Consumer-to-Business (C2B) and Consumer-to-Consumer (C2C).
5. E-governance refers to the use of modern Information and Communication Technologies such as Internet, smart phones, mobiles, local networks, etc. by government to improve its effectiveness, efficiency and service delivery.
6. E-learning is the use of electronic media and ICT to enable people to learn anytime and anywhere by providing course material, trainings, guidance from experts and conducting examinations.

EXERCISE

A Choose the correct option for each of the following.

1. Which of the following communication devices can be included under ICT?
   (a) Mobile phones (b) Radio (c) Networks (d) All of these
2. Which of the following is not a category of e-commerce?
   (a) B2B (b) C2B (c) C2C (d) None of these
3. In which of the following categories of e-commerce companies do business with each other?
   (a) B2B (b) C2B (c) B2C (d) C2C
4. Which of the following categories of e-commerce utilizes shopping-cart software?
   (a) B2B (b) C2B (c) B2C (d) C2C
5. In which city is the Centre for E-Governance (CEG) set up by the Government of India?
   (a) Mumbai (b) New Delhi (c) Kolkata (d) Chennai

B Fill in the blanks using the words given below.

ICT	e-governance	C2B	fraud	E-Learning

1. E-commerce is also referred to as a subset of ________________.
2. In the ________________ category of e-commerce, a consumer posts his project online with a detailed business proposal.
3. E-commerce sites need to implement extra security features to prevent __________.

4. Through ________________, government services are made available to citizens electronically.
5. ________________ allows you to study at any time and at any place.

C State whether the following statements are true (T) or false (F).

1. Today, distance learning is possible because of ICT. ☐
2. For e-commerce, you have to go to an electronics store to buy and sell goods. ☐
3. You can do online shopping only during daytime. ☐
4. The IT Act 2000 provides legal status to the information and transactions carried on the Internet. ☐
5. E-learning can be done outside the classrooms. ☐

D Expand the following.

1. ICT 2. VOICE 3. SARITA 4. CEG 5. C2B

E Answer the following questions.

1. What do you mean by ICT?
2. Give two advantages and two disadvantages of ICT.
3. Write any two initiatives that the government has taken to promote e-governance in India.
4. Write any two advantages of e-learning.
5. Name the various categories of e-commerce.

FA

Research Project

List out four e-learning and e-commerce websites. Explore and describe the convenience that they provide.

Teacher's Notes

(a) Discuss about ICT and its various applications in different spheres of our lives.
(b) Discuss how e-commerce has made shopping easy.
(c) Discuss what all things should be kept in mind to avoid online fraud.

WORKSHEET AND PROJECTS–2

FA

WORKSHEET

A Choose the correct option for each of the following.

1. Initialization is the value from where the loop ______________.

   (a) Starts (b) Ends (c) Continues (d) None of these

2. Termination is the value at which the loop ______________________.

   (a) Starts (b) Ends (c) Continues (d) None of these

3. The default index value or the step value for a FOR...NEXT loop is ___________.

   (a) 0 (b) 1 (c) –1 (d) Any of these

4. Which of the following is an umbrella term that includes any communication device or application?

   (a) E-commerce (b) E-governance (c) ICT (d) None of these

5. What is the term used for putting the information for communication in a code that is not understood by all?

   (a) Authenticating (b) Encrypting (c) Decoding (d) Authorizing

6. Which of the following types of media are included in the e-learning modules?

   (a) Audio (b) Video (c) Images (d) All of these

7. What are the components of loop?

   (a) Initialization (b) Termination (c) Body of the loop (d) All of these

8. If the loop does not terminate, it is called an _____________ loop.

   (a) Endless (b) Never ending (c) Constant (d) None of these

9. Which of the following services and applications can be included in ICT?

   (a) Broadband services (c) e-commerce

   (b) Videoconferencing (d) All of the above

10. In which of the following categories of e-commerce, individual consumers put up items for sale through auctions?

    (a) B2B (b) B2C (c) C2C (d) C2B

B Unscramble the words to fill in the blanks.

1. _____________ means repeated execution of a statement or a set of statements. (OPLNGOI)
2. A ____________________ is used to keep a track of the number of times the loop is executed. (ONOCLTR ARVILEAB)
3. The ____________ command does not work with WHILE...WEND loop. (TEXI)
4. ______________ is the use of electronic media and ICT to enable people to learn anytime and anywhere. (ENEARLGNI)

5. _______________ is the buying, selling and exchange of goods and services over computer networks. (EMRCMECOE)
6. __________________________ is the most widely used security technology used by the web browsers. (REECUS OTSCSKE AYLRE)
7. ____________ of the loop refers to the statements that are to be executed repeatedly. (YBDO)
8. Step up/down specifies how the ____________ moves forward or backward. (OOLP)
9. In e-commerce, all the transactions are performed ______________. (EYLLLEACCATINOR)
10. ______________ refers to technologies that provide access to any type of information through telecommunications. (CTI)

C State whether the following statements are true (T) or false (F).

1. A control variable is used to keep a track of number of times the loop is executed. ☐
2. E-commerce sites need to implement extra security features to prevent online frauds. ☐
3. The block of statements between WHILE and WEND constitutes the termination statements. ☐
4. The new value of the control variable is compared against the final value specified in the FOR statement. ☐
5. To shop online, payment can be done through credit cards only. ☐

D Answer the following questions.

1. Write a program to print the product of any 10 natural numbers which are accepted from the user. The program should terminate if the sum becomes a multiple of 5.
2. Write a program to print table of 19 using the FOR...NEXT loop.
3. Write a program to print all the even numbers from 100 to 10 using WHILE...WEND loop.
4. Why e-commerce is becoming a multibillion dollar source of revenue?
5. Give two advantages and two disadvantages of e-governance.

Projects

Research the e-governance projects taken up by the central government of India and make a detailed PowerPoint presentation on any two projects.

6 Introduction to HTML

Learning Objectives

By the end of this chapter you should be able to
- understand HTML—a markup language.
- understand HTML tags, elements and attributes.
- know the structure of an HTML document.
- create and view an HTML document.
- define BODY Element <BR> tag.

Introduction

You have studied about the Internet, web pages, websites and web browsers. You also must have visited various websites using browsers like Internet Explorer, Google Chrome, Opera, Mozilla Firefox, etc. Each website consists of multiple web pages linked to each other through hypertext.

In this chapter you will learn how to create a website using HyperText Markup Language (HTML). It is easy to learn and use. Also, no prior knowledge of programming is required for it.

HTML was invented by Tim Berners Lee in 1990 and its first version called HTML 1.0 was released in 1991. Some other versions are HTML 3.2, HTML 4.01, XHTML and the latest HTML 5 was released in 2011.

HTML—A MARKUP LANGUAGE

Hyper**T**ext **M**arkup **L**anguage or HTML is the computer language used to create documents, called web pages, on the World Wide Web. These web pages, which can be viewed in a web browser, include both text and graphics. HTML is basically used to define the structure and layout of a web page. It defines how the content of the page is to be presented or displayed in the browser.

Let us understand the terms **HyperText** and **Markup**.

HyperText means highlighted text. This highlighted text or image is linked to any other web page, thus creating a hyperlink. Each web page of a website has hyperlinks so that you can browse from one page to another.

HTML is also a markup language, a language consisting of markup tags. These tags describe how the content will be displayed on the web page. For example, <b> tag displays the text in bold. You will learn about HTML tags in the next section.

Two tools are required for creating HTML documents. For creating and saving a web page, you need an **HTML Editor** and for viewing it you need a **web browser**. The purpose of a web browser is to read HTML documents and display them as web pages. To display the web pages in the browser, you write the HTML code in an HTML Editor. **Notepad** is a very basic text editor which is excellent for HTML coding. Apart from this, WordPad and Text Edit are also used as HTML editors. As the viewer of a web page you cannot see the HTML code in the browser. Instead you only see the result of the markup tags used in the code.

Before we start coding in HTML, let us discuss various components that make up the HTML code: tags, elements and attributes.

HTML Tags

HTML tags are used to identify HTML elements. A **tag** is a piece of code that instructs the browser how to display a particular text or image. A tag name is a keyword surrounded by angular brackets (< and >). For example, <b> is the tag to display the text in bold. Generally, HTML tags come in pairs. The first tag in the pair is called the **ON** tag or the **Opening** tag. The second tag is preceded by a forward slash (/) before its name. This tag is called **OFF** tag or the **Closing** tag. The content is enclosed between the opening tag and the closing tag. Hence, the general format of the tag is:

<tag name>content</tag name>

For example,

```
<b>MOTHERLAND</b>
```

The above code will display the word MOTHERLAND in bold. That is, it will appear as

MOTHERLAND

when you view the web page in the browser.

HTML Elements

A web page is made up of HTML elements. The opening tag, closing tag and the content in between together form an HTML **element**. In other words, an HTML element is everything between the opening and the closing tag, including the tags. In the above example, <b>, MOTHERLAND and </b> form an HTML element.

There are two types of elements in HTML: Container elements and empty elements.

(a) **Container Elements**: These elements have both opening (or ON) and closing (or OFF) tags. For example, <b>, </b>, <u>, </u>, <font>, </font>, etc. are container elements.

(b) **Empty Elements**: These have an opening tag but do not have a closing tag. The empty elements usually perform a particular function. For example, <br>, also known as the line break tag, is an empty element that displays the text in a new line. <hr> is another empty element that draws a horizontal line in the browser. It is also known as horizontal rule.

HTML Attributes

Attributes provide additional information about the elements. An HTML tag may have several attributes that specify the additional effects to be applied to the content enclosed between the tags. For example, you may like to specify the font style, colour and alignment or apply borders to your table or image and so on. These attributes are always specified in the opening tag. For example, if you want to have the text (say MOTHERLAND) in red colour, you will give the following code:

<font color = "red">MOTHERLAND</font>

In the above example, color is the attribute of the font tag.

STRUCTURE OF AN HTML DOCUMENT

The various components that make up an HTML document are elements, tags and attributes. Each HTML document starts with an <html> tag and ends with an </html> tag. A browser will interpret the entire code written between these tags as an HTML document.

It is the HTML element that defines the document as an HTML file. It is a container element. This element contains only the <head> and <body> elements. They, in turn, can contain other elements. A standard HTML document is divided into two distinct sections: **HEAD** and **BODY**.

Head

The <head> provides information about the document page and is the first element contained inside the <html> element. The <head> element is a container element that includes identification and supplementary information about the document. Most of this information is not displayed as no text is put inside the head element. It contains the <title> element which specifies the title of the web page that you are creating.

Title

The <title> element is a container element because it has an opening (<title>) and closing (</title>) tag. In between these tags, the title is written. This title is displayed in the title bar of the browser window.

Body

This section contains the main content of the web page which includes text and graphics. The text enclosed in the <body> element is displayed on the web page according to the tags and attributes in which the respective content is enclosed.

To sum up, the basic structure of an HTML document will be as follows:

<html>

<head>

```
    <title>.................</title>
</head>
<body>
.................
................
</body>
</html>
```

Points to Remember While Writing HTML Code

HTML is a very simple language but while writing the code in an HTML document, the following points should be kept in mind:

1. The tag names and attribute names are not case sensitive. For example, <TITLE> and <title> are the same. However, as a convention, lower case is generally used to write the tags in an HTML document. Also, remember that the values of the attributes may be case sensitive.
2. There is no relevance of spaces between the tags. For example, the following three statements will give the same result:

   (i)
   ```
   <b> MOTHERLAND</b>
   ```

   (ii)
   ```
   <b>          MOTHERLAND          </b>
   ```

   (iii)
   ```
   <b>
   MOTHERLAND
   </b>
   ```

   However, there should be no space before, after or in between the tag names, that is, between < and > in a tag. That means the following statements are incorrect:

   ```
   <t i t l e>
   <    title>
   <title    >
   <  title    >
   ```

3. The HTML elements can be nested. This is done in order to apply more than one effect to a particular text or graphic. Care has to be taken that the element that is opened first will be closed later. Consider the following example in which you want to underline the text and also display it in bold.

   ```
   <b> <u>MOTHERLAND </u> </b>
   ```

Note that in the above example, <b> tag was typed first and then the <u> tag. The closing of these tags is always done in the opposite order. Here, first the </u> tag was typed and then the tag </b>.

4. It is strongly recommended that you create the HTML document in a proper order with line breaks (using the Enter Key) and indents (using the Tab key). Even though no change in the browser window is seen, as it does not matter how you structure the HTML document, it definitely helps in understanding, modifying and debugging the code.

CREATING AN HTML DOCUMENT

As mentioned before, you need an HTML editor to create an HTML document. In fact, you can type the code in any word processor like WordPad, MS Word, Notepad, etc. In this chapter, we will be using Notepad to write the HTML code.

1. Click **All Programs** from the **Start** menu.
2. From the **Accessories** submenu, select **Notepad**. The Notepad window will appear.
3. Type the HTML document as shown in Figure 6.1 below:

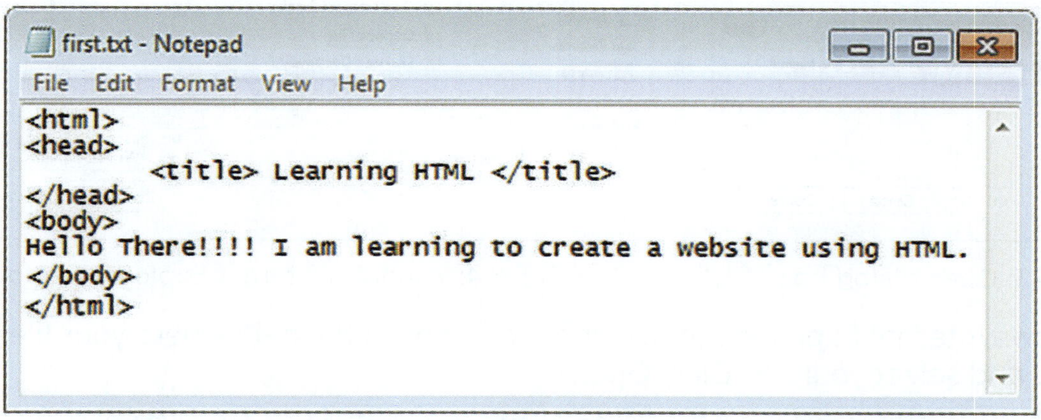

Fig. 6.1: Notepad window

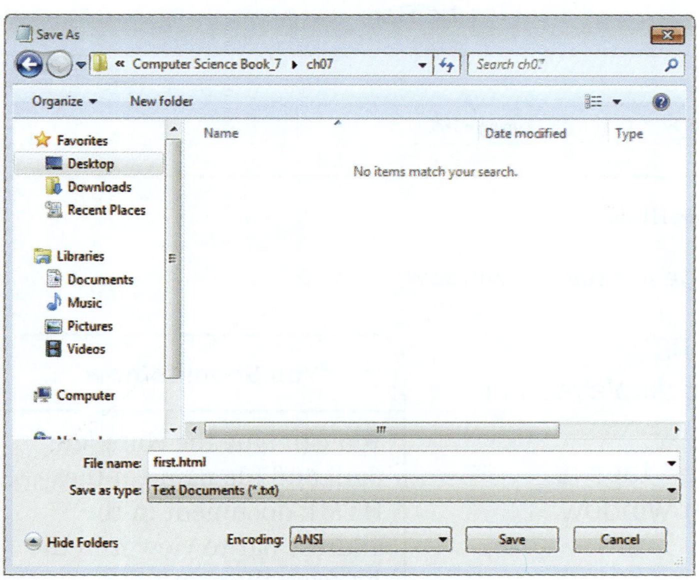

Fig. 6.2: Save As dialog box

4. To save the file, select **Save As** option from the **File** menu. The **Save As** dialog box appears.
5. Choose the location where you want to save your file. Type the name with an extension *.htm* or *.html* in the **File name** text box. Click the **Save** button.

VIEWING HTML DOCUMENTS IN A WEB BROWSER

To view an HTML document, open any web browser (Internet Explorer). Thereafter, follow the steps given below:

> **You Should Know**
>
> If the menus are not displayed in the Internet Explorer, press **Alt** key to view the menu bar.

1. Select **Open** option from the **File** menu.
2. The **Open** dialog box is displayed. Click the **Browse** button.

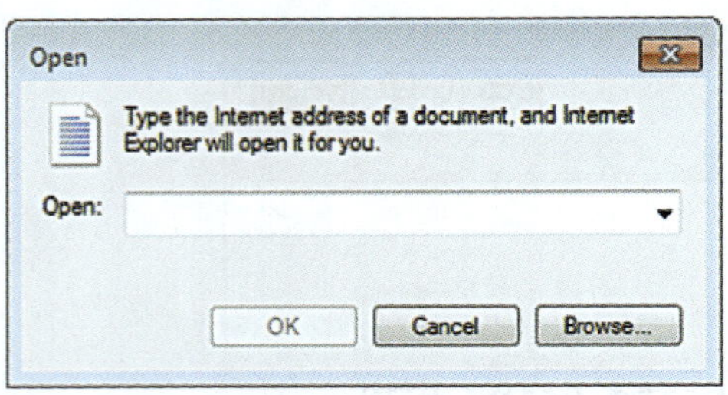

Fig. 6.3: Open dialog box

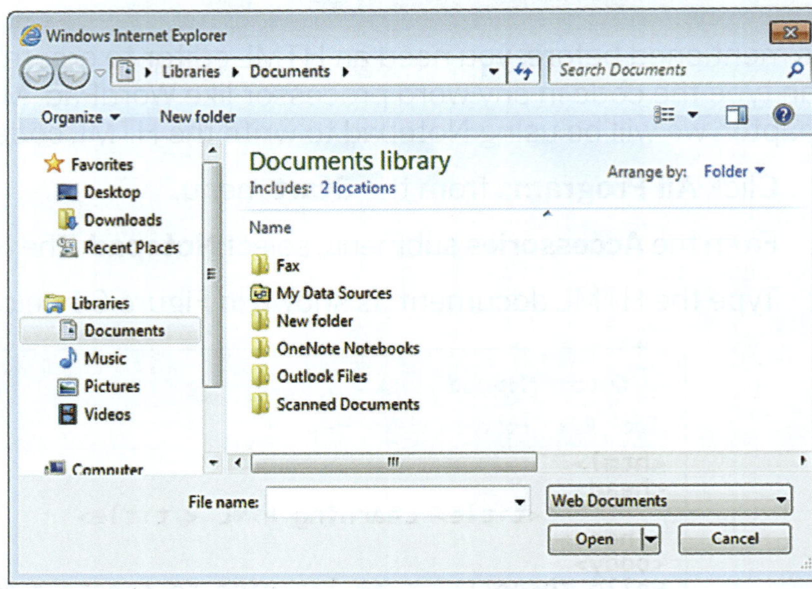

Fig. 6.4: Windows Internet Explorer window

3. Windows Internet Explorer window appears. Choose the path where your file has been stored and select your file. Click **Open**.
4. The **Open** dialog box will reappear. Click **OK** and you will see the HTML document in the browser (Internet Explorer).

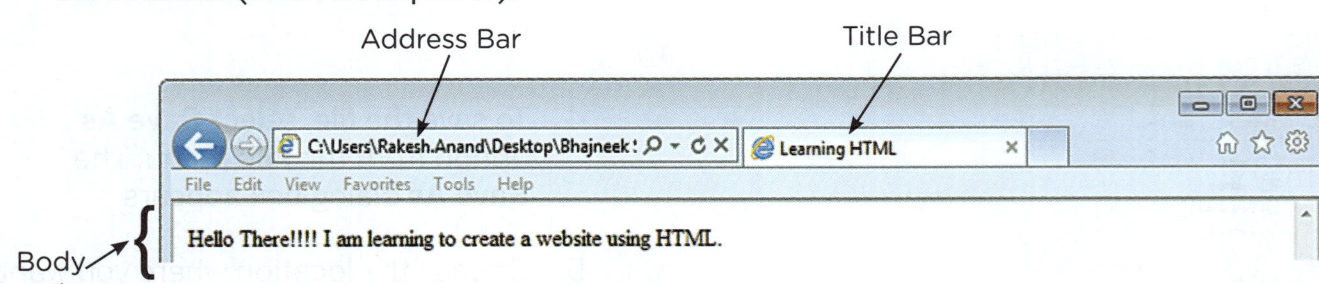

Fig. 6.5: Web page in browser window

From the above output, you infer the following:

(a) The complete path with the file name is displayed in the address bar.

(b) The text between the <title> and </title> tags is displayed on the title bar of the browser window.

> **You Should Know**
>
> You can type the complete path and file name of the HTML document in the address bar to view it in the browser directly.

(c) The content given within the body element is displayed in the body part of the browser.

Practice Time 1

Kunjal wants to create a simple web page on Fast Foods. Give her the step-by-step instructions to complete the task.

SOLUTION

1. Open **Notepad**.
2. Type the following HTML code:

```
<html>
<head>
        <title> Fast Foods</title>
</head>
<body>
Fast foods are becoming increasingly popular due to various reasons. It is fast to cook and easy-to-eat food, and our taste buds love them. Fast food is actually very harmful. It causes obesity and other lifestyle-related diseases. Fast food is harmful because it is fried in oil, which increases cholesterol levels in our body. Also, raw materials in fast foods don't have any nutritional value.
</body>
</html>
```

3. Select **Save As** option from the file menu. Type the name of the file in the File name text box, say 'fast food.html'.
4. Open **Internet Explorer** or any other browser.
5. Select **Open** option from the **File** menu.
6. The **Open** dialog box is displayed. Click **Browse**.
7. Select the file 'fast food.html' and click **Open**.
8. In the **Open** dialog box, click **OK** to view the web page.

BODY ELEMENT

The <body> element is one of the basic HTML elements. As it has both ON and OFF tags, it is a container element. The entire content (text and graphics) that has to be displayed on the web page is enclosed between the opening and closing tag of the <body> element. You might like to have desired properties of the web page that you are creating. For example, you may want to specify the background colour, margins, text colour, etc. All these properties of a web page can be set through the attributes of the body element. The <body> element has a number of attributes to control and format the page display. Some of these attributes are discussed below:

bgcolor

This attribute is used to set the background colour of the document. The value of this attribute can be a colour name or a RGB hexadecimal code. For example,

<body bgcolor = "red"> or <body bgcolor = "#223344">

You Should Know

All colours are made up of three primary colours—red, green and blue. These colours are represented as hexadecimal values. In a hexadecimal value, the first two digits represent the amount of red, the second two digits represent the amount of green and the last two digits represent the amount of blue contained in the colour.

background

This attribute is used to have an image in the background of an HTML document. The value of this attribute is the complete path and file name of the image file that you want to insert as the background. For example,

```
<body background = "C:\desktop\a.jpeg">
```

text

This attribute is used to set the text colour of the document and its value can be the name of the colour or a hexadecimal RGB code. For example,

```
<body text = "yellow">          or      <body text= "#006600">
```

leftmargin, topmargin, rightmargin and bottommargin

These attributes are used to set all the four margins—top, bottom, left and right margins of a web page. The value of these attributes is numeric and the unit is pixels. For example,

```
<body leftmargin = "80">  or  <body topmargin = "95">
```

Consider the following example that uses the body element with its attributes. Type the following HTML code in Notepad, save the document as *politics.html* and then open it in a browser.

You Should Know

You can use more than one attribute for an element by separating each attribute with a space. For example,

```
<body text="green" bgcolor="yellow" topmargin="80">
```

HTML code

```
<html>
<head>
        <title> Politics in India</title>
</head>
<body bgcolor="Blue" text = "yellow" leftmargin="60" topmargin= "75"
rightmargin="60">
India is the largest democracy in the world with the largest number of political parties
taking part in the election campaign. In the 1996 national elections, almost 600 million
people voted and an average of 26 candidates competed for each of the 543 territorial
constituency seats. Elections are held at national level and state level. Elections are also
held for city, town and village councils. There are different political issues in Indian politics,
```

```
at national level and at regional or state level. Some communities just demand more
economical and social rights for their communities, while others demand more autonomy
for their cultures within the Indian states. With all its problems India survives as a single
state with democratic character.

</body>
</html>
```

Politics.html will appear as shown below in the web browser:

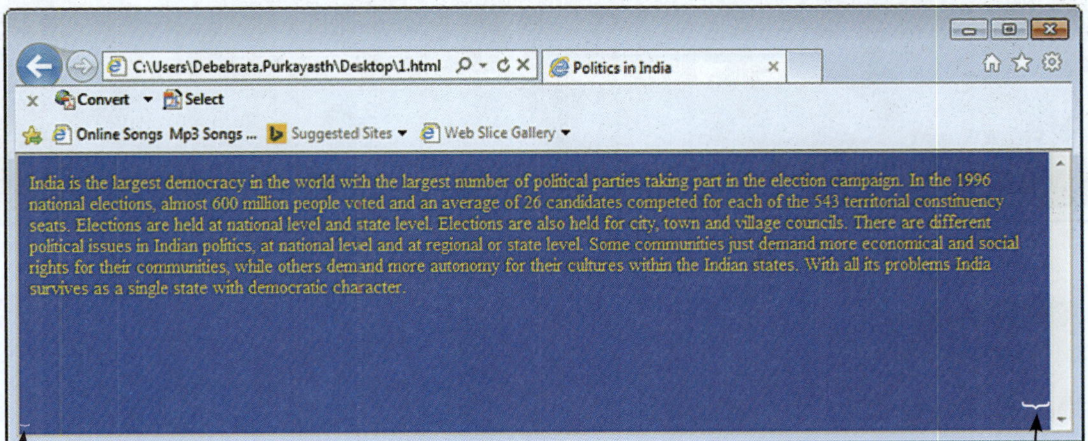

Fig. 6.6: Web page with body attributes

If you use the background attribute instead of bgcolor and give the complete path with file name as its value, the browser will place the image specified in the value as the background.

HTML code (with background attribute)

```
<html>
<head>

    <title> Politics in India</title>

</head>
<body background="file:///C:/Users/Mohini/Desktop/images.jpg" text = "yellow"
leftmargin="60" topmargin= "75" rightmargin="60">

India is the largest democracy in the world with the largest number of political parties
taking part in the election campaign. In the 1996 national elections, almost 600 million
people voted and an average of 26 candidates competed for each of the 543 territorial
constituency seats. Elections are held at national level and state level. Elections are also
held for city, town and village councils. There are different political issues in Indian politics,
at national level and at regional or state level. Some communities just demand more
economical and social rights for their communities, while others demand more autonomy
for their cultures within the Indian states. With all its problems India survives as a single
state with democratic character.

</body>
</html>
```

Browser Window

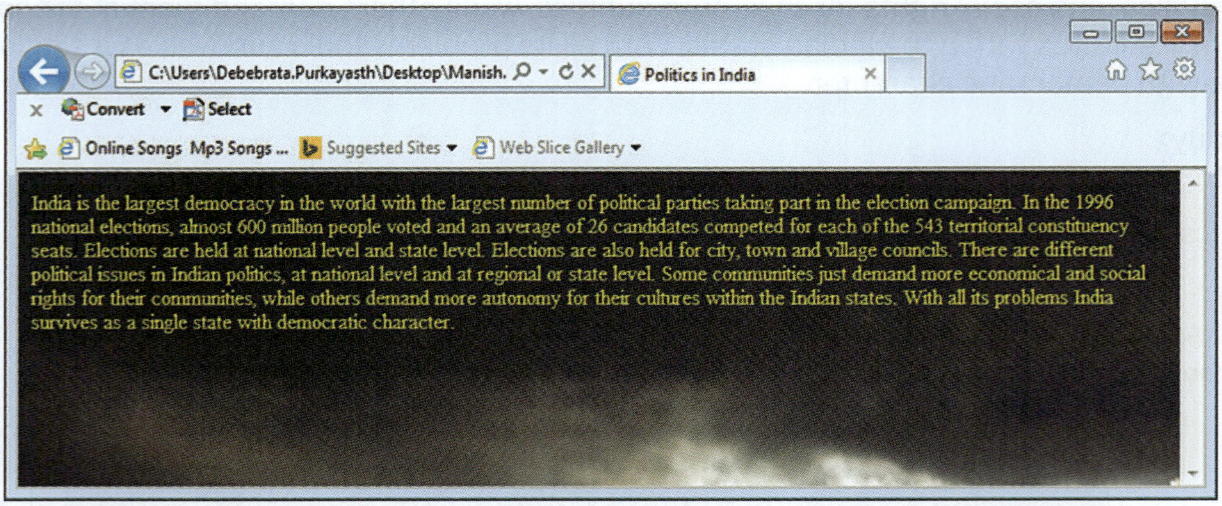

Fig. 6.7: Web page with background image

 element

Type the following code in Notepad.

```
<html>
<head>

        <title> Understanding line breaks </title>

</head>
<body>

        O wild West Wind,
        thou breath of Autumn's being,
        Thou, from whose unseen presence the leaves dead are driven,
        like ghosts from an enchanter fleeing,

</body>
</html>
```

Save the file and view it in the browser. You will see that the entire text is displayed in a single line.

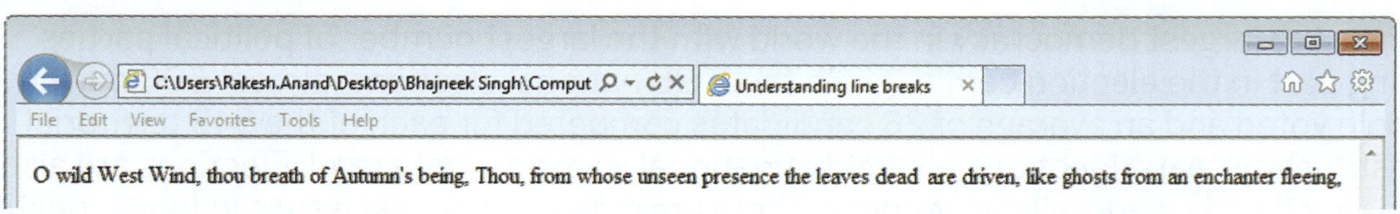

Fig. 6.8: Display of content in web browser

This is because the browser does not recognize the formatting features of a text editor. So, pressing an **Enter key** for a new line in the code has no effect in the browser. The <br> element does the required job in such cases. It is used to insert line breaks. That is, if you want your text to appear in a new line or want some blank lines between the text,

element is used. This is an empty element as it does not have an OFF tag.

Now type the above code containing <br> element after every line of text content. When you save the file and view it in the browser, you will see the text with line breaks.

```
<html>
<head>
        <title> Understanding line breaks </title>
</head>
<body>
        O wild West Wind, <br>
        thou breath of Autumn's being, <br>
        Thou, from whose unseen presence the leaves dead are driven, <br>
        like ghosts from an enchanter fleeing, <br>
</body>
</html>
```

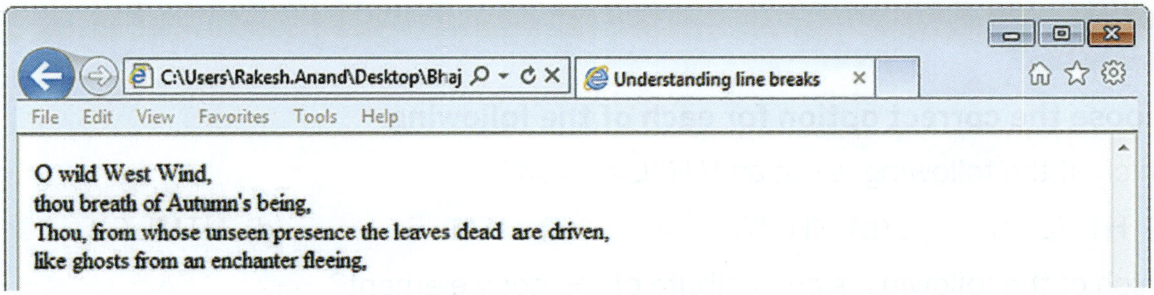

Fig. 6.9: Text with <br> element

You can also use the <br> tag to have multiple line breaks. Insert 4–5 <br> tags after the first line of the text and view the page in the browser. Do you see more number of line breaks?

Quick Recap

1. Each website consists of multiple web pages linked to each other through hypertext.
2. **H**yper**T**ext **M**arkup **L**anguage or HTML is the language used to create documents, called web pages, on the World Wide Web.
3. A browser is used to view web pages. Some examples of browsers are Internet Explorer, Google Chrome, Opera, Mozilla Firefox, etc.
4. HTML was invented by Tim Berners Lee in 1990. Its first version, called HTML 1.0, was released in 1991 and the latest version HTML 5 was released in 2011.
5. HTML defines how the content of the page is to be presented or displayed in the browser. HTML code is written in HTML editor.
6. A tag is a piece of code that instructs the browser how to display a particular text or image. A tag name is a keyword surrounded by angular brackets (< and >).

7. HTML tags generally come in pairs. The opening tag, closing tag and the content in between together form an element.
8. Elements are of two types—container elements and empty elements.
9. Container elements are the elements that have both opening and closing tags.
10. Empty elements are the elements that have an opening tag but do not have a closing tag.
11. The tag names and attribute names are not case sensitive.
12. HTML files are saved with an extension *.htm* or *.html*.
13. A standard HTML document is divided into two distinct sections: HEAD and BODY.
14. The <head> element includes identification and supplementary information about the HTML document.
15. The <body> element contains the main content of the web page which includes text and graphics. Some attributes of <body> element are bgcolcor, background, leftmargin, topmargin, rightmargin and leftmargin.

EXERCISE

A Choose the correct option for each of the following.

1. Which of the following is not an HTML version?

   (a) HTML 1.0 (b) XHTML (c) HTML 5 (d) HTML 6

2. Which of the following is an attribute of the body element?

   (a) bgcolor (b) background (c) leftmargin (d) All of the above

3. What instructs the browser how to display a particular text or image?

   (a) Tag (b) Element (c) Attribute (d) None of the above

4. Which of the following is an empty element?

   (a) <html> (b) <body> (c)
 (d) <head>

5. Which attribute of the body tag is used to set the top margin of the web page?

   (a) Top (b) margintop (c) topmargin (d) topandmargin

B Fill in the blanks using the words given below.

tag attributes website Tim Berners Lee *.htm* or *.html*

1. ____________ invented HTML.
2. A ____________ consists of multiple web pages linked to each other through hypertext.
3. HTML files are saved with an extension ________________________.

4. A __________ is a piece of code that instructs the browser how to display a particular text or image.
5. __________ are the properties associated with each tag.

C **State whether the following statements are true (T) or false (F).**

1. HTML can include both text and graphics. ☐
2. HTML tags are always in pairs. ☐
3. The tag names and attribute names in HTML are case sensitive. ☐
4. An ON tag has a forward slash before its name. ☐
5. Empty elements do not require an OFF tag. ☐

D **Answer the following questions.**

1. Differentiate between a container element and an empty element.
2. Name any two web browsers.
3. How is bgcolor different from background attribute of the body tag?
4. Name two distinct parts of an HTML document.
5. Write the attributes of the body tag with their functions.

Lab Activity

FA

1. Sahil wants to create a web page on Rulers of India. Help him do so. Set all the page margins as 60 pixels. Also, insert a suitable background image of the web page. The title of the page should be 'Rulers of India'.
2. Help Shreya create a colourful web page on Artists of India.
3. Sukanya wants to create a website on Types of Plants. Help her do so. The background colour should be green and the text should be in red colour.

Research Project

FA

Create a web page on the previous year's achievements of your school for your school website using HTML. Explore different web page layouts on the Internet and try using them in your creation.

Teacher's Notes

(a) Discuss all the HTML tags with their attributes.
(b) Discuss the need of a text editor.

• 7 Displaying Text in HTML

Learning Objectives

By the end of this chapter you should be able to
- understand <hr> and <comment> elements.
- learn about the <center> element.
- learn about the various text elements in HTML:
  - a. Paragraph <p> element
  - b. Heading <hn> element
  - c. Font element
  - d. Physical markup elements (Bold, underline and italic)

Introduction

In the previous chapter, you studied the basic structure of an HTML document. You also created a web page using basic elements of HTML, that is, head, title and body.

The information to be displayed in a web browser should be presentable and appealing to the viewer. The headings, paragraphs, titles, subtitles, etc. should be well structured. In this chapter you will learn the basic elements to display the HTML text in various formats in a web browser.

Let us discuss elements that help in better presentation of information on the web page such as <hr>, <comment>, <font>, <p> and <center> elements.

HORIZONTAL RULE (<HR>)

The <hr> element is used to create a horizontal line on the web page. This is also called **Horizontal Rule** in HTML. It is an empty element as it has no OFF (or closing) tag. The <hr> element has the following attributes:

Size: Size specifies the thickness of the horizontal line in pixels. For example, the following statement will draw a line that has a width of 8 pixels in the browser window.

<hr size="8">

> **You Should Know**
>
> The default value of the size attribute of <hr> element is 2 pixels.

Width: This attribute takes the horizontal width of the line as its value. This value can be provided in two ways:

- *In pixels:* For example, the statement <hr width="100"> will draw a line which is 100 pixels wide.
- *In percentage of page width:* For example, <hr width="60%"> will draw a line that will cover 60% of the width of the web page horizontally.

> **You Should Know**
>
> A pixel is equal to dividing an inch into 72 points.

Align: It specifies the side of the web page according to which the line will be aligned. So, the value of this attribute can either be left, center or right.

For example,

<hr align="right"> will right align the line.

Color: It specifies the colour of the line. The value of this attribute can be either the name of a colour or a hexadecimal RGB code.

For example,

<hr color="green"> will draw the line in green colour.

Noshade: This attribute does not have any value. Specifying it along with the <hr> element displays a solid line without any shading in the browser.

For example,

<hr noshade>

> **You Should Know**
>
> In HTML 5, <hr> element represents a thematic break between paragraph-level elements. No visible line is drawn in the browser.

To sum up all the attributes that we have learnt, let us draw a horizontal line in the browser which is red in colour, is center aligned and covers 50% of the page width. The command required will be as follows:

<hr size="50%" align="center" color="red">

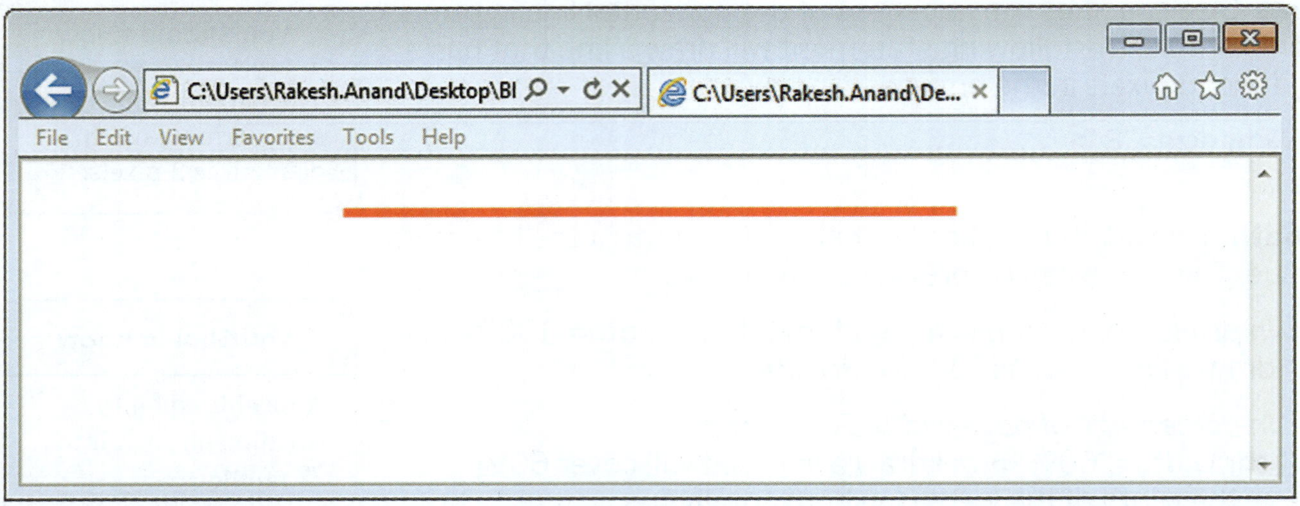

Fig. 7.1: Red horizontal bar

COMMENT ELEMENT (<!-->)

A comment is a statement given in HTML code which is meant to have only a reference to a particular code. It is ignored by the browser and hence is not displayed. You use comments just to write small explanations of the HTML code, which helps in better understanding and easy modification of the document by anyone in the future.

The syntax of the comment tag is

<!--and-->

For example, consider the statement

<!--This is a comment entry-->

In the above command, the statement 'This is a comment entry' will not be displayed in the browser.

CENTER ELEMENT (<CENTER>)

The center element is used to place the text in the center of the web page between the left and the right margins. In other words, the text or image enclosed between <center> and </center> is aligned in the center of the web page. It is a container element. For example,

<center>I AM IN THE CENTER.</center>

> **You Should Know**
>
> The <center> element has become obsolete and is not available in HTML 5. Instead, we use CSS (Cascading Style Sheets) in the code.

TEXT ELEMENTS IN HTML

There are some basic elements that help you to display text in the browser like paragraph, font, heading, etc. These elements make the web page appear structured and different sections of the page are easily distinguishable.

Paragraph <p>

The paragraph element is used to display multiple lines of text, that is, a paragraph in HTML. It is defined by <p> and </p> tags. When the text enclosed between these two tags is displayed in the browser, a blank line is inserted before and after the enclosed text.

Align is the attribute of the paragraph element that is used to align it in the center, left or right of the web page. Hence, the value of the align attribute can be either of the following:

- center : aligns the text in the center
- left : aligns the text to the left side of the web page
- right : aligns the text to the right side of the page
- justify : aligns the text from both left and right side of the page

The syntax of the <p> element is

```
<p align="value">
```

where value can be left, right, center or justify.

As an example, type the following HTML code in Notepad, save the document as an HTML file and open it in the browser.

```
<html>
<head>
    <title>Learning alignments</title>
</head>
<body>
    <p align="left">
    Positive thinking requires a lot of mental workout. The more you work for it, the better you will be at it. Although it is not possible to think positive all the time, you should try that majority of your thoughts reflect good and happy things. It will certainly make you more positive and a more happy person in life.
    </p>
    <br>
    <p align="right">
    Generally, people don't think positive because they might not be aware of the right tools for becoming a positive person. You must learn skills like building up your self confidence, encouraging yourself and others for adopting a positive attitude, good habits, doing meditation, exercising regularly and above all, being in the company of positive people. You should also try to bend more towards spiritualism.
```

```
    </p>
    <br>
    <p align="center">
    You will definitely start loving life by thinking of life as an adventure. Every time you step
    out of your house, just think that you are going out for an adventure. Think about how
    the possibilities are endless. There are possibilities to meet new people, to help the
    needy, to reach your workplace at time and even to impress your boss by your work.
    </p>
    <br>
    <p align="justify">
    It is very important that you change your thoughts by developing good habits and
    adopting a positive attitude. Do not let anything overpower you such that it becomes
    an obsession. It is easier to break a habit when you first notice it. So, instead of waiting
    for years and years to leave that habit, you should take immediate measures to stop
    it. Otherwise, it will become more and more difficult for you to come out of your
    obsession. Surveys have shown that obsession is one of the most dangerous thing to
    happen for oneself and for others.
    </p>
</body>
</html>
```

In the browser, the HTML document will be as shown below:

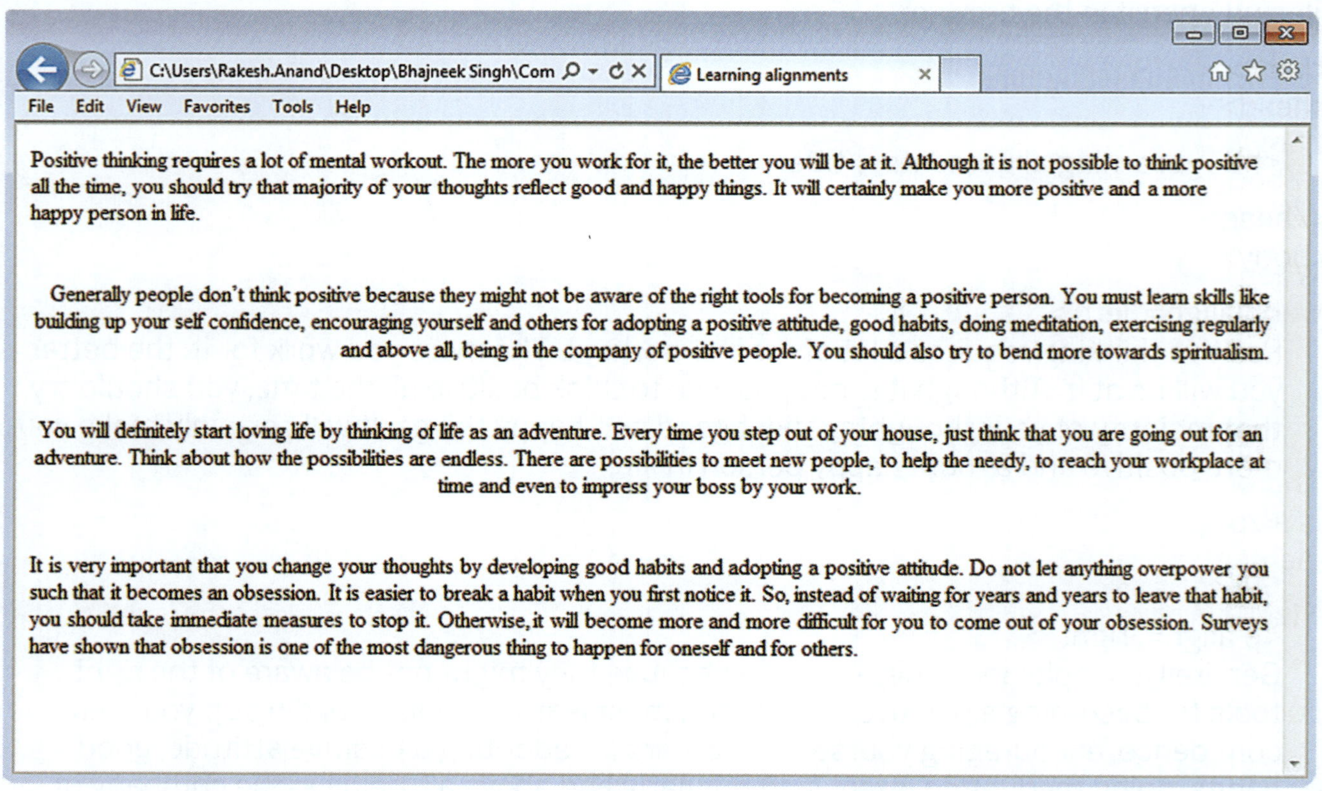

Fig. 7.2: Values of align attribute

Heading <hn>

The heading element of HTML displays different levels of headings in an HTML document. It is a container element and the text enclosed between the ON and OFF tags is displayed differently from the main text.

HTML provides six heading levels, H1 to H6. H1 displays the heading in the largest size of 24 points whereas H6 displays the smallest size of 8 points. The syntax for using heading element is as follows:

```
<hn>heading text</hn>
```

In the above statement, n is a heading level and it can take values from 1 to 6.

As an example, type the following HTML code and view it in the browser.

```
<html>
<head>
<title>Use of heading styles</title>
</head>
<body>
<h1>There is no substitute for hard work</h1>
<h2>There is no substitute for hard work</h2>
<h3>There is no substitute for
hard work</h3>
<h4>There is no substitute for
hard work</h4>
<h5>There is no substitute for
hard work</h5>
<h6>There is no substitute for
hard work</h6>
</body>
</html>
```

When viewed in a browser, the web page looks as shown.

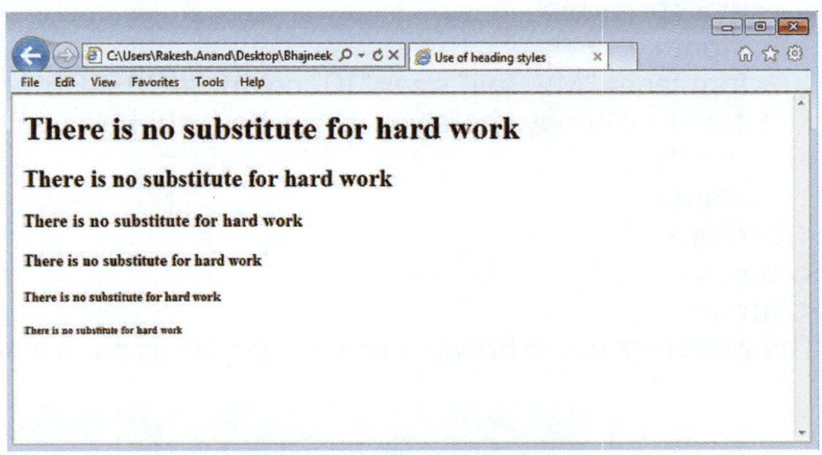

Fig. 7.3: Displaying different heading styles

Font Element (<font>)

The <font> element is used to display the text in a particular font style, size and colour. It is a container element containing <font> and </font> tags. The three attributes of <font> element are as follows:

Size: It is used to specify the size of the text. The smallest font size is 1 and the largest font size is 11.

For example,

```
<font size="5">FANTASTIC HOLIDAY</font>
```

Color: This attribute is used to set the colour of the text. The value of this attribute can either be the name of the colour or the RGB colour code in hexadecimal. For example,

```
<font color="red">FANTASTIC HOLIDAY</font>
```

Or

```
<font color="FF0000">FANTASTIC HOLIDAY</font>
```

Face: It is used to specify the typeface or the name of the font. For example,

```
<font face="arial">FANTASTIC HOLIDAY</font>
```

To understand the various attributes of the font element, write the following HTML code in Notepad and see the corresponding web page in the web browser.

```
<html>
<head>
<title>Changes in font (size, text and colour)</title>
</head>
<body>
<center>
    <font face="Monotype Corsiva" size="11" color="pink">
    <B>Be Strong</B>
    <br> <br> <br>
    </font>
    <font face="MV Boli" size="10" color="#C054BB">
    People will always hate you, break you; but how you handle them, is what <B>Makes
    You</B>
    </font>
</center>
</body>
</html>
```

The web page in the browser window will be as shown below:

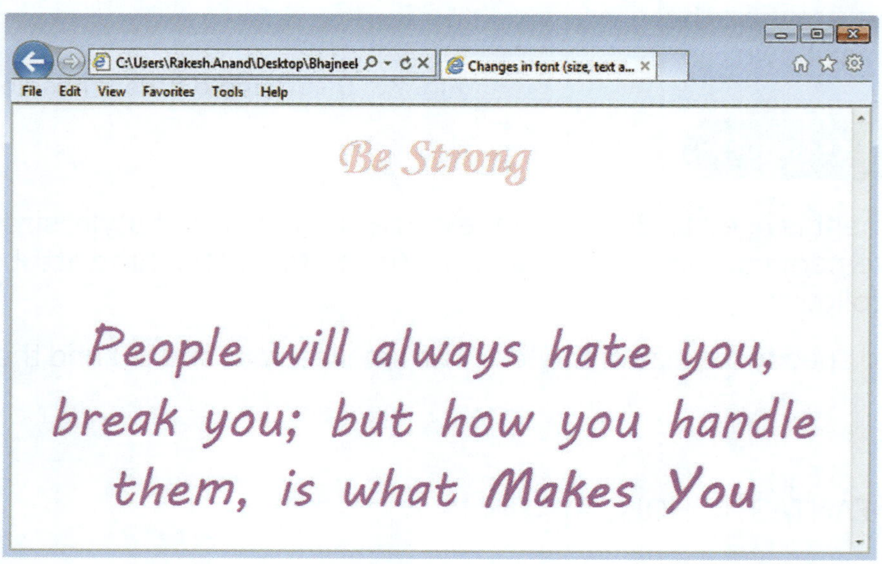

Fig. 7.4: Font face, color and size

Physical Markup Elements

The physical markup elements (bold. italic and underline) change the appearance of the text. All of these are container elements.

Bold: The bold element is used when you want to emphasize the text. Enclose the text that is to be displayed in bold between <b> and </b> tags. For example,

<b>SILENCE PLEASE</b>

Underline: This element underlines the text enclosed between <u> and </u> tags. For example,

<u>SILENCE PLEASE</u>

Italics: The text enclosed between <i> and </i> tags is displayed in italics. For example,

<i>SILENCE PLEASE</i>

Type the code given below in Notepad and see the effect of physical markup elements in the browser.

```
<html>
<head>
<title>Font Style</title>
</head>
<body>
    <b>SUCCESS</b>
    <br> <br>
    <u>There is no shortcut to success.</u>
    <br> <br>
    <i>Always remember</i>
</body>
</html>
```

The above code when viewed in the browser looks as shown:

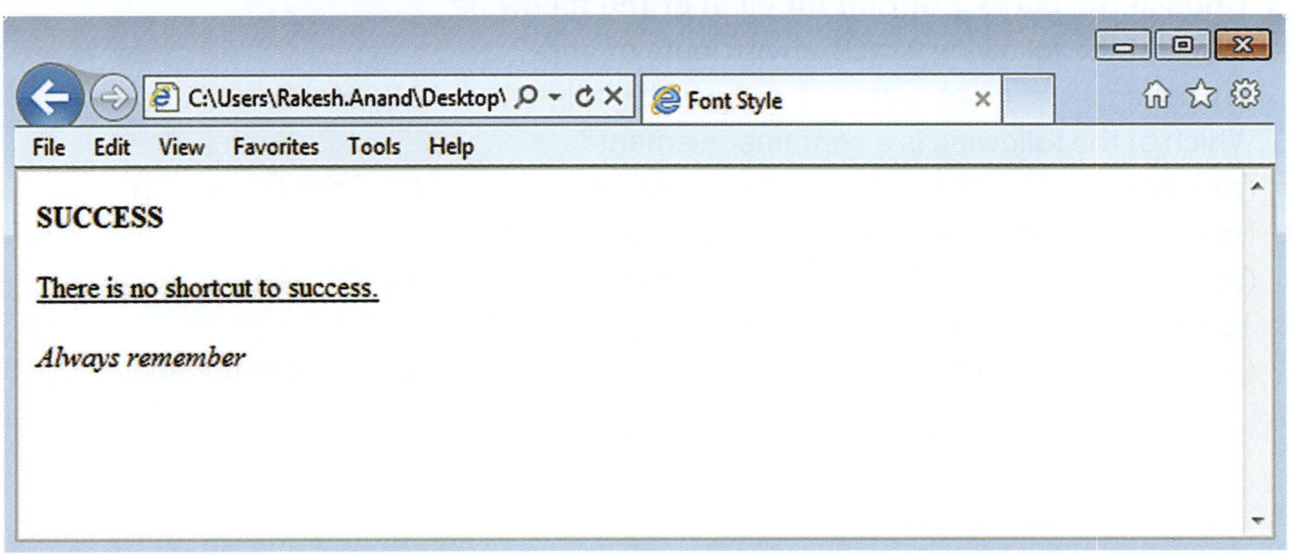

Fig. 7.5: Bold, Underline and Italic

You can nest or combine these tags if you want to apply multiple effects to a particular text. For example, if you wish to underline text and also make it bold, you can write the following statement:

<b><u>SILENCE PLEASE</u></b>

Quick Recap

1. The <hr> element is used for creating a horizontal line on the web page.
2. The attributes of <hr> element are size, width, colour, align and noshade.
3. A comment given in HTML code is ignored by the browser and is not displayed. You use comments just to write small explanations of the HTML code, which helps in better understanding and easy modification of the document by anyone in future.
4. The comment tags are <!--and-->.
5. The paragraph element is used to display multiple lines of text.
6. Paragraph element is defined by <p> and </p> tags.
7. Align is the attribute of the paragraph element that is used to align it in center, left or right of the web page.
8. The heading element of HTML displays different levels of headings in an HTML document.
9. The font element is used to display the text in a particular font style, size and colour.
10. The attributes of font element are face, size and colour.
11. The physical markup elements (bold, italic and underline) change the appearance of the text.

EXERCISE

A Choose the correct option for each of the following.

1. Which of the following is NOT an attribute of <hr>?
   (a) color (b) size (c) height (d) noshade
2. Which of the following is a container element?
   (a) <hr> (b) <comment> (c) <u> (d) Both (b) and (c)
3. How many levels of headings are possible in HTML?
   (a) 4 (b) 5 (c) 6 (d) 7
4. Text written after which of the following tags is not shown in the browser?
   (a) <!— (b) <!- (c) <-! (d) None of the above

5. Which tag will be used to display text in italics?
   (a) <itl> (b) <i> (c) <u> (d) <italics>

B Identify the tag/element from the list given below.

<u> <hr> <font> <center> comment element

1. To display the text in the center of the web page. ____________
2. To draw a horizontal line in the browser ____________
3. The element that is ignored by the browser ____________
4. To underline the text ____________
5. To display the text in a particular size ____________

C State whether the following statements are true (T) or false (F).

1. <hr> element can draw a line only in black colour. ☐
2. There are 7 attributes of the font element. ☐
3. Color is the attribute of font element. ☐
4. You can left align a paragraph. ☐
5. <b> is an empty element. ☐

D Answer the following questions briefly.

1. Write the advantages of using comments in the HTML code.
2. Write the HTML code to display your school's name and address in italics, underline the text and give it yellow colour on the web page.
3. Write the statement to draw a solid line on the web page. The line should be of size 10 pixels, in red colour and center aligned.
4. Identify the errors in the following statements:
   i. <font color="orange" align="center"> ii. <p align=right>
5. Write an HTML code to prepare a web page on World Environment Day. Try to use all the tags learnt in this chapter.
6. What is the use of noshade attribute in the <hr> element?
7. List all the attributes of font element.
8. What values can the align attribute of <p> element have?
9. Explain the two ways, giving examples, in which the color attribute of the <hr> element can be given values.
10. Give the two ways in which the horizontal length of the line can be specified.

FA

Lab Activity

1. Create the web page that gives the benefits of examination. Create a suitable layout of the web page with appropriate font colour, size and face. Make the page look presentable.
2. Meeta wants her students to create a web page containing one paragraph each on any two of their hobbies. Each paragraph should be of a different colour and center aligned from the left and right side of the page. There should be a heading—'Hobbies' at the top. The name of each hobby should be the sub headings.
3. Sushant has a keen interest in creating web pages. It is his friend Raunak's birthday and he wants to create a web page containing a few lines on their friendship. Since his friend's favourite colour is yellow, so he wants the background of the page to be yellow. The heading 'Happy Birthday Raunak' should be in bold face and underlined. He also wants the line to appear in the center of the page and a horizontal line after each line of text. The text should be in red colour and the horizontal line in blue colour. At the bottom right of the page, he wants to write his name. Help him create the web page.
4. Create a web page on 'My Family'. Choose a suitable font style, size and colour of the text for each member of the family.

FA

Research Project

Find out the HTML version on your system. Does your browser support all HTML 5 elements? Also, find out the additional key features that HTML 5 provides as compared to the previous one.

Teacher's Notes

(a) Discuss various elements covered in this chapter and their attributes.
(b) Demonstrate the effect of all the values of the align attribute of the <p> element.
(c) Encourage students to create web pages using different font styles, colours and sizes.
(d) Demonstrate all the levels of the heading element with an example.

WORKSHEET

A Choose the correct option for each of the following.

1. Which of the following is an incorrect code statement?
   (a) < body>
   (b) <body>
   (c) <b> Hello </b>
   (d) <b><u> Hello </u></b>
2. Which of the following are components of an element in HTML?
   (a) ON tag
   (b) OFF tag
   (c) Content between ON and OFF tag
   (d) All of the above
3. Which of the following attributes is used to insert an image in the background?
   (a) Bgcolor (b) backgroundcolor (c) background (d) None of the above
4. In which year was the first version of HTML released?
   (a) 1990 (b) 1991 (c) 1992 (d) 1993
5. What are the properties associated with each tag called?
   (a) Element (b) ON (c) Attribute (d) None of the above
6. Which of the following cannot be the value of the align attribute of <p> element?
   (a) Right (b) Bottom (c) Left (d) Center
7. In which of the following ways can the horizontal width of the line in a web page be specified?
   (a) In pixels
   (b) In percentage
   (c) Both (a) and (b)
   (d) Neither (a) nor (b)
8. Which of the following is not an attribute of <font> element?
   (a) Color (b) Style (c) Size (d) Face
9. Which of the following is a container element?
   (a) <h4> (b)
 (c) <hr> (d) None of the above
10. In <hn> tag, what is the range of values of n?
   (a) 2–8 (b) 1–8 (c) 2–6 (d) 1–6

B Unscramble the words to fill in the blanks.

1. A ________________ is used to view a web page. (BWE SWRBERO)
2. ________________ is the latest version of HTML. (TLMH 5)
3. ________________ element is used to insert line breaks. (b>r<)
4. The HTML code is written in an ________________. (MHTL RDEIOT)
5. ________________ is also called horizontal rule. (RH)

C State whether the following statements are true (T) or false (F).

1. HTML tags are enclosed in angular brackets. ☐
2. You can view an HTML document by typing the complete path and file name in the address bar. ☐
3. Empty elements have both ON and OFF tags. ☐
4. <hr> is a container element. ☐
5. The text enclosed between <!--and--> is not displayed in the browser. ☐

D Identify the address bar and title bar in the following figure

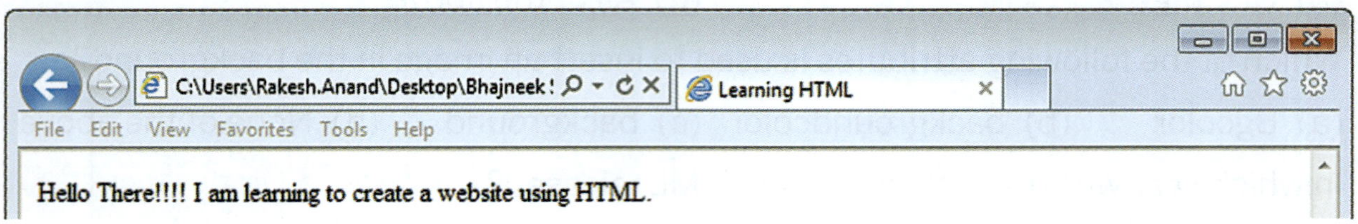

E Application-based questions

1. Aarav wants to have blue colour as the background of his page. Give the command to do so without using the colour name.
2. Nikita wants to have 50 pixels as left and right margins of her page and a picture in the background. Write the HTML statement to do so.
3. What is the error(s) in the following statement:

   <body background="file:///C:/Users/Mohini/Desktop/images.jpg" text = "red" left margin="60" top margin= "75" right margin="60">

F Answer the following questions.

1. Explain the structure of an HTML document.
2. What is the use of body tag? How can you insert an image in the background of an HTML document?
3. What is the difference between <p> and <br> elements?
4. Name the three physical markup elements.
5. What is the use of comment element in HTML?

Projects

1. Form a web page on "Rivers of India". Find out information about all the major rivers of India and display information about each river in a different style and colour. Mention your name at the bottom of the web page.

8 More on Flash 8

Learning Objectives

By the end of this chapter you should be able to
- import image files.
- modify an instance of a symbol.
- group outline and fill of an object.
- use Eyedropper tool.
- transform objects.
- use gradients.
- work with text in Flash.

Introduction

You have learnt quite a bit of Macromedia Flash 8 in Class 6. You had explored the **Tools Panel**, **Timeline** and also applied animations to objects using frame-by-frame animation, motion tweening and shape tweening.

In this chapter, you will study some more tools and advanced features of Flash 8. You will also learn to create gradients, enhance symbols and animate text.

IMPORTING IMAGE FILES

Flash 8 allows you to import and use images created in other applications. You can import JPEG, GIF, PNG images and various other file formats into Flash. To do so, follow the steps given below:

1. Select **Import** option from the **File** menu.
2. Click **Import to Stage** from the submenu. The **Import** dialog box appears.
3. Select the drive and folder where your graphic file is saved. Select the file to be inserted and click **Open**.
4. The image will be added to the Stage.

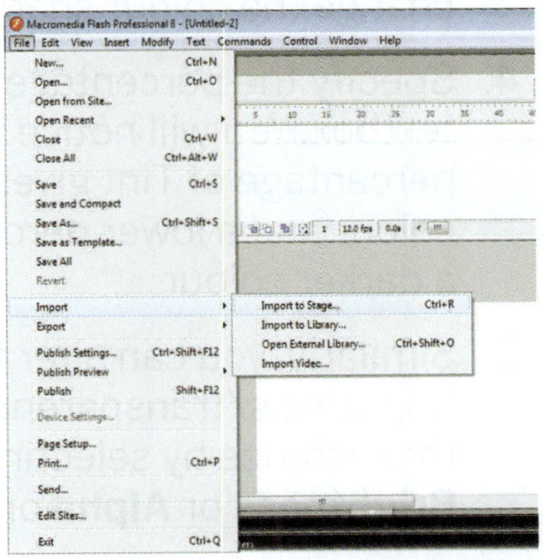

Fig. 8.1: Import to Stage option

You can work with this image in the same way as you work with other objects. These imported images are added to the Flash library as **assets**. An **asset** is a non-Flash item that you import and store for future use. You can convert these assets to symbols and store them in your **Flash library**.

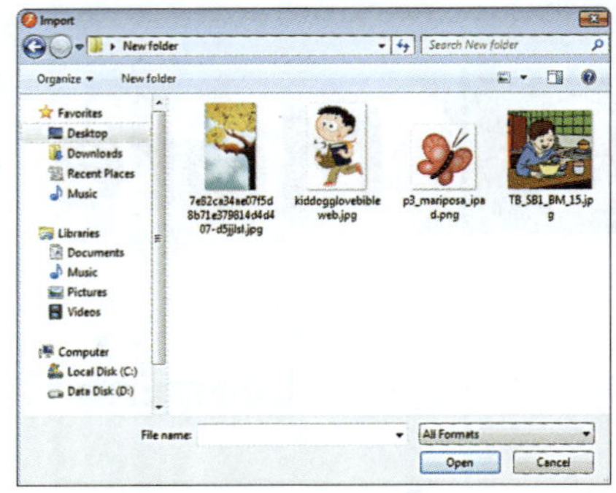

Fig. 8.2: Import dialog box

Quick Way

The shortcut key to import a picture in Flash is **Ctrl+R**.

To import an image directly into the library you can choose **Import to Library** from the **Import** submenu.

You Should Know

The graphic files that you want to import must be at least 2 pixels * 2 pixels in size.

MODIFYING THE INSTANCE OF A SYMBOL

You have already learnt how to create a symbol from a drawing and store it in the Flash library. You also know that you can create an instance (or occurrence) of a symbol to use it on the Stage. Each time you insert a symbol, you create an instance of that symbol. Once you have inserted a particular instance, Flash allows you to modify its properties by changing its colour or brightness. Follow the steps given below to modify an instance:

1. Select the **Arrow** tool from the **Tools Panel** and select the instance to be modified.
2. In the **Property Inspector** window, click the drop-down menu arrow for the **Color** in the Color list box.
3. You will find the following options: None, Brightness, Tint, Alpha and Advanced. Select the **Tint** option to change the colour shade.
4. Specify the percentage in the textbox. You will notice that a higher percentage of Tint gives a lighter colour and a lower percentage gives a darker colour.
5. Similarly, you can alter the brightness/transparency of the instance by selecting the **Brightness** or **Alpha** option.

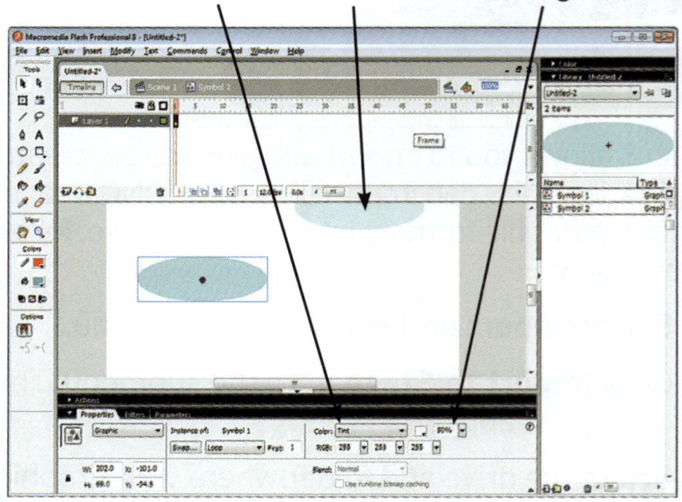

Fig. 8.3: Changing the colour shade of an instance

GROUPING OUTLINES AND FILL

You have understood that when you draw an object in Flash, two distinct objects are created—one is the outline and the other is the fill. In order to move both the objects together, you need to group them and make the two parts a single object. The steps to group the outline and the fill are as follows:

1. Click the **Arrow** tool from the **Tools Panel**.
2. Click and drag to select both the outline and the fill.
3. Select **Group** option from the **Modify** menu.
4. If you want to ungroup the outline and the fill, select **Break Apart** from the **Modify** menu.

Quick Way

The shortcut key to group the objects is **Ctrl+G**. To break apart the grouped objects, the shortcut key is **Ctrl+B**.

Fig. 8.4: (a) Outline and Fill grouped together

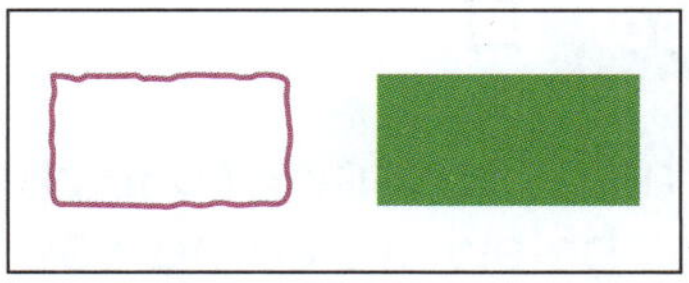

Fig. 8.4: (b) Outline and Fill ungrouped

EYEDROPPER TOOL

The **Eyedropper** tool is used to copy the outline and fill properties from one object and immediately paste them to another object. It is useful in situations where you have created your own custom colours and gradients for outline or fill colour. Instead of recreating them again, you would like to copy and then reuse them in multiple objects. You can pick up colours and style from the existing lines, strokes and fills and can then apply these colours and styles to other objects. You can pick up a colour from one object using the **Eyedropper** tool and fill this colour in another object using the **Paint Bucket** tool.

The steps to use the **Eyedropper** tool are as follows:

1. Select **Eyedropper** tool from the **Tools Panel**. The pointer changes to an eyedropper.
2. Click the outline or filled area whose properties you want to copy.
3. (i) If you click the stroke or outline, the tool automatically changes to an **Ink Bottle** tool.
   (ii) If you click the filled area, the tool automatically changes to a **Paint Bucket** tool with its **Lock Fill Modifier** turned on.
4. Click the line or fill where you want to apply the copied properties.

In the figure, the outline properties of the oval are copied using the **Eyedropper** tool and applied to the line in the adjacent figure.

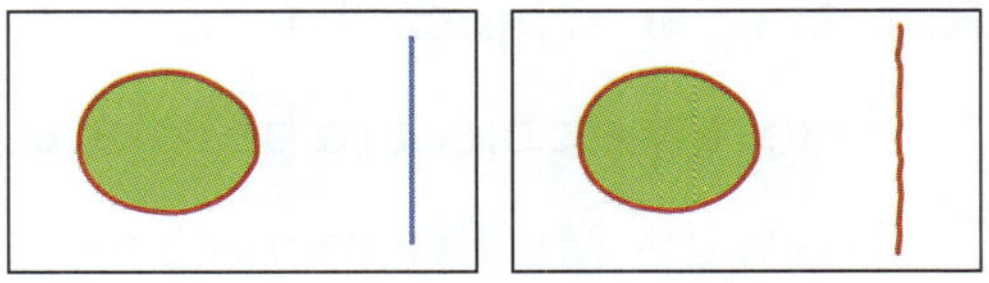

Fig. 8.5: Eyedropper tool

> **You Should Know**
>
> The **Eyedropper** tool also allows you to apply an image as a fill in combination with **Paint Bucket** tool.

TRANSFORMING OBJECTS

Transforming an object means to modify the object by changing its shape, size, colour, position and orientation on the Stage. If a gradient was applied to the object, you can change that too in different ways. In this section, you will learn various methods of transforming an object.

Free Transform Tool

Free Transform tool helps to move, scale, rotate, compress, stretch or skew an object on the Stage. In the steps below, we compress the drawing using the **Free Transform** tool.

1. Draw an object on the Stage. You can even import a picture if you wish to.
2. Select the object and click **Free Transform** tool.
3. Double-click on the object so as to select both outline and fill.
4. As you click on the object, you will see a **Central handle**, also called the **Transformation Point**, of the selected object in its centre.
5. As you move the pointer over different parts of the selection, it changes to indicate which transformation function is available. For example, to move the object, the pointer changes to a cross whereas to rotate an object, the pointer changes to a curved arrow.

> **Quick Way**
>
> The shortcut key to use Free Transform tool is **Q**.

Moving an Object: To move an object from one place to another on the Stage, follow the steps given below:

1. Select the object that you want to move.
2. When you position the pointer over the selected object, the pointer changes to a cross (×).
3. Click and drag the object to a new position and then release the left mouse button.

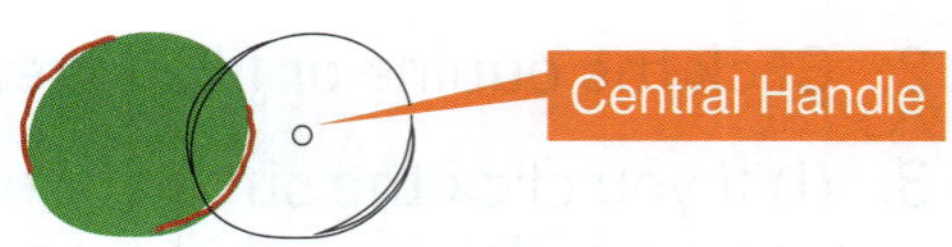

Fig. 8.6: Moving an object

Rotating an Object: The steps to rotate an object are as follows:

1. Select the object to be rotated.
2. From the **Modify** menu, select **Transform** option.
3. Select **Rotate and Skew** from the submenu.

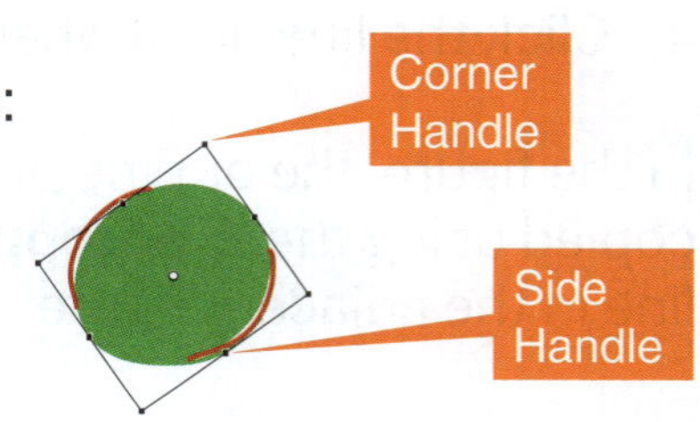

Fig. 8.7: Rotating an object

4. Click the corner handle of the object. A curved arrow called the **Rotation Handle** ( ) appears.
5. Drag this **Rotation Handle** by the desired angle to rotate the object. You will see the outline of the object as you rotate.
6. To end the rotation, release the mouse button and click anywhere outside the selected object.

Quick Way

To rotate a selected object, select the Free Transform tool and position the mouse pointer on any of the four corner handles. When the pointer changes to a curved arrow, click and drag to rotate the object.

Flipping an Object: Flipping an object means to invert it either horizontally or vertically. The steps to flip an object are as follows:

1. Select the object that you want to flip.
2. Select **Transform** from **Modify** menu.
3. Select **Flip Vertical** or **Flip Horizontal**. Accordingly, the selected object will be flipped.

Fig. 8.8 (a): Original image

Fig. 8.8 (b): Flipped image

In the figure, the image on the left is flipped horizontally. Notice the flipped image in Fig. 8.8 (b).

Scaling an Object: Scaling an object means to change the size of the object. To scale the selected object, click on its corner handles and drag it diagonally or horizontally in the desired direction. Release the mouse button when the desired size is obtained.

You Should Know

The Free Transform tool cannot transform symbols.

GRADIENTS

A gradient is a multicoloured fill in which one colour slowly changes to another. These gradients can be used to fill closed objects on the Stage.

Creating a New Gradient

Flash allows you to create two types of gradients—**Linear** and **Radial**. A linear gradient changes colour from the starting point to the end point in a straight line whereas in a radial gradient the change of colour is in the outward direction, in concentric circles, starting from the central point. The figure shows linear and radial gradients.

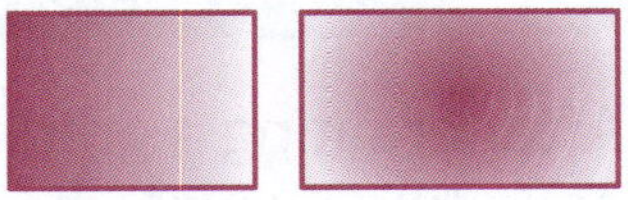

Fig. 8.9: Linear and Radial Gradients

To create a new gradient, follow the steps given below:

1. Select an object on the Stage.
2. Select **Color Mixer** option from the **Window** menu. The **Color Mixer Panel** is displayed on the top right corner of the Flash window.

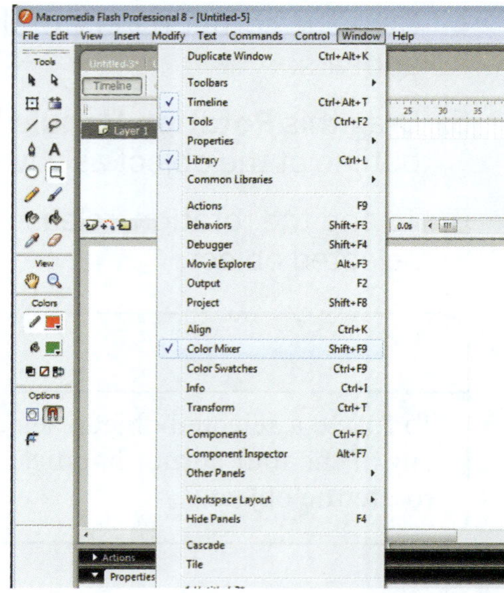

Fig. 8.10: Window menu

Quick Way
The shortcut key to open the Color Mixer is **Shift+F9**.

3. Click the drop-down arrow of the **Type** list box and choose either of the gradients — Linear or Radial.
4. Click and drag the **Left Color Marker** and **Right Color Marker** to choose the desired colours. You will see that the change of colour is reflected in the selected object also. A new gradient has been created.

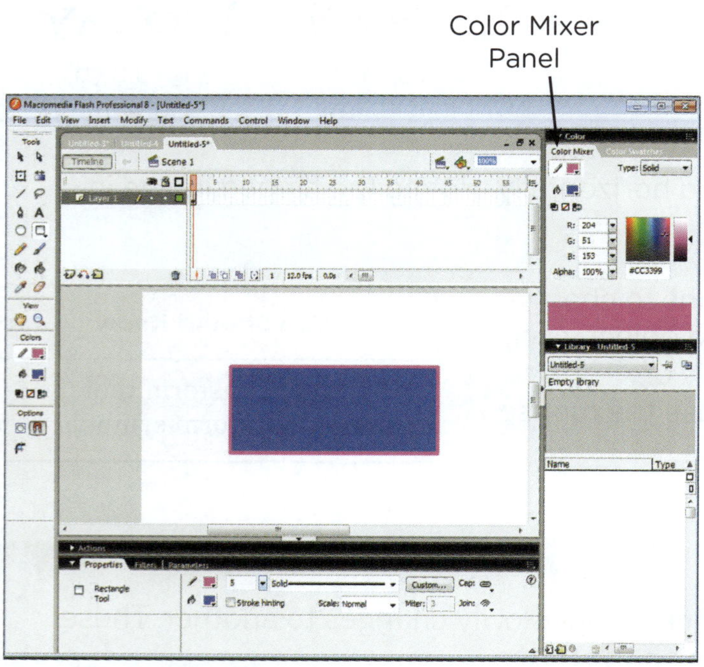

Fig. 8.11: Color Mixer option

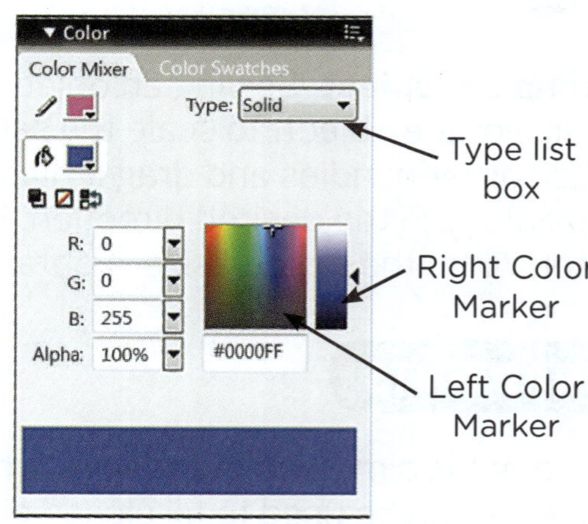

Fig. 8.12: Color Mixer Panel

Gradient Transform Tool

After creating a gradient, Flash 8 gives the option to transform the applied gradient by adjusting its size, direction, rotation or center. To modify the gradient fill of an object, first select the **Gradient Transform** tool. Then, click inside the object that has gradient as fill. The transformation of linear and radial gradient is discussed below.

Linear Gradient: See the figure showing linear gradient. The two vertical lines on either side of the object indicate the direction of the fill. The line on the right has a **Gradient Rotate Handle** (◌) and a **Width Adjustment Handle** (←→).

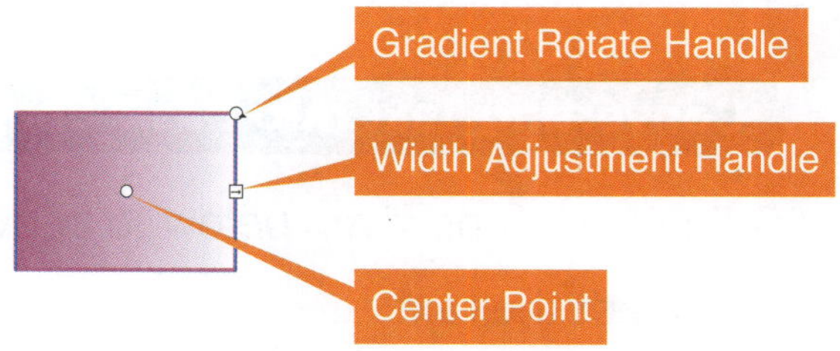

Fig. 8.13: Linear fill with handles

The gradient fill can be changed in the following ways:

(a) The **center point** of the gradient is the point where the colour mixing is in equal proportion. To change the center point of the gradient fill, bring the mouse pointer above the center point. When the cursor changes to a four arrow cursor (✛), click and drag the center point.

(b) To change the width of the gradient fill, position the mouse pointer over the **Width Adjustment Handle**. The pointer will change to a double-headed arrow (←→). Drag the adjustment handle to left or right in order to increase or decrease the gradient width. You will see that there is no change in the size of the object. Only the gradient is resized.

Fig. 8.14: Changing the width of the gradient

(c) To rotate the gradient fill, position the pointer over the **Rotation Handle** (◌). The pointer changes to (◌). Now drag the **Rotation Handle** clockwise or anticlockwise by the desired angle.

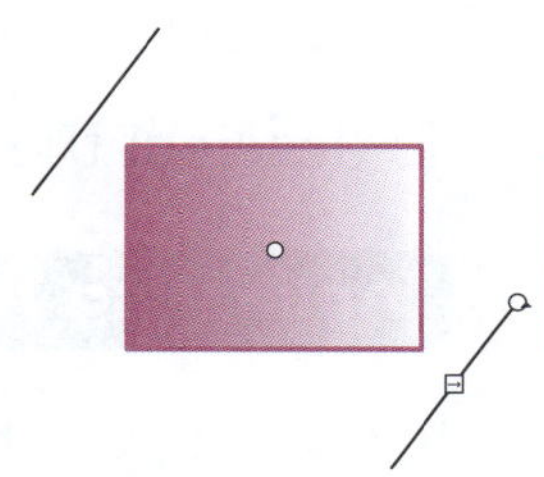

Fig. 8.15: Rotating the gradient fill

Radial Gradient: Select the **Gradient Transform** tool and click on an object filled with a radial gradient. An ellipse appears around the selected object as shown below:

You can perform any one or all of the following actions:

(a) Drag the **Center Point** to adjust the center of the gradient.
(b) Drag the **Adjustment Handle** to increase or decrease the radius of the gradient.
(c) Drag the **Diagonal Resize Handle** to change the gradient size proportionately.
(d) Drag the **Rotation Handle** clockwise or anticlockwise to rotate the gradient at the desired angle.

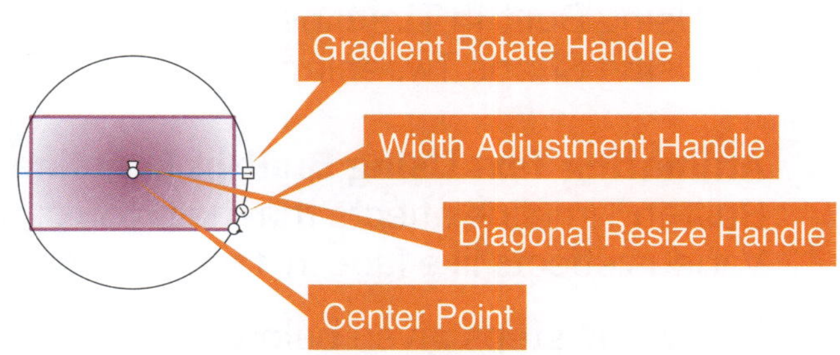

Fig. 8.16: Radial Gradient

WORKING WITH TEXT IN FLASH

You have already learnt about the text tool in Class 6 which is used for inserting text on the Stage. You applied formatting effects like font colour, size and style to the entered text. After the text has been added to the Stage, various text effects can be applied but before you animate text or reshape a text character, you need to first convert the text into a basic shape. After this, you can use the Selection tool to reshape it. You can even fill characters with gradients.

You Should Know

Once you have converted a text character into a shape, you cannot edit it as text.

Converting Text Into Basic Shapes

Follow the steps given below to convert the text into a basic shape:

1. Select the text.
2. Select **Break Apart** option from the **Modify** menu. You will see that a single text block is broken into multiple text blocks and each character has its own separate text block.

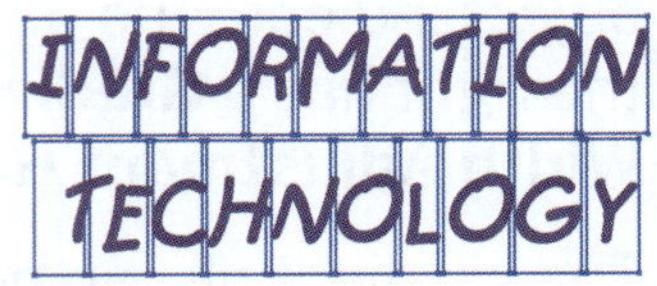

Fig. 8.17: Broken text

3. Again select **Break Apart** from the **Modify** menu. Now, the characters can no longer be considered as text. So, no text formatting effects, that is, font colour, size, style, etc. can be applied. Each individual character is independent. You can resize or reshape these shapes like any other shape by moving the pointer to the edge of any character and dragging it. You can even fill colour or gradient into this reshaped character with another colour/gradient using the **Paint Bucket** tool. For example, the alphabet I and Y have been formatted as shown in the figure.

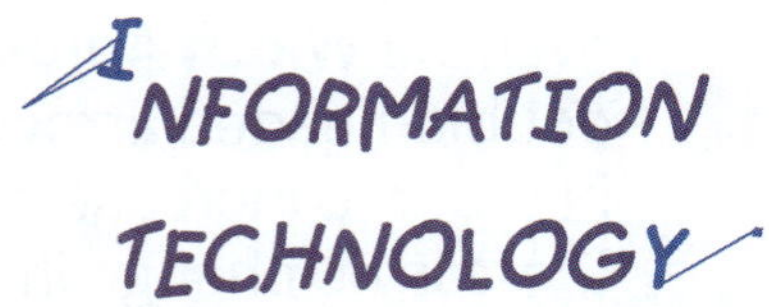

Fig. 8.18: Text converted to basic shapes

To deselect the shapes, click outside the converted text block.

Animating Text

In Class 6, you had animated text using frame-by-frame animation. In that process, each character was added in a different frame. In this chapter, you will animate text using two new methods:

- Using Built-in Timeline Effects
- Using Shape Tweening

Animating Text Using Built-in Timeline Effects: Flash 8 provides you the option to use Built-in Timeline effects that help you create animations by selecting just a few options. Various effects like fade in, fade out, explode, etc. can be applied using this feature of Flash 8.

Follow the steps given below to understand how to do this:

1. On a new Flash document, click **Text** tool.
2. Type any word, say ANIMATIONS@@@ on the Stage.
3. Right click the text and select **Timeline Effects** from the **drop-down** menu.
4. From the **Effects** submenu, choose the desired effect, say **Blur**.
5. The **Blur** dialog box appears. The dialog box shows the preview of the selected animation with default settings like Effect Duration, Resolution, Scale, etc. You can change the settings if you want and then click **OK**. The Timeline window will now show frames and animations.

6. Save the file and press the **Enter** key to play the movie.

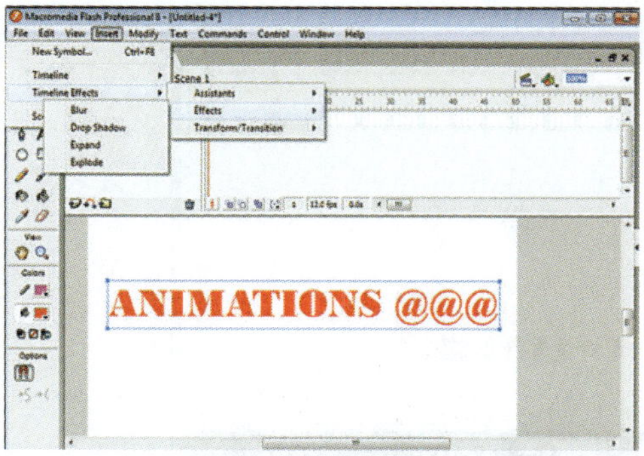

Fig. 8.19: Timeline Effects Option

Fig. 8.20: Blur dialog box

> **Quick Way**
>
> Press **Ctrl+Enter** to preview the animation in a separate window.

Animating Text Using Shape Tweening: This is another method to animate text. Follow the steps given below to apply shape tweening to the selected text:

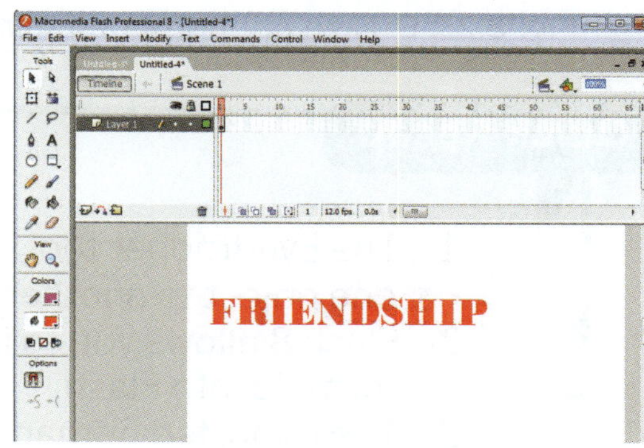

Fig. 8.21: Text in frame 1

1. Open a new Flash document.
2. Select Frame 1. Use the **Text** tool to write FRIENDSHIP.
3. Click the **Arrow** tool in the **Tools Panel**.
4. Select the text and choose **Break Apart** option from the **Modify** menu.
5. Again select **Break Apart** from the **Modify** menu.
6. Select frame 55 and insert a keyframe by pressing F6.
7. Delete the old text.
8. Select **Text** tool and type IS LIFE. You can apply the desired font colour, size and style to the text.
9. With frame 55 still selected, click the **Arrow** tool and select the latest typed text.
10. Select **Break Apart** from the **Modify** menu twice.
11. Select any frame between frame 1 and frame 55.
12. From the **Property Inspector** window, click the arrow next to **Tween** option. From the drop-down menu select **Shape**.

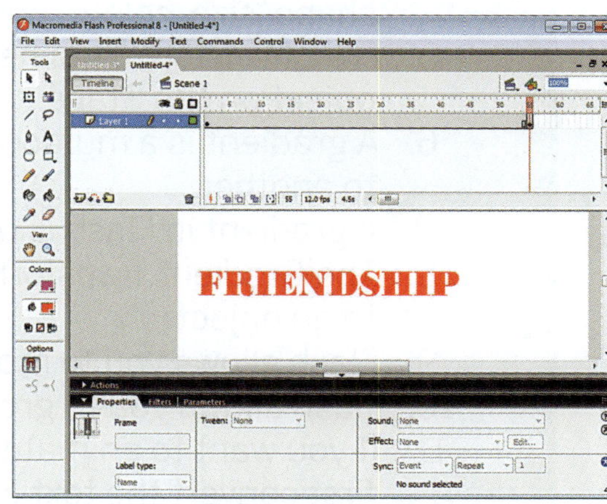

Fig. 8.22: Keyframe at frame 55

> **You Should Know**
>
> Before playing the movie, make sure that Frame 1 is selected.

13. Save the file and press **Enter** to play the movie.

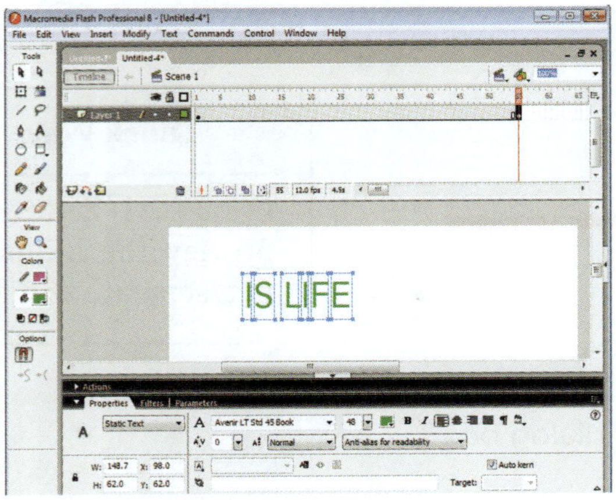

Fig. 8.23: Broken or ungrouped text

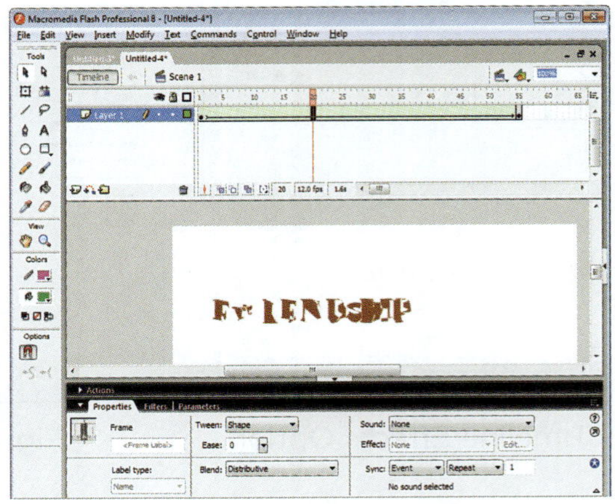

Fig. 8.24: Animated text with Shape Tweening

Quick Recap

1. The Eyedropper tool is used to copy the fill and outline properties from one object to another.
2. Flash 8 allows you to import JPEG, GIF, PNG and various other file formats into Flash.
3. The imported bitmap images are added to the Flash library as assets.
4. Transforming an object means to modify the object by changing its shape, size, colour, position and orientation on the Stage.
5. Free Transform tool helps to scale, rotate, compress, stretch or skew an object on the Stage.
6. A gradient is a multicoloured fill in which one colour slowly changes to another.
7. A gradient in Flash is of two types—linear and radial.
8. The Gradient Transform tool is used to transform the gradient applied to an object.
9. Flash allows you to modify the properties of an instance.
10. Flash allows you to group and ungroup outline and fill of an object.
11. If you want to animate text or reshape a text character, you have to first convert the text into basic shape. Then you can animate text using Built-in Timeline options or Shape Tweening.

EXERCISE

A Choose the correct option for each of the following.

1. Which of the following is considered as transforming an object?

   (a) Rotation (b) Flipping (c) Moving (d) All the above

2. Which of the following menu items contains the Transform option?
   (a) Modify (b) Window (c) File (d) Image
3. Which of the following tools is used to edit the gradient?
   (a) Gradient (b) Transform (c) Gradient Transform (d) None of the above
4. What is the shortcut key to ungroup selected objects?
   (a) Ctrl+G (b) Ctrl+B (c) Alt+G (d) Alt+B
5. Which of the following file formats can be imported into Flash?
   (a) *.jpeg* (b) *.gif* (c) *.png* (d) All of the above

B Fill in the blanks using the words given below.

Scaling Rotation Handle assets Ink Bottle transformation point

1. If you copy the outline using an Eyedropper tool, the tool automatically changes to an ________ tool.
2. The imported images are added to the Flash library as ________ .
3. ________ an object means to change the size of the object.
4. The central handle of the selected object is also called ________ .
5. You will drag the ________ in clockwise or anticlockwise direction to rotate a gradient fill.

C State whether the following statements are true (T) or false (F).

1. An Eyedropper tool is used to copy properties of one object to another. ☐
2. An asset cannot be converted into a symbol. ☐
3. Scaling an object means to change the size of the object. ☐
4. You cannot modify the instance of a symbol in Flash. ☐
5. If you want to animate text or reshape a text character, you have to first convert the text into basic shape. ☐

D Give one word for each of the following.

1. It helps to scale, rotate or skew an object on the Stage. ________
2. A multicolour fill. ________
3. This tool helps to copy a fill and is used along with the Eyedropper tool. ________
4. It is a type of gradient in concentric circles. ________
5. Shortcut to group the selected objects. ________

E Answer the following questions.

1. In which situations is an Eyedropper tool used?
2. Write the steps to import an image into Flash. Assume that the name of the file is *image.jpeg* and is stored in C:\Desktop.
3. What is a gradient? How is linear gradient different from a radial gradient?
4. Write the steps to group the outline and fill of an object. Why is it required?
5. Write the steps to convert text into basic shapes.

FA

Lab Activity

1. Somil wants to import a picture *flower.jpeg* into Flash but does not know how to do the task. Give him the steps to complete his task.
2. Gaurangi is fond of jewellery designing. She has saved a symbol of a ring in the Flash library. She wants to change the colour and brightness of the symbol. Help her to complete the task.
3. Prabhnoor wants to write the names of his five friends, convert the text into symbols and then animate them using Timeline effects. Help him to complete the task.
4. Saumya, a teacher in a playschool, wants that when she narrates a nursery rhyme in the class the lyrics should be projected on the screen of the interactive board. Take any nursery rhyme and animate the text using Shape Tweening.

FA

Research Project

Write a short poem on yourself and then apply various animation effects to it. Explore different aspects of Shape Tweening.

Teacher's Notes

(a) Discuss all the tools of the Tools Panel and their uses.
(b) Demonstrate to the students how to apply animations to text using Timeline Effects and Shape Tweening. The teacher may first demonstrate frame-by-frame animations that the students had studied in Class 6.

9 Animations with Layers

Learning Objectives

By the end of this chapter you should be able to

- use Timeline.
- use layers in Flash 8.
- create an animation using Motion Tween and Shape Tween.
- use Onion Skin tools.
- use the Masking feature in Flash.
- use the Motion Guide.
- use filters in Flash.

Introduction

In Class 6, you have learnt to create some basic animations.

You animated an object using Frame-by-Frame animation, Motion Tweening and Shape Tweening.

This chapter will introduce you to a new concept of layers and then apply animation effects to objects in different layers.

TIMELINE

In a Flash window, **Timeline** is a fixed pane above the workspace where you actually work with frames. The objects in various frames are controlled, sequenced and organized through the Timeline to form an animated movie. The figure below shows various parts of a Timeline.

You are familiar with all the parts of the Timeline. Let us have a quick glance at its main components.

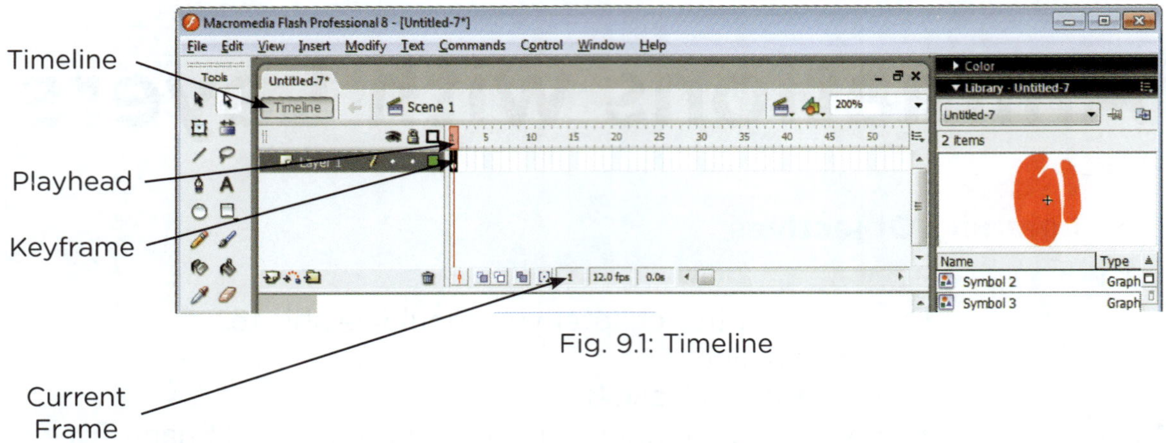

Fig. 9.1: Timeline

Playhead: It is the red rectangle with a red vertical line. It is always on the current frame and so indicates the current status of the movie.

Frames: These are represented as a series of vertical rectangles on top of the Timeline. Every fifth frame has light grey fill and is marked with a frame number, which is written at the top of the Timeline. To insert a frame in your movie, press **F5**.

Current Frame: It is the textbox that gives the current frame number.

Keyframe: Frames with black dots are keyframes. A keyframe is a critical point in the animation. It is the point where any change in the object is reflected. To insert a keyframe, press **F6**.

LAYERS IN FLASH 8

In Macromedia Flash 8, layers are analogous to transparent sheets placed on top of each other. These layers hold objects on them. The distribution of multiple objects in different layers helps in better organization of the content, especially in large animated movies. For example, you can keep a set of backgrounds in one layer, animated cartoon characters of the movie in another layer and text content on a separate layer.

In the areas of a layer that do not contain any object or content on them, you can see through the content in the layers below. You can set the order of layers to set the order of objects in a movie. You can draw, import, edit and animate objects in one layer without affecting the objects on another layer.

Each movie contains a single layer by default. Flash 8 allows you to add multiple layers. Each layer has its own row of frames and keyframes. You can hide, unhide, lock, rearrange, delete and even customize these layers as per your convenience.

The figure shows the Timeline with layers.

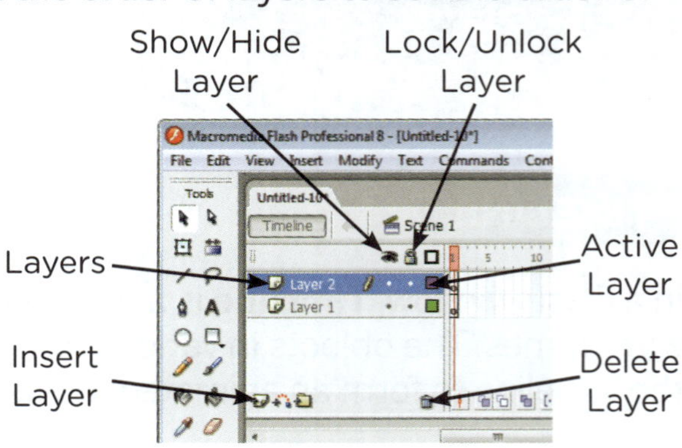

Fig. 9.2: Timeline with layers

Let us have a look at some basic operations with layers.

Inserting a Layer: Follow the steps given below to insert a layer:

1. Click **Insert** menu and select **Timeline** option.
2. From the submenu, select **Layer**. A new layer will be inserted on top of the previous layer.

Quick Way

To insert a new layer, click the **Insert Layer** button at the bottom left of the **Timeline**.

Renaming a Layer: If the layers in your movie have relevant names, it is easy to manage and remember them. To rename a layer, double-click on the layer name. The cursor will appear. Type the new name and press the **Enter** key.

Selecting a Layer: By selecting a particular layer, you are making that layer active. Just click on the layer name and the desired layer will be active and highlighted in the Timeline. The active layer is indicated with a **pencil** icon.

Deleting a Layer: To delete a layer, select the layer and click the **Delete Layer** button on the bottom left of the Timeline. Once the layer is deleted, all objects on that layer are also automatically deleted.

Rearranging Layers: The layers in Flash 8 can be rearranged, that is, the order in which they are arranged can be altered. To do so, click on the name of the layer and drag it to the required position.

Hide and Show Layers: Hiding a layer helps you to view the contents on other layers. Flash gives you the option to hide layers individually and also to hide all layers of the movie at one go. Follow the steps given below to hide/unhide the layers:

1. Click the **Eye button** ()above the layer names in the Timeline. A **Red Cross** () appears in front of the layer name. You will see that none of the objects of the hidden layer are visible on the Stage.
2. To unhide a layer, click on the **Red Cross** () in front of the layer name. The objects of that layer will be visible again on the Stage.

Lock a Layer: When a layer is locked, no modifications to the objects of that particular layer can be done. A layer can be locked by clicking on the **black dot** under the **Lock** button ().

You Should Know

The **Layer Properties** dialog box provides you with the options to set various properties of the layers like name, type, colour, etc. To open the **Layer Properties** dialog box, select the Timeline option from the **Modify** menu. Thereafter, select **Layer Properties** from the submenu.

CREATING ANIMATIONS USING MOTION TWEENING AND SHAPE TWEENING

Let us now apply animation effects using both motion tweening and shape tweening. In the example given below, two layers are used to create an animated movie. On one layer, shape tweening is applied while on the other layer motion tweening is applied.

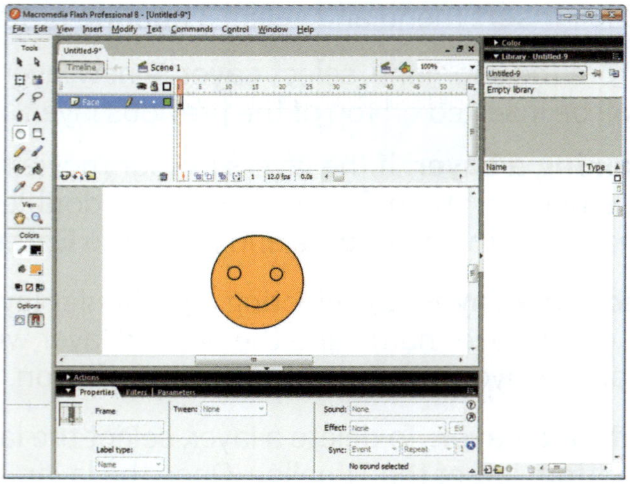

Fig. 9.3: Happy face

1. Open a new Flash document.
2. The new document has by default a single layer named **Layer1**. Double-click on this layer to rename it with a suitable name, say *Face*.
3. Click Frame 1. Select the **Oval** tool. Set the **Fill Color** to orange and draw a happy face as shown in the figure.
4. Insert a new layer by clicking the **Insert Layer** button. Rename this layer as *Snake*.
5. Click Frame 1 of the *Snake* layer. Draw a snake at the bottom right of the Stage using the **Brush** tool as shown in the figure.

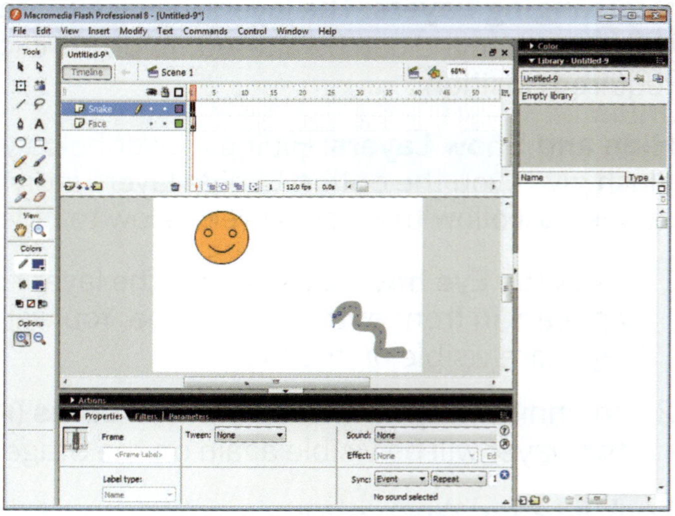

Fig. 9.4: Snake

6. Click Frame 50 of the *Face* layer. Press **F6** to insert a keyframe.
7. Staying on Frame 50 of the *Face* layer, change the shape of the object using the **Arrow** tool. You also have the option of deleting the object and creating a new one. You can change any property of the object from the **Property Inspector** window. In our example, we have made a sad face.
8. To create a shape tween in the *Face* layer, select any frame between Frame 1 and Frame 50. In the **Property Inspector** window, click the arrow next to **Tween** list box and select the **Shape** option.
9. Click the *Snake* layer to make it active. Select Frame 50 of this layer and press **F6** to insert a keyframe.

10. To create a motion tween in this layer, staying on Frame 50, use the **Free Transform** tool to move the snake near the face, that is, to the top left corner of the Stage. Select any frame between Frame 1 and Frame 50 of this layer. Right click on the timeline and select **Create Motion Tween** option from the drop-down menu.
11. Save the movie as *facesnake.fla*.
12. Press **Enter** key to play the movie.

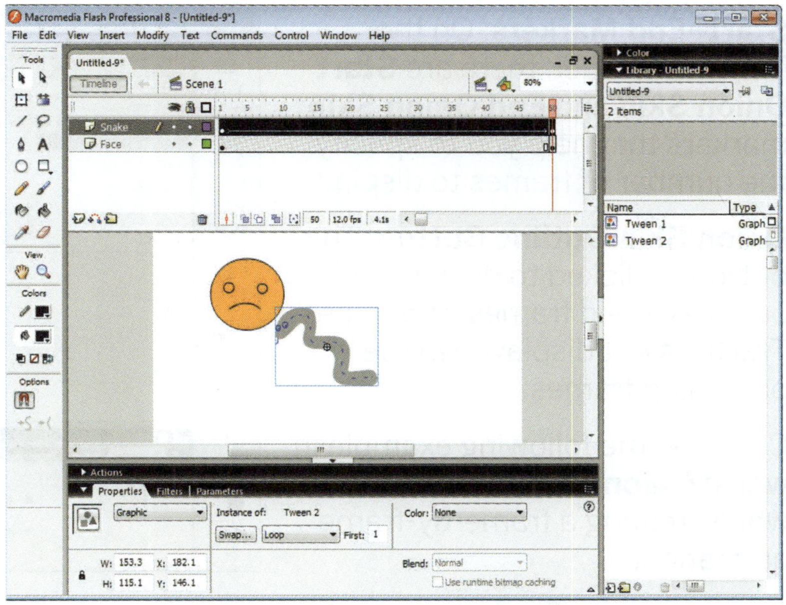

Fig. 9.5: Stage and Property Inspector

ONION SKIN TOOLS

The **Onion Skin** tools provide you with the **Onion Skin** feature of Flash 8. This feature allows you to see the position of an object over several successive frames. It helps you to compare the previous and the next frames and accordingly adjust the objects in the current frame. This feature gives the best effect in frame-by-frame animation.

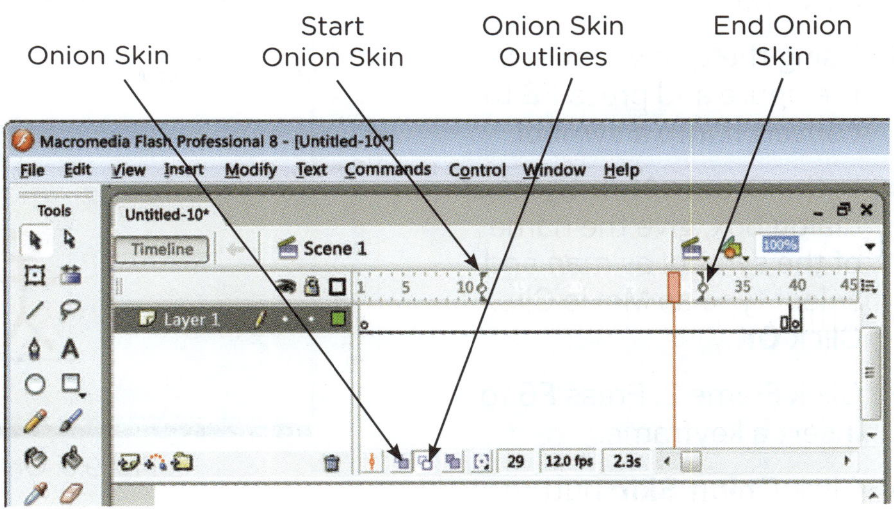

Fig. 9.6: Onion Skin tools

The set of **Onion Skin** tools is at the bottom of the Timeline as shown in the figure.

By default, the **Onion Skin** feature is turned off and one frame of animation sequence appears on the Stage at a particular time. The frame so displayed is corresponding to the position of Playhead in the Timeline. To apply the **Onion Skin** feature in your movie, you should know the following tools:

Onion Skin Button: Click the **Onion Skin** button to enable the **Onion Skin** feature. Now you will be able to view multiple frames on the Stage at one particular time. The frame under the Playhead then appears in dark colour while the surrounding frames are in lighter colour.

Start–End Markers: On the Timeline header, there are **Start Onion Skin** and **End Onion Skin** markers that help you to specify the number of frames to display.

Onion Skin Outline Button: This button is clicked to display only onion-skinned frames as outlines. The fill is not displayed in the preceding frames.

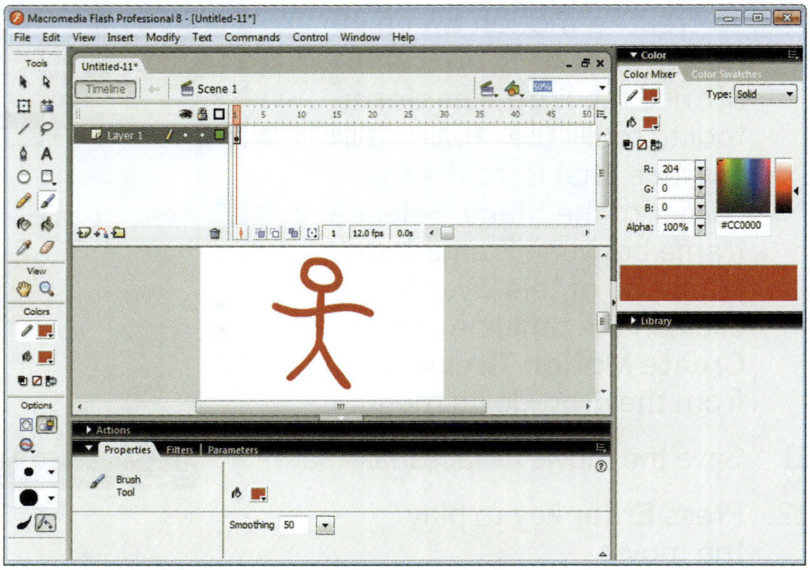

Fig. 9.7: Using Onion Skin tools

Consider the following example in which **Onion Skin** feature is used while creating a frame-by-frame animation:

1. Open a new Flash document.
2. Create the figure on the Stage using the **Brush** tool as shown.
3. Using the arrow tool, select the figure and press **F8** to convert it into a symbol.
4. In the **Create New Symbol** dialog box, give the name of the symbol as *man* and select type as Movie Clip. Click **OK**.
5. Click Frame 2. Press **F6** to insert a keyframe.

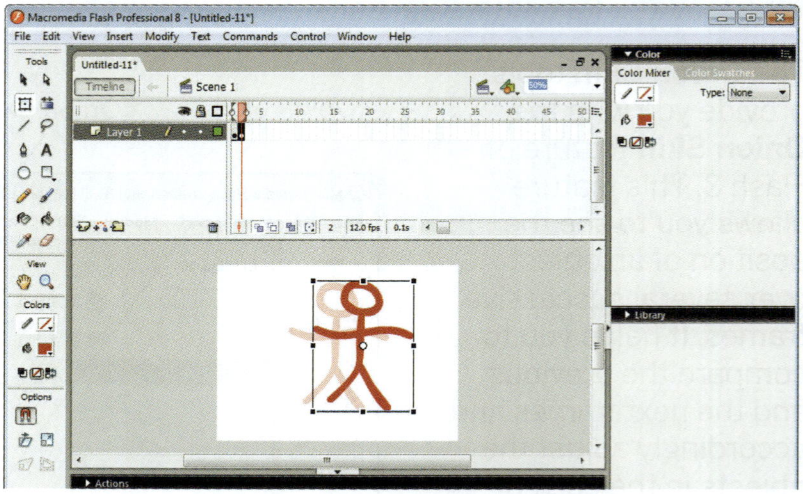

Fig. 9.8: Onion Skin feature

6. Click **Onion Skin** button to enable the Onion Skin feature. Now, if you try to change the object on the Stage, you will see the traces of the last frame. This will help to position the object in the current frame in a better way. Click the **Free Transform** tool and drag the position of the object a little towards right of the Stage. Also, press F6 after inserting each new frame to make all of the frames as keyframes.
7. Click all frames till Frame 10 and repeat the process given in Step 6.
8. Click and drag the **Start–End markers** to set the number of frames that you want to see in the Onion Skin mode.
9. Save the file and press **Enter** to view the animation.

Fig. 9.9: Start and End markers

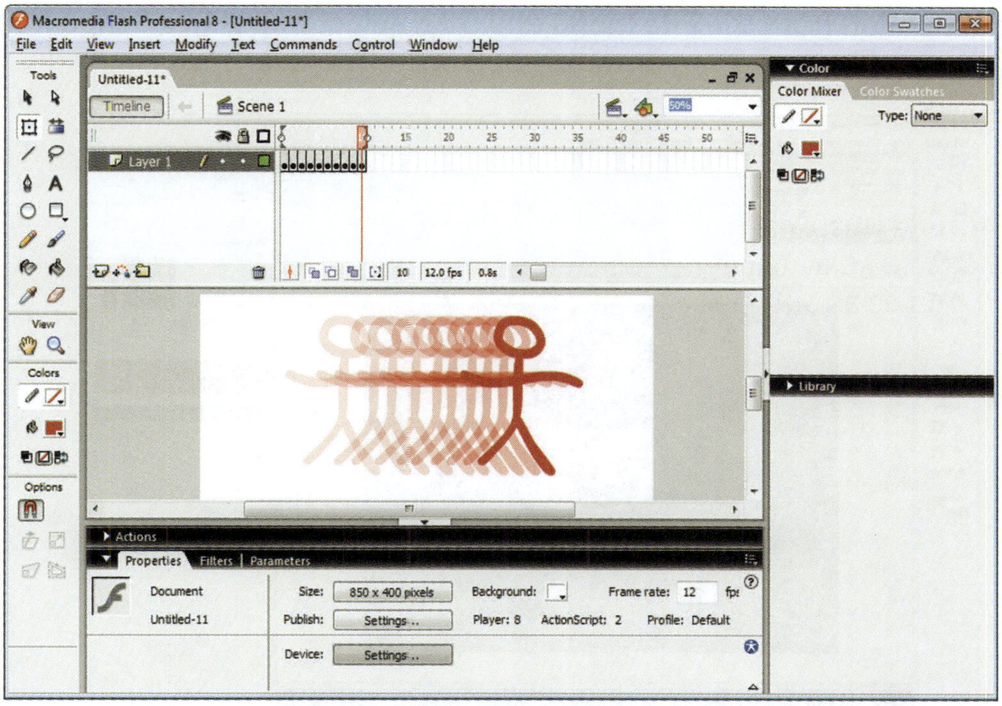

Fig. 9.10: Onion Skin tool applied to the object on the Stage

MASKING FEATURE IN FLASH

Masking is a special feature of Flash using which you can selectively block areas of a layer. These blocked areas are not visible in the movie. So, you can use masking to hide objects under mask. The mask acts as a hole or a window through which you can see the contents of the underlying layer. The rest of the mask layer hides everything. This feature is particularly useful in creating spotlight effects or magnifying glass effects.

Creating a Masked Layer

Follow the steps given below to create an animation by masking:

1. Open a new Flash document. By default, it has a single layer with the name **Layer 1**.
2. Double-click on Layer 1 and change the name of the layer to *winner*.
3. In the **Properties Inspector** window, click the arrow next to **Background** and select dark blue colour from the color palette.

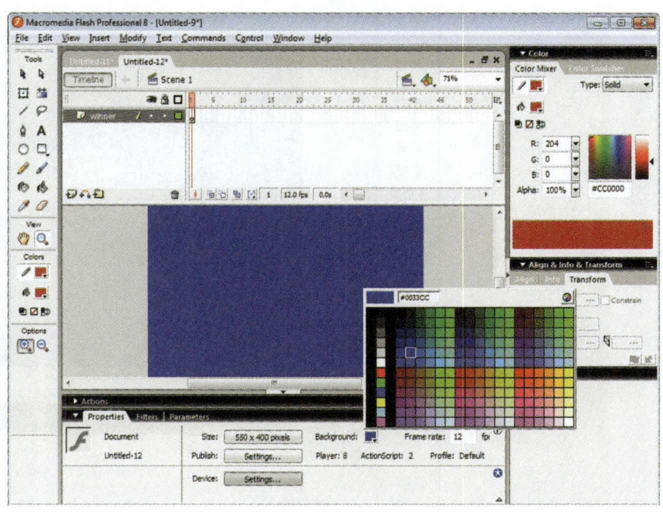

Fig. 9.11: Background colour selection from Property Inspector

4. Select **Import** option from the **File** menu and then select **Import to Stage** from the sub-menu. Alternatively, you can draw any object on this layer.

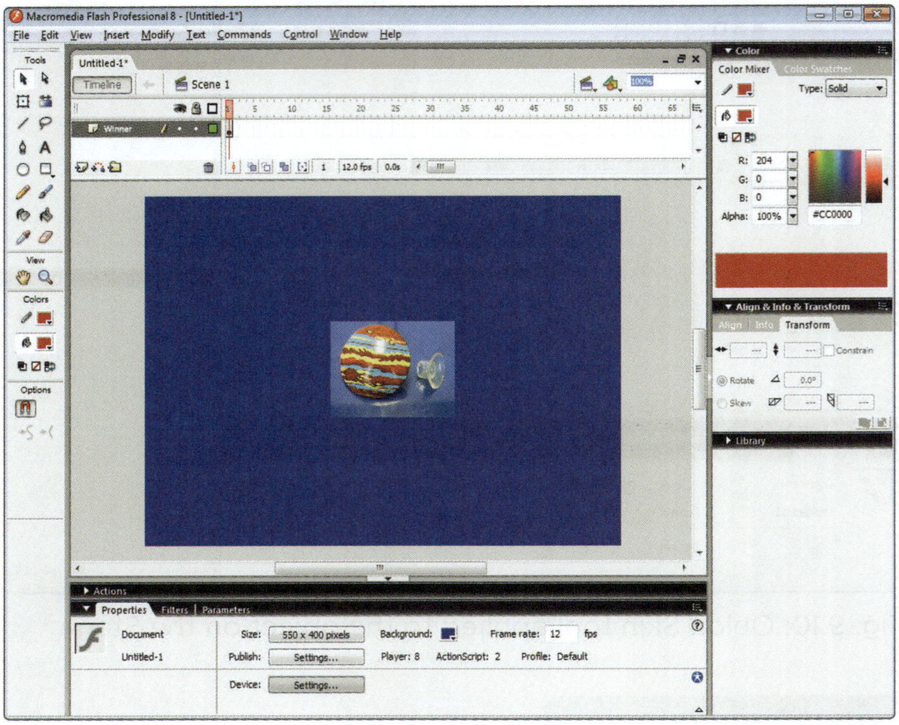

Fig. 9.12: Image on Layer 1

5. Click **Insert Layer** button to add a new layer.
6. Double-click on this layer and rename it as *curtain*.

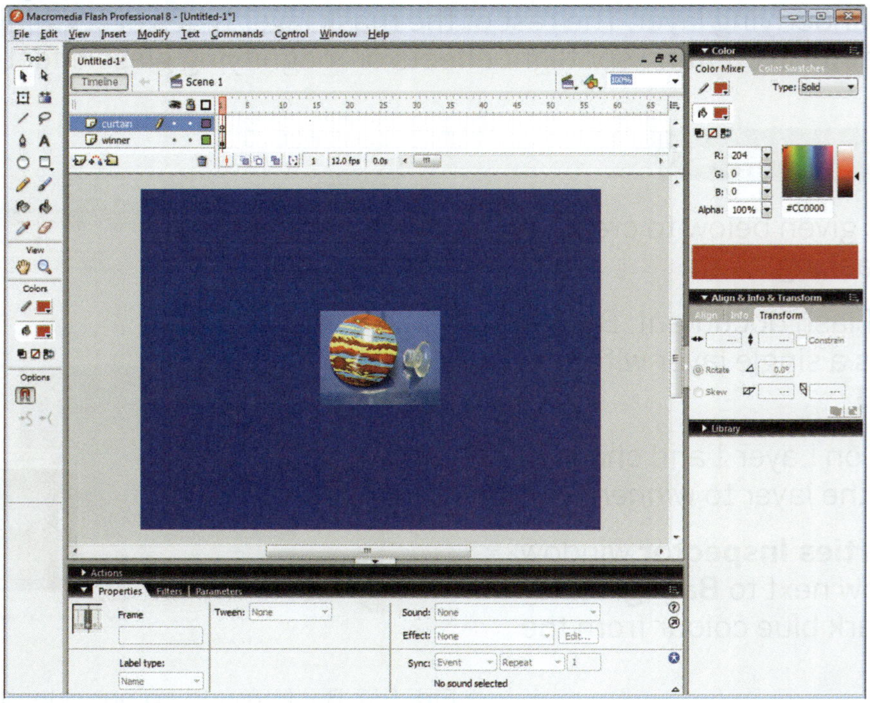

Fig. 9.13: Layer 2 inserted

7. Click Frame 1 of *curtain* layer. Draw an oval at the left side of the Stage using the **Oval** tool. The oval should be slightly bigger than the picture on the Stage.

8. Click Frame 40 of Layer 1, that is, *winner* and press **F6** to insert a keyframe.

9. Similarly, click Frame 40 of Layer 2, that is, *curtain* and press **F6** to make it a keyframe.

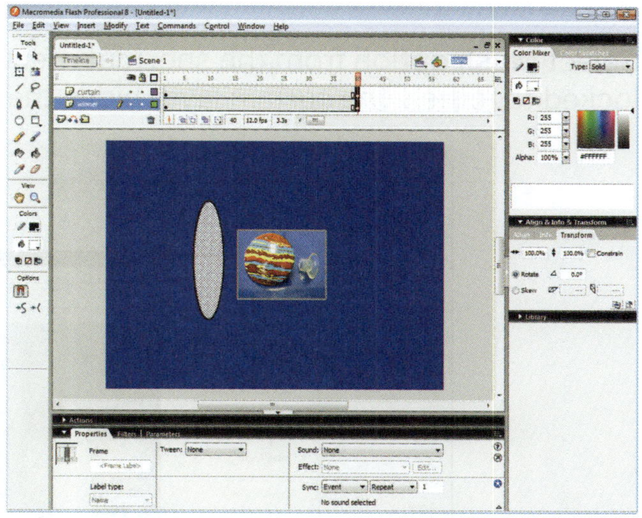

Fig. 9.14: Oval inserted in Frame 1

10. With the *curtain* layer selected, drag the oval to the right end of the Stage.

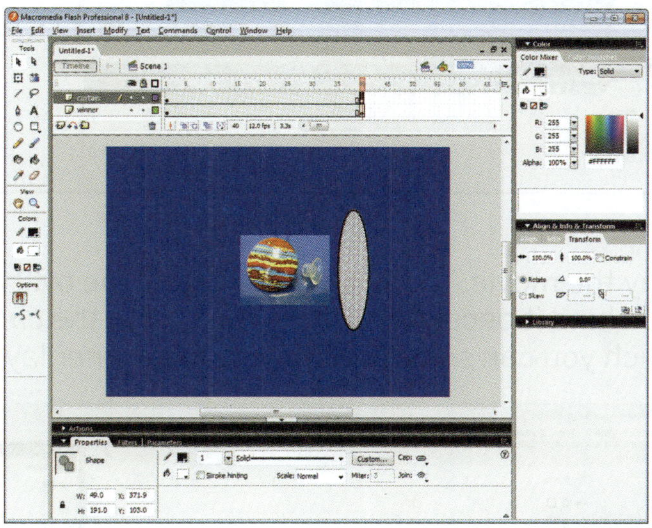

Fig. 9.15: Oval at the right end of the Stage

11. To create motion tween in the *curtain* layer, click any frame between Frame 1 and Frame 40. Right click and choose **Create Motion Tween** option.

12. Right click on the layer name that is to be masked, that is, *curtain* layer.

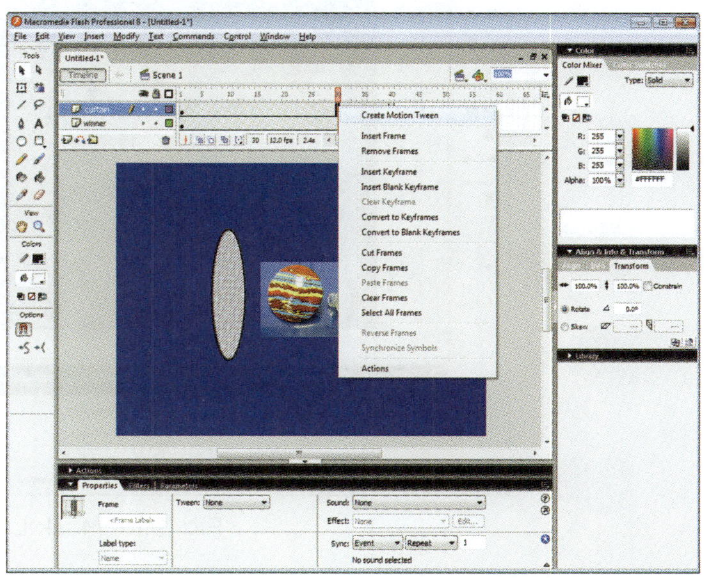

Fig. 9.16: Create Motion Tween option

13. Select **Mask** option from the shortcut menu. The *winner* and *curtain* layers are now locked together. The *curtain* layer hides the *winner* layer.

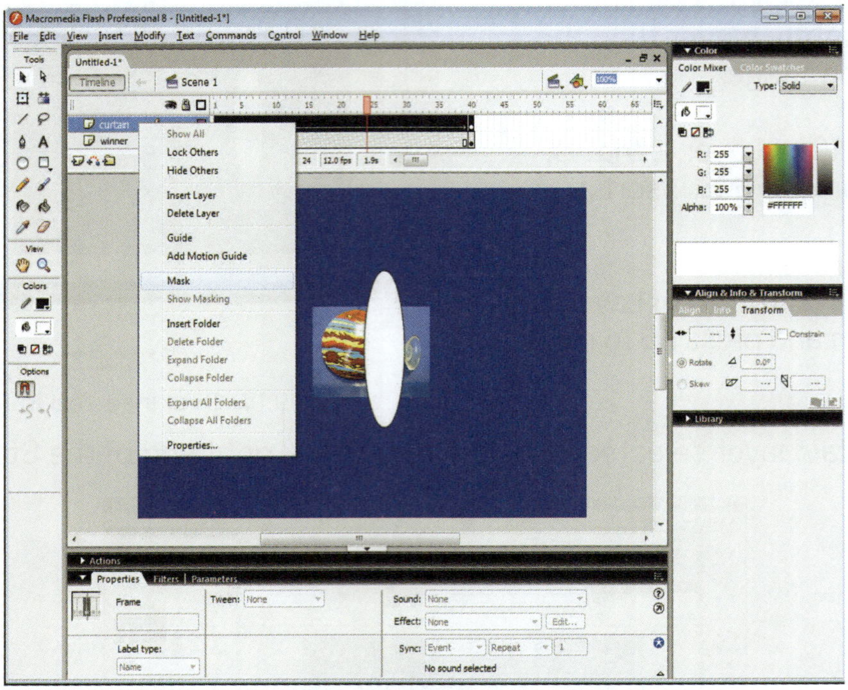

Fig. 9.17: Mask option

14. Save the file and play the movie. You will notice that as the oval moves across the screen, the picture behind it becomes visible. The oval in the *curtain* layer acts like a window through which you can see the picture of the *winner* layer.

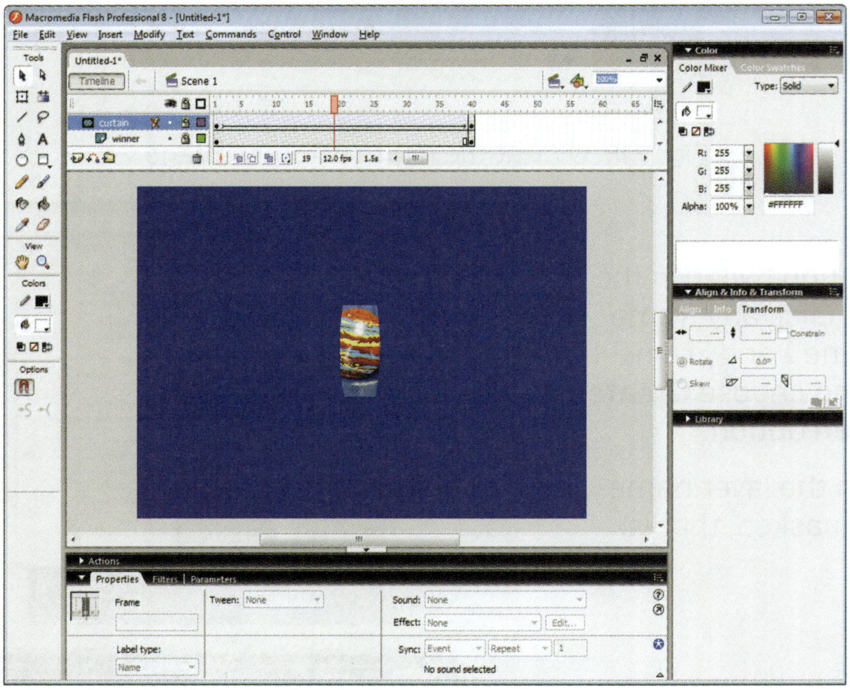

Fig. 9.18: Mask Layer

Practice Time 1

Anuj has recently learnt masking in class. He wants to create an animation to reveal text on the Stage through masking. Help him to complete the task.

SOLUTION

1. Create a new Flash document.
2. Select the **Text** tool. Change the font properties of the text as desired in the **Property Inspector** window.
3. Click on Frame 1 on Layer 1 and type the text, ***INCREDIBLE INDIA***.
4. Double-click on Layer 1 and rename it as *text*.
5. Click on Frame 30 on the same layer and press **F6** to insert a keyframe.
6. Click **Insert Layer** button at the bottom of the **Timeline**. A new layer is inserted. Double-click and rename it to *mask*.
7. Click on Frame 1 of the *mask* layer.
8. Using the **Rectangle** tool, draw a rectangle on the left side of the Stage. The rectangle should be slightly larger than the text.
9. Click on Frame 30 on the *mask* layer and press **F6** to insert the keyframe.
10. Using the **Free Transform** tool, drag the rectangle towards the right end of the Stage.
11. Right click on any frame between Frame 1 and Frame 30 on the *mask* layer. Choose **Create Motion Tween** option from the shortcut menu.
12. To create the mask, right click on the mask layer. Select **Mask** from the shortcut menu.
13. Save the file and press **Enter** to play the movie.

MOTION GUIDES

In the previous sections, when you created motion tween animations, the object used to move along a straight line. Motion guide is a feature in Flash 8 that is similar to motion tween but in this case, the object can be animated along a definite hand-drawn path. This path is called **guide layer**. This is the path along which an object moves. Follow the steps given below to create an animation using motion guide.

1. Open a new Flash document.
2. Double-click on **Layer 1** and rename it as *ball*.
3. Click **Oval** tool from **Tools Panel** and draw a ball on the top left corner of the Stage. You can choose the colour of the ball from the **Properties Inspector** window.
4. Right click on Frame 1 and select **Create Motion Tween** option.
5. Click Frame 30 and press **F6** to insert a keyframe.

6. Click **Add Motion Guide** button in the Timeline window. You will see that a motion guide layer named *ball* is created above the *ball* layer.

7. With the guide layer selected, click **Pencil** tool and draw the path for the ball to move on the Stage.

8. Select *ball* layer. Click any frame between 1 and 30.

9. Click **Snap** checkbox in **Property Inspector**, if it is not enabled. Now, the registration point of the object will be snapped to the motion path.

10. With the *ball* layer still selected, click Frame 1.

11. Place the *ball* on the path in such a manner that the registration point of the ball is exactly above the start of the path.

12. Click Frame 30 of the *ball* layer.

13. Place the *ball* such that the registration point of the ball is above the end of the path.

14. Save the file and play the movie. You will see that the ball moves along a definite path, called the motion guide.

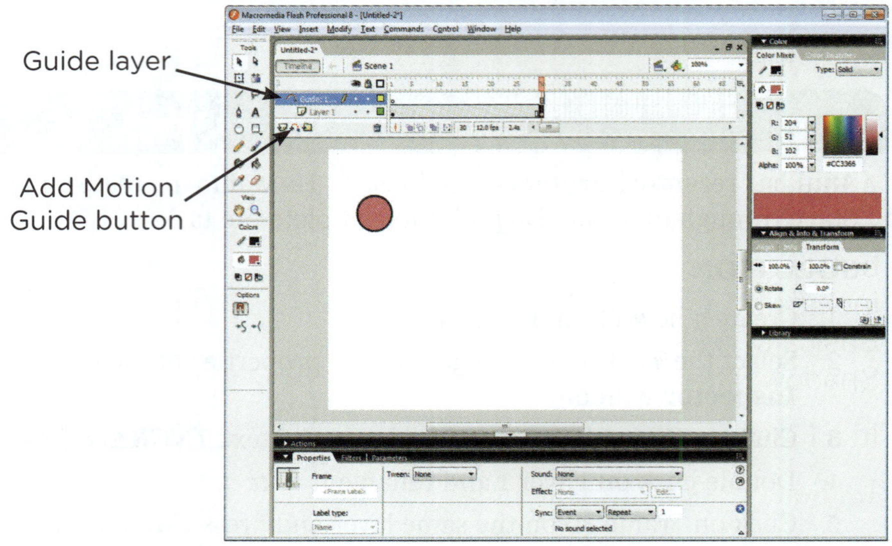

Fig. 9.19: Guide layer

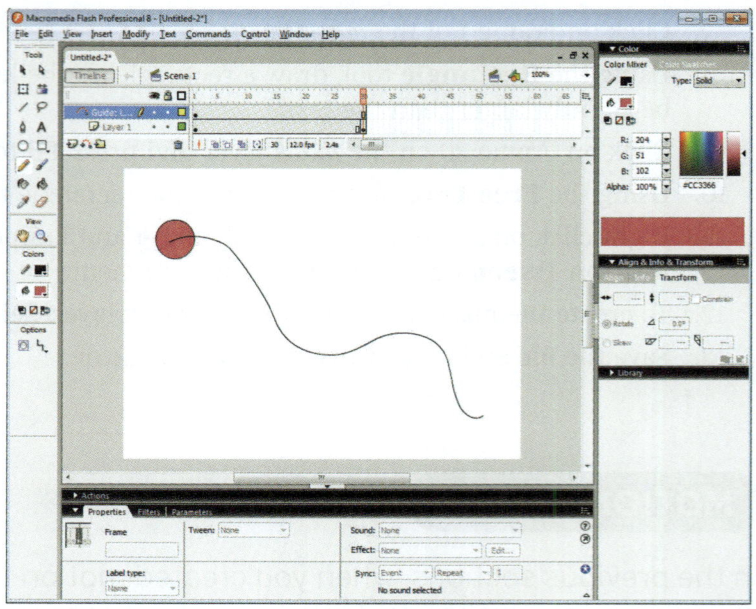

Fig. 9.20: Path for the ball

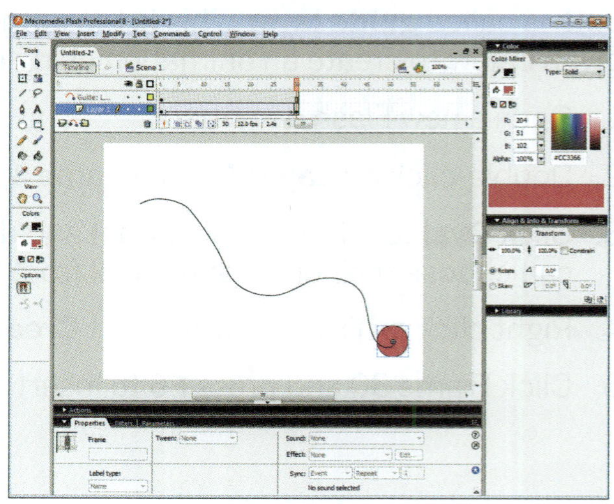

Fig. 9.21: Ball at the end of the path

FILTERS IN FLASH

A filter is a special tool provided by Flash 8 that helps to enhance the graphics of your movie. These filters are built-in visual effects and can be applied to text, movie clips and buttons only. They cannot be applied to graphic symbols. The filters provided by Flash include Drop shadow, Blur, Glow, Bevel, Gradient Glow, Gradient Bevel and Adjust Color. Basically, a filter manipulates the pixels of the graphical object. For example, the Drop Shadow filter will appear to have a shadow behind it.

In a Flash document containing text, follow the steps given to apply a filter to your text.

1. Select the text using the **Arrow** tool.
2. Click the **Filters** tab at the bottom of the Flash window.

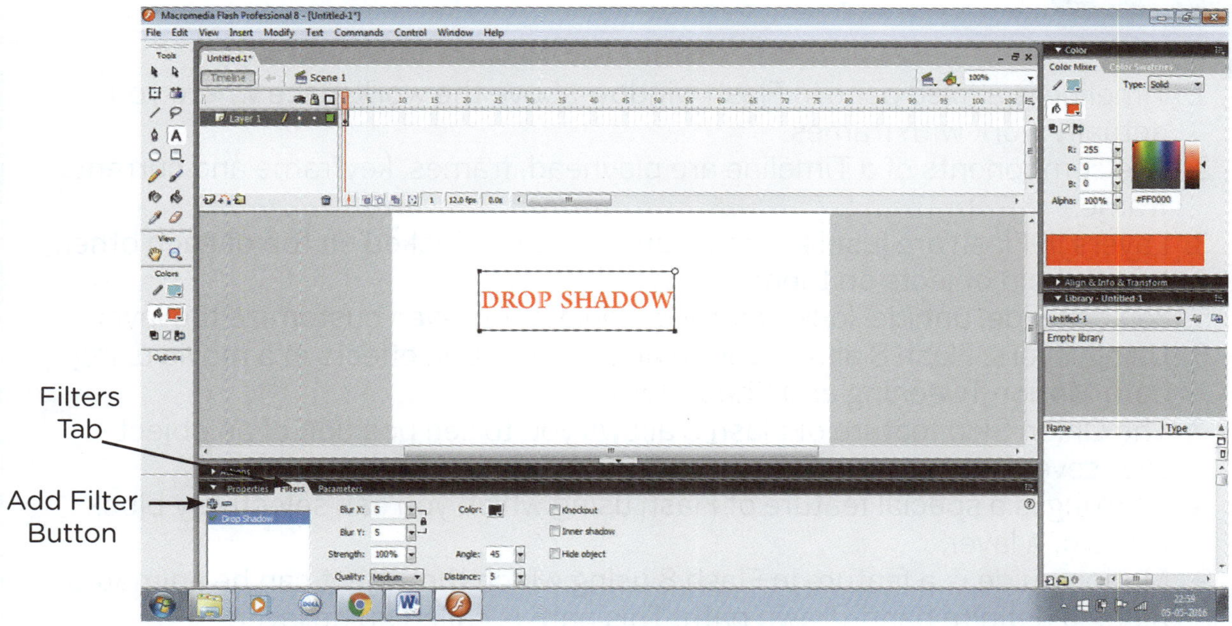

Fig. 9.22: Filters Tab

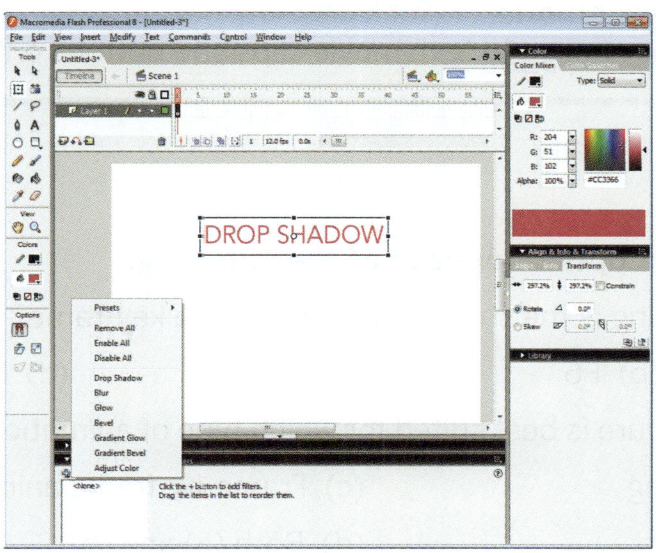

Fig. 9.23: Add Filters sub-menu

3. Click **Add Filters** button on the **Filters** tab.
4. Select the type of filter that you wish to apply, say **Shadow**.
5. The options for the selected filter will appear in the **Filters panel**. Set the various options like Blur X, Blur Y, Angle, Distance and Strength of the shadow.
6. You will see that the selected filter is applied to the text on the Stage.

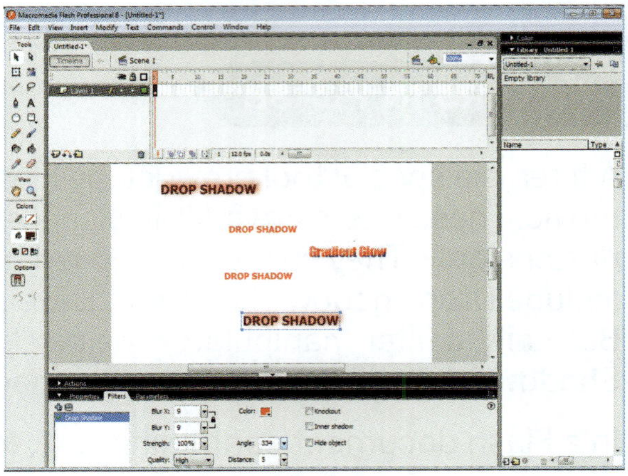

Fig. 9.24: Text with different filter effects

Quick Recap

1. Timeline is a fixed pane in Flash window above the workspace where you actually work with frames.
2. The components of a Timeline are playhead, frames, keyframe and current frame.
3. Layers in Flash are just like transparent sheets stacked on top of each other.
4. Layers hold objects on them.
5. You can hide, unhide, lock, rearrange, delete and even customize the layers.
6. Using layers, Flash 8 allows you to apply animation effects in a movie using both Motion Tweening and Shape Tweening.
7. The Onion Skin feature of Flash 8 allows you to see position of an object over several successive frames.
8. Masking is a special feature of Flash using which you can selectively block areas of a layer.
9. Motion guide is a feature in Flash 8 using which the object can be animated along a definite hand-drawn path. This path is called guide layer.
10. A filter is a special tool provided by Flash 8 that helps to enhance the graphics of your movie.
11. Filters can be applied to text, movie clips and buttons only.

EXERCISE

A Choose the correct option for each of the following.

1. Which of the following is the shortcut key to insert a keyframe?

   (a) F1 (b) F6 (c) F5 (d) F7

2. The Onion Skin feature is best suited for which type of animation?

   (a) Motion Tweening (c) Frame-by-frame animation

   (b) Shape Tweening (d) Both (a) and (b)

3. Which of the following features in Flash 8 are similar to motion tween?
   (a) Masking (b) Motion guide (c) Onion Skin (d) None of the above
4. Using which of the following feature the object can be animated along a definite path?
   (a) Masking (b) Motion guide (c) Onion Skin (d) None of the above
5. What is the default name of the layer in a new Flash document?
   (a) L1 (b) Layer 1 (c) NewLayer (d) New Layer1

B Fill in the blanks using the words given below.

Layers	locked	Onion Skin	mask	motion guide

1. ________________ are analogous to transparent sheets stacked on top of each other.
2. When a layer is ________________, no modifications to the objects of that particular layer can be done.
3. The ________________ feature allows you to see position of an object over several successive frames.
4. The ________________ acts as a hole or a window through which you can see the contents of the underlying layer.
5. The definite hand-drawn path through which the object is animated is called ________________.

C State whether the following statements are true (T) or false (F).

1. By default, each movie contains a single layer. ☐
2. Each layer has its own row of frames and keyframes. ☐
3. When the eye button is clicked, a yellow cross appears in front of the layer name. ☐
4. A layer can be locked by clicking the black dot under the Lock button. ☐
5. You cannot give a name to a Flash layer. ☐

D Give one word for each of the following.

1. These hold objects on them. ____________
2. A frame where change actually occurs. ____________
3. This button is used to hide a layer. ____________
4. This button is clicked to display only onion-skinned frames as outlines. ____________
5. The red rectangle with a vertical line in the Timeline. ____________

E Answer the following questions.

1. What is the benefit of using layers in Flash?
2. How can you hide a layer in Flash?
3. Explain Onion Skin feature of Flash 8.
4. Define a motion guide. Write the steps to create a motion guide for an object.
5. What is a filter in Flash? Name any five filters provided by Flash 8.

FA

Lab Activity

1. Paridhi wants to create an animation in which a bird flaps its wings and flies from bottom left of the Stage to the top right corner of the Stage. As the bird moves the sun opens and closes its eyes. Help her to complete the task.
2. Stuti wants to learn mask layers. She wants to display a star with the Glow filter effect under a mask. How will she create the animation?
3. Ravish wants to show a man walking towards his house. The colour of the house changes as soon as he goes near the house. Help him to create the animation.
4. Write the names of your five friends and apply different filter effects to each name.
5. Create an animation in which the shuttlecock moves in a defined motion path.
6. Gurneet wants a boy to throw a ball on the screen but he wants to see the relative position of the ball in successive frames. Help him to complete the task.

FA

Research Project

You have learnt many features of Macromedia Flash 8 in Classes 6 and 7. Take any small story, such as the famous story of the hare and the tortoise. Create a 3–4 minute animated movie that depicts the story. You can use any type of animation to do so. The animated movie should also preferably contain subtitles. Also, you can either import the picture of main characters of the story or draw them using drawing tools in Flash.

Teacher's Notes

(a) Explain the usage of layers to students giving suitable examples. Also, demonstrate all the operations on layers covered in this chapter.

(b) Discuss in class all the features—Onion Skin, Masking Layer, Filters, Motion Guide

10 Introduction to Windows Movie Maker

Learning Objectives

By the end of this chapter you should be able to
- start Windows Movie Maker.
- know the components of Windows Movie Maker interface.
- create a movie.

Introduction

When multiple pictures and audio-video clips are joined together, we get a movie. Movie Making is becoming increasingly popular these days.

In this chapter, you will learn basics of Windows Movie Maker 2012. Since it is a free software, it can be downloaded from various websites but before downloading, you have to check the operating system installed on your computer. It is a streamlined video-editing application that allows you to capture, import and edit audio-video content to create and share movies. You can even add titles and narrations to your movie. Further, Windows Movie Maker 2012 supports almost all video (MOV, MPEG-4, WMV, etc.) and audio (WAV, AU, MP3, etc.) formats.

STARTING WINDOWS MOVIE MAKER

To start Windows Movie Maker, select **Windows Movie Maker** from the **Start** menu. The home page of Windows Movie Maker, better known as Windows Movie Maker User Interface, appears.

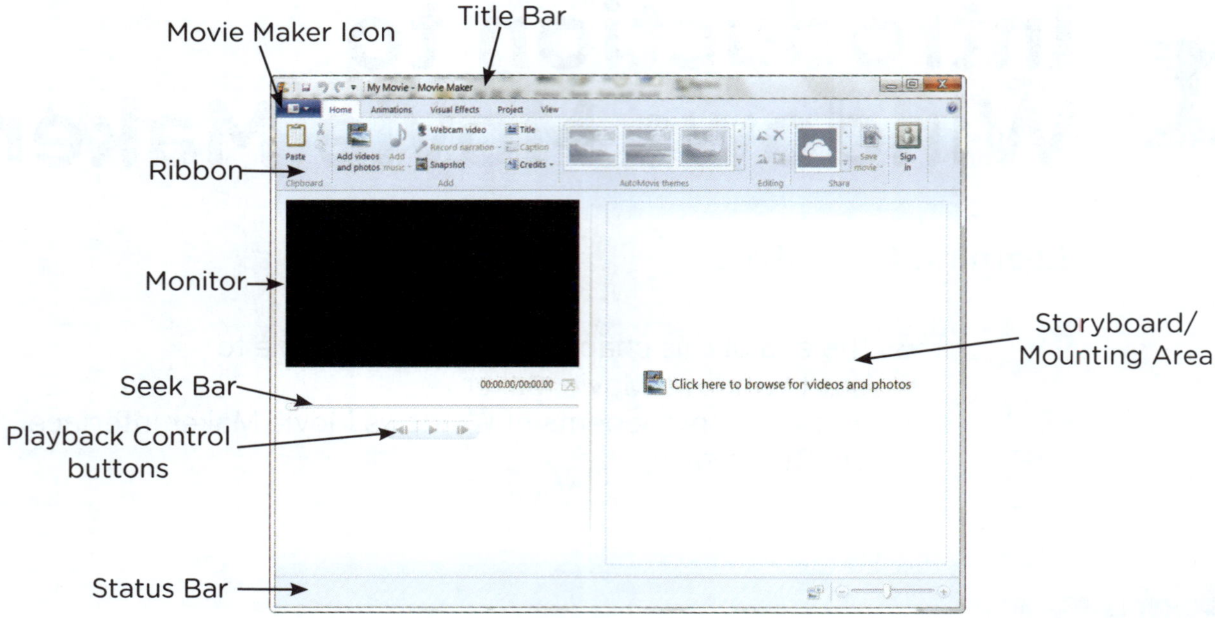

Fig. 10.1: Windows Movie Maker User Interface

COMPONENTS OF WINDOWS MOVIE MAKER USER INTERFACE

The Windows Movie Maker User Interface contains the following components:

1. Movie Maker Icon
2. Title Bar and Ribbon
3. Storyboard
4. Monitor
5. Status Bar

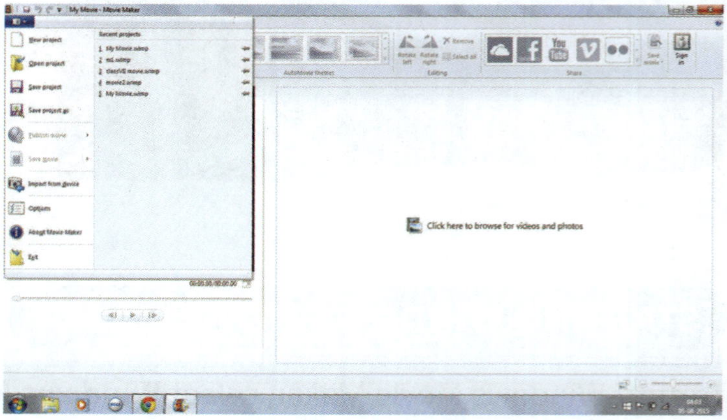

Fig. 10.2: Movie Maker Icon

Movie Maker Icon: The **Movie Maker** icon is present on the extreme left of the ribbon in Windows Movie Maker User Interface. When you click on this icon, a drop-down menu appears that contains basic commands to create, open and save movie projects, publish and save movies, import files, etc. On the right side of the drop-down menu, the names of the recent movie projects are displayed.

You can directly click on the name to open the respective movie project. You can also set different options for your movie project using the Movie Maker icon.

Title Bar and Ribbon: As in the case of all other Windows, the **Title Bar** of Windows Movie Maker User Interface also contains **Quick Access Toolbar**, the file name, application name and window control buttons on the right.

Below the title bar, the **Ribbon** contains various tabs—**Home**, **Animations**, **Visual Effects**, **Project** and **View**. These tabs contain commands to perform various tasks while creating or editing a movie.

Below the ribbon, the User Interface is divided into two sections—first one on the left contains the **Monitor** with **Playback Control** buttons, **Timer** and **Seek Bar**. The second section on the right contains the **Storyboard**.

Monitor: The **Monitor** section of the Windows Movie Maker User Interface is used to preview individual photographs, video clips, titles, credits or an entire movie project.

Below the monitor, there are **Playback Control** buttons that help you to navigate through the movie project. You can play, pause, rewind or forward the movie through these buttons. You can view individual clips and can also take still picture of the current frame that is displayed on the monitor from the selected clip. As the movie is played, the **Seek Bar** progresses forward. You can start playing the movie from any place by clicking on the Seek Bar.

Just below the monitor, on the right side, you have the timer display that displays the time elapsed and the total duration of the movie in **hours:minutes:seconds.hundredths of a second (h:mm:ss.hs)**.

The **Preview Full Screen** button, next to the **Timer**, is used to preview the movie on full screen.

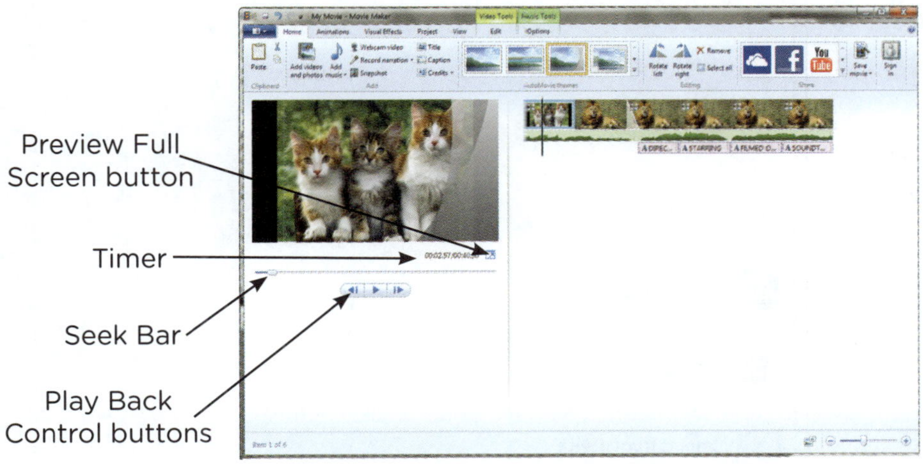

Fig. 10.3: Monitor

> **Quick Way**
>
> The shortcut key to have a full screen preview of the current movie project is **F11**.

Storyboard: The **Storyboard**, also called **Mounting Area**, is used to add and view the sequence of clips and/or photographs in your movie. If required, you can also rearrange the order of these clips. Through the storyboard, you can also view video effects, transitions, audio tracks, etc. that you have added to your movie.

The storyboard contains a button in the centre, **Click here to browse for videos and photos**. You can click this button to add videos and photographs to your movie.

Status Bar: The Status Bar displays information of the current movie project like total number of items (video clips and photographs) added to the movie and the currently selected clip's/photograph's number.

You Should Know

If you want to change the size of the video clips/ photographs that are being displayed on the Storyboard, click **Change Thumbnail Size** button present on the right of the Status Bar.

CREATING A MOVIE

To create a movie, you have to start a new project. A movie project is a file that contains information about the arrangement of various pictures, video/audio clips and effects used to make a movie.

Once you open Windows Movie Maker 2012, you can directly start creating the movie. If Windows Movie Maker is already open and you want to start working on a new project, click the Movie Maker Icon and select **New project** option from the drop-down menu.

Once you have started a new project, creating a movie consists of the following steps:

(a) Adding videos and photos
(b) Adding titles and credits
(c) Saving the movie

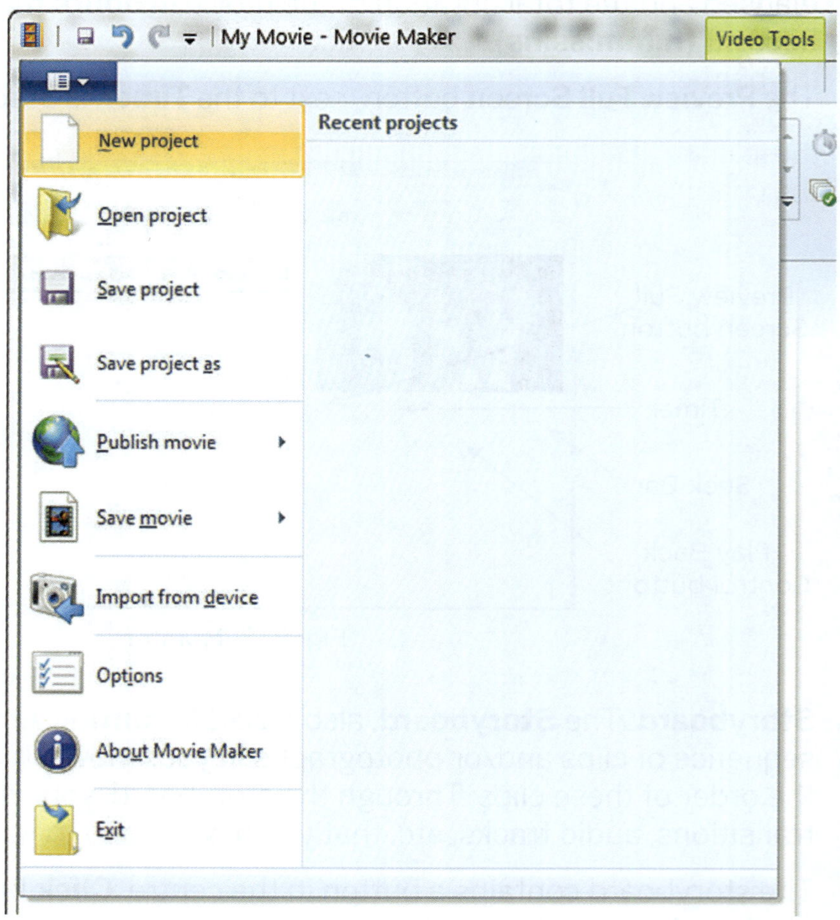

Fig. 10.4: New project option

Adding Videos or Photos

1. Click **Add videos and photos** button from the **Home** tab or from the **Storyboard**. The **Add Videos and Photos** dialog box appears.
2. Select the drive and folder where the video/picture is stored.
3. Select the video or picture file from the displayed list.
4. Click the **Open** button.

You will see that the selected clip or picture is added to the **Storyboard**. Also, as you add any of the photographs or video clips, the **Video Tools Edit** tab gets added to the **Ribbon**. This tab contains commands to edit the photographs or video clips that you have added in your movie. You will learn about these commands as you proceed further in the chapter.

Add Videos and photos

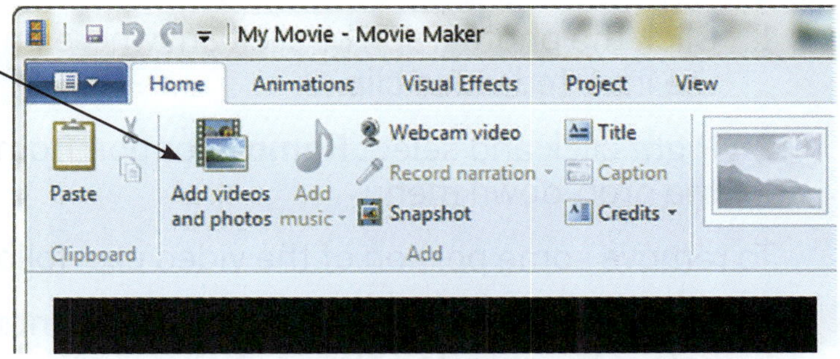

Fig. 10.5: Adding videos and photos command

Fig. 10.6: Add Videos and Photos dialog box

Video Tools Edit tab

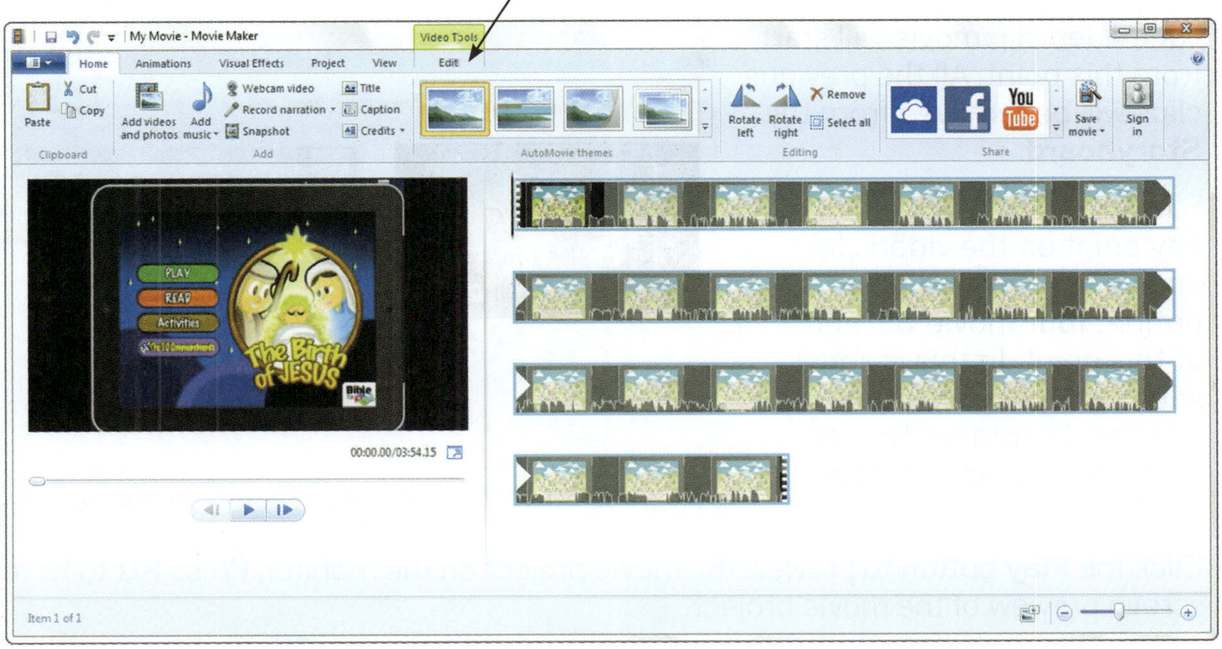

Fig. 10.7: Video added to the Storyboard

To remove a complete video clip or a photograph from the **Storyboard**, follow the steps given below:

1. Click the photograph or click anywhere on the inserted video clip.
2. Right click and select **Remove** option from the drop-down menu.

Quick Way

To delete the photograph or the entire video clip, click on the photograph or video clip and press the **Delete** key from the keyboard.

To remove some portion of the video clip, follow the steps given below:

1. Click at the position from where you want to start the selection. The cursor will appear before the selected clip.
2. Right click and select **Set start point** option from the drop-down menu.

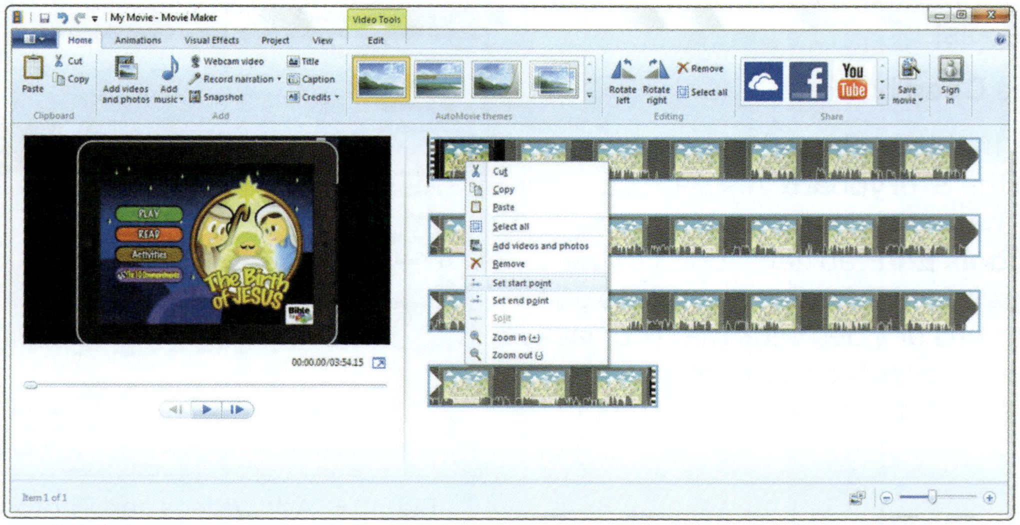

Fig. 10.8: Set start point and Set end point options

3. Your video clip movie will start from this point. All the previous clips will be removed from the **Storyboard**.
4. Similarly, right click at any point on the video clip and select **Set end point** option. Your movie will end at this point. In this manner, your movie now contains just the desired portion of the video clip as shown in the figure.

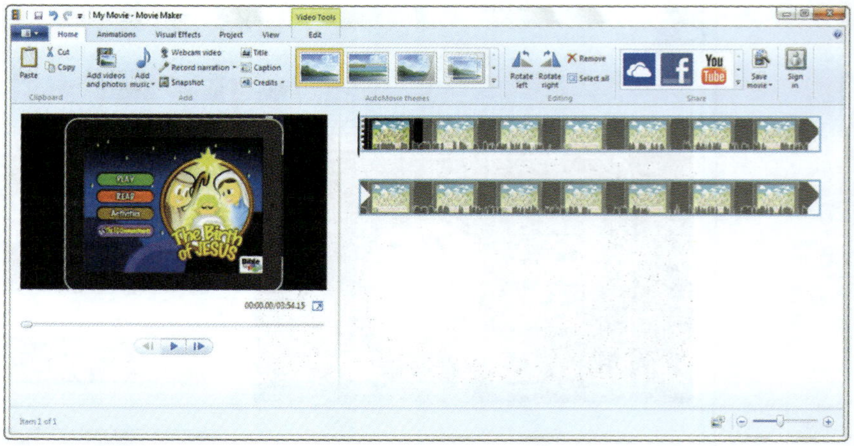

Fig. 10.9: Trimmed video clips in the movie project

5. Click the **Play** button to preview the movie project on the monitor. Press **F11** to have a full screen preview of the movie project.

Quick Way

You can click the **Set start point** and **Set end point** buttons on the **Video Tools Edit** tab to select a portion of a video clip.

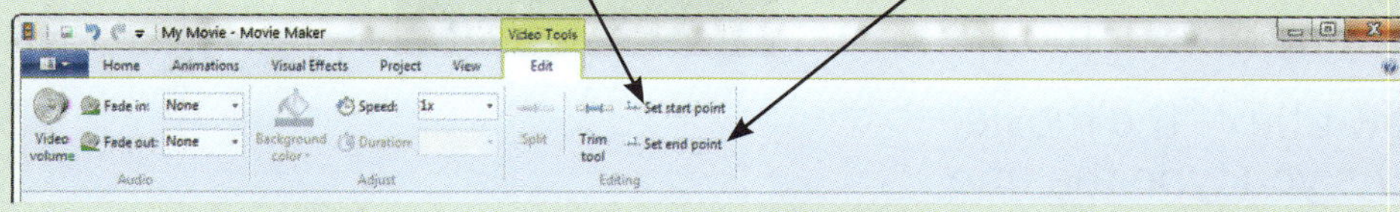

Video Tools Edit tab

The shortcut key to preview a video clip on the monitor is **Spacebar**. You can again press **Spacebar** to stop playing it.

To reorder the sequence of clips and photographs in a movie on the storyboard, click and drag the photograph/video clip that you want to move from one position to another.

Adding Titles and Credits

Titles and Credits are texts like title of your movie, names of the people associated with the movie, date of creation, etc. that are given in the movie.

Titles can be added at the beginning, end or in between the movie. They can also be added overlaying a particular clip or photograph. Such text is known as caption. Credits can only be placed at the end of the movie. To add titles and credits, you have three buttons in the **Add** group of buttons on the **Home** tab.

Fig. 10.10: Title, Caption and Credits buttons on the Home tab

(a) **Title**: Adds a new title before the selected item in a new frame before the selected frame.
(b) **Caption**: Adds text that is displayed over the selected video or photograph frame.
(c) **Credits**: Adds new frame containing blank credits

You Should Know

Many single pictures run in succession in a movie. A single picture or a still shot, that is part of a larger video or movie, is called a frame.

Adding Titles

The steps to add a title to the movie are as follows:

1. Click on the clip before which you want to add the title.
2. On the **Home** tab, click **Title** command in the **Add** group of buttons. You will see that the title clip is added on the Storyboard. It is also displayed on the monitor with the cursor to type the title. The default title of the movie is same as the name of the movie project file. Since the file has not been saved yet, so the default file name (*My Movie*) appears

on the title frame of the movie project. Also, as the title frame is added to your movie, the **Text Tools Format** tab gets added to the ribbon. The commands in this tab help you to put various text effects to the title frame of your movie.

3. Type the new title of the movie as desired. As you type the title on the monitor, the new title also appears below the title frame on the Storyboard.

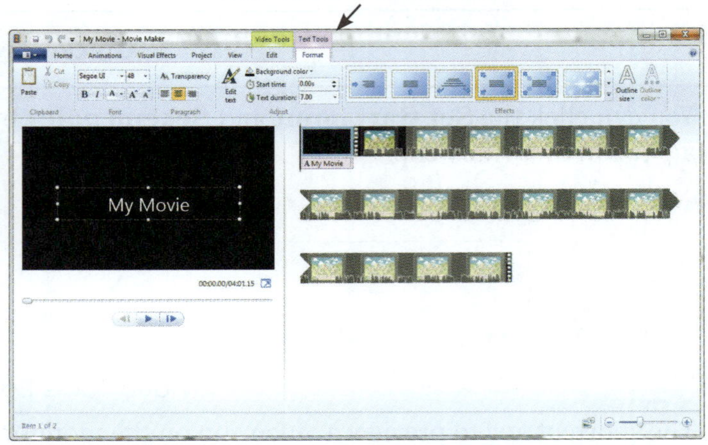

Fig. 10.11: Title frame with default movie name

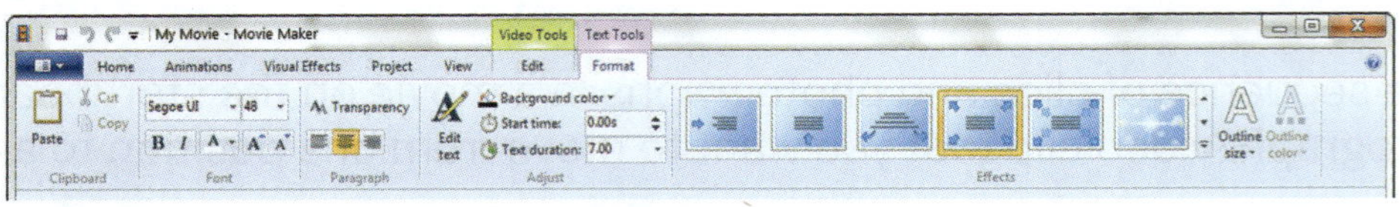
Fig. 10.12: Text Tools Format tab

   a. Select the desired font style, size, color, etc. from the **Font** group of buttons.
   b. Select the desired alignment of the text from **Paragraph** group of buttons.
   c. The default background colour of the title frame is black. If you want to change the background colour of the title slide, click the arrow near the **Background color** button in the **Adjust** group of buttons. Select the desired background colour from the **Color Palette**.
   d. Set the time in seconds after which you want the caption to appear in the movie in the **Start time** text box.
   e. To set the time duration for the title to be displayed, specify the time (in seconds) in the **Text duration** text box in the **Adjust** group of buttons.

4. You can also choose any of the text transition effects from the **Effects** gallery of icons. If you keep your mouse pointer on any of the effects, you will see the tool tip with the name of the effect and simultaneously, a preview of that particular effect is also seen on the monitor.

5. Click on the title frame on the Storyboard when finished.

6. Click on the **Play** button below the monitor to view the text effects applied to the title frame.

> **You Should Know**
>
> Click the **Edit text** button in the **Adjust** group of buttons to edit the title text.

Adding Captions

Captions are the texts that are added on the inserted video clip or photograph. To add a caption to your movie, follow the steps given below:

1. Select the clip on which you want to add captions.
2. Click **Caption** command from the **Add** group of buttons on the **Home** tab.

3. The currently active clip with the cursor in the text area appears. Also, the **Text Tools Format** tab gets active.
4. Type the caption on the monitor. You will see that the same caption is added below that particular frame on the Storyboard.
5. Select the font size, style, color from the **Font** group of buttons on the **Text Tools Format** tab.
6. To apply various effects to the caption, select any of the effects from the **Effects** gallery of icons on the **Text Tools Format** tab. If you place your mouse pointer on any of the buttons, you will see the tool tip with the name of the effect and also a preview of the effect on the monitor.
7. Set the time, in seconds, after which you want the caption to appear in the movie in the **Start time** text box.
8. Set the **Text duration** for which you want to display the text in **Adjust** group of buttons.
9. Click the clip on the Storyboard when finished.
10. Click the **Play** button to view the caption with applied effects.

Fig. 10.13: Caption to be typed

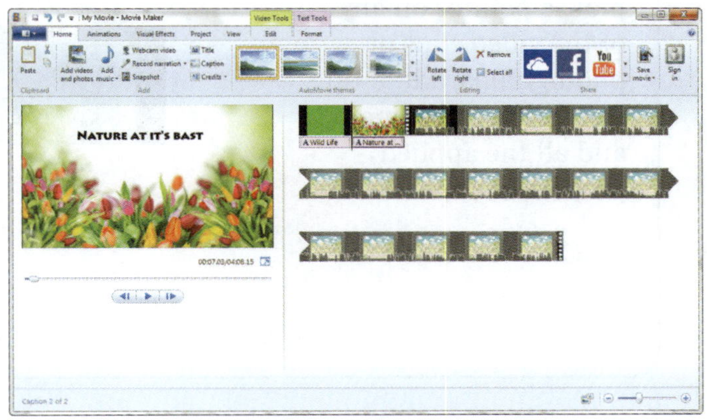

Fig. 10.14: Captions added to the movie

Adding Credits

Credits are always added at the end of the movie. While including the credits, we specify the names of the people who have contributed to the making of the movie like the director, producer, actors, singers, etc. To add credits to the movie, follow the steps given below:

1. Click the arrow next to **Credit** command in the **Add** group of buttons on the **Home** tab. The drop-down menu appears.
2. The various options provided by Windows Movie Maker 2012 for adding the **Credits** are as follows:
   - Credits
   - Starring
   - Soundtrack
   - Director
   - Location

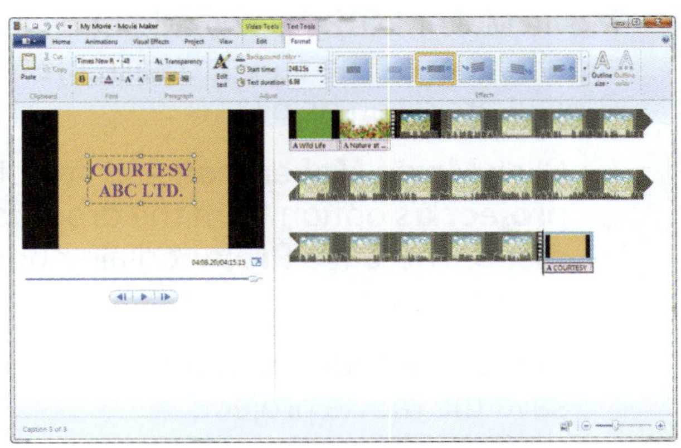

Fig. 10.15: Credits added to the movie

Select the desired option and type the text on the monitor. The same text appears below the respective credit frame on the Storyboard.

3. You can apply the desired text effects from the **Text Tools Format** tab as you had applied while adding titles and captions.
4. The credit frame is added at the end of the movie. Click the frame on the Storyboard when finished.
5. Click the **Play** button to view the credits with applied effects.

You Should Know

If you place your mouse pointer on any of the video clips or photographs, a tool tip displaying the name and all the applied properties appears.

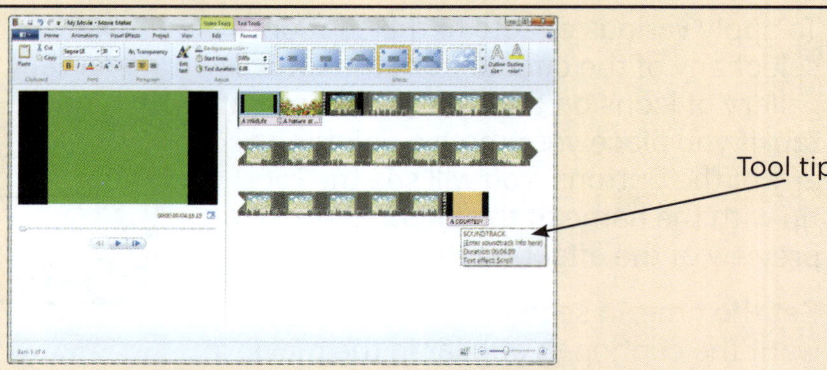

Tool tip displaying the properties of the video clip/photograph

SAVING A MOVIE

You can save the movie in two ways—**As a Project** or **As a Movie.**

When the movie is saved as a project, it is saved with the extension *.wlmp*. This movie project saved can be opened in Windows Movie Maker 2012 for any additions and modifications. The steps to save the Movie Project are given below:

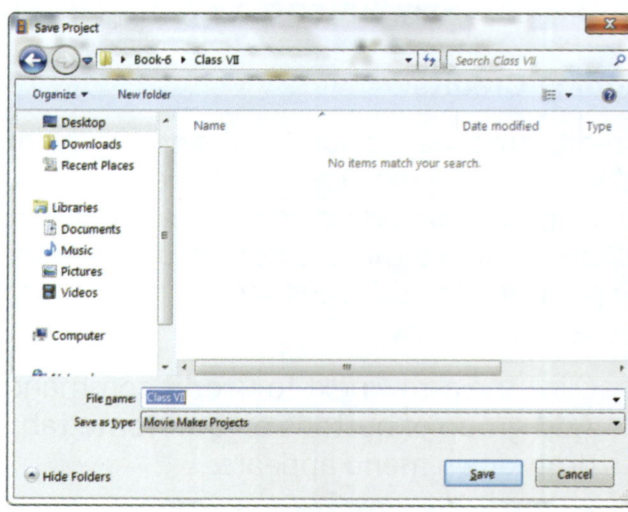

Fig. 10.16: Save Project dialog box

1. Click **Movie Maker icon** and select **Save project as** option from the drop-down menu. The **Save Project** dialog box appears.
2. Select the folder in which you want to save the movie project.
3. Specify the name of the file and click the **Save** button. The movie project file with the extension *.wlmp* is saved. You will notice that this saved project is also added in the **Recent Projects** list in the **Movie Maker** drop-down menu.

When the movie project that you are working on is saved as a movie, it is saved in a video format (for example, MPEG-4, MOV, etc.) that can run on any media player like Windows Media Player, VLC Media player, etc. You cannot make further modifications in a file that is saved in any video format. Such a process is also known as **rendering a movie**. To save the current movie project in a video format, follow the steps given below:

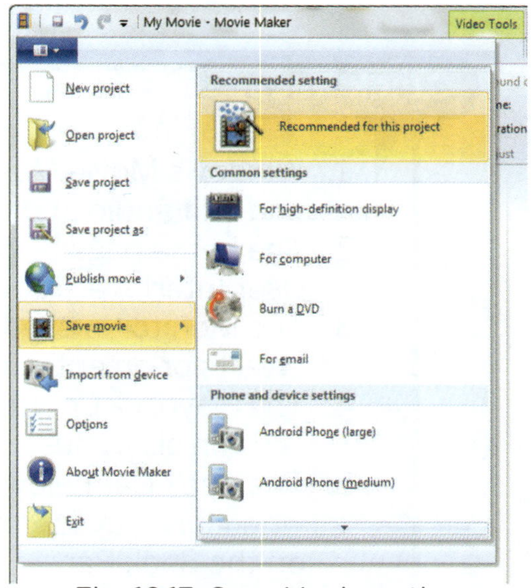

Fig. 10.17: Save Movie option

1. Click **Movie Maker** icon.
2. Click **Save movie** option and from the submenu select **Recommended for this project** option. The **Save Movie** dialog box appears.
3. Specify the folder where you want to save the movie.
4. Specify the name of the file in the File name text box.
5. Select the type of video format in which you want to save the movie. The default format of the movie is *.mpeg-4*.
6. The **Movie Maker** progress bar appears that shows the status of the movie being saved or rendered.
7. Once the movie is saved, a dialog box stating that the video file is created is displayed.

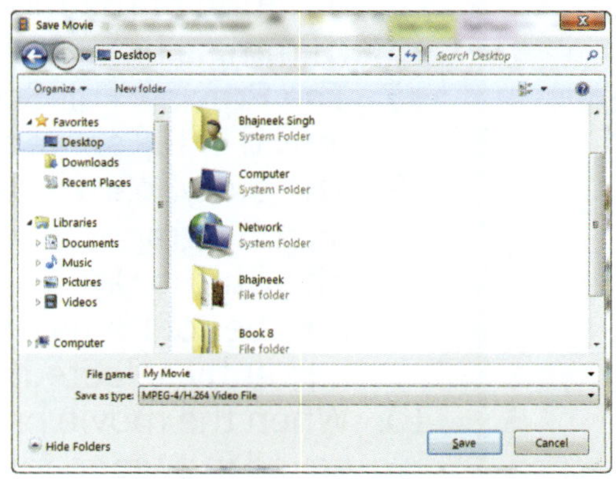

Fig. 10.18: Save Movie dialog box

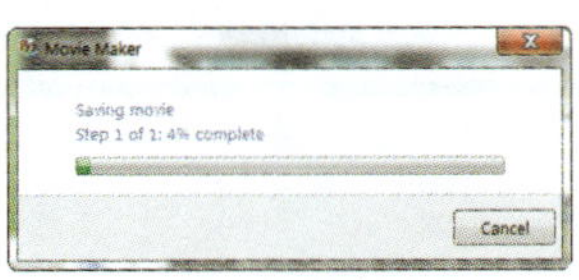

Fig. 10.19: Movie Maker progress bar

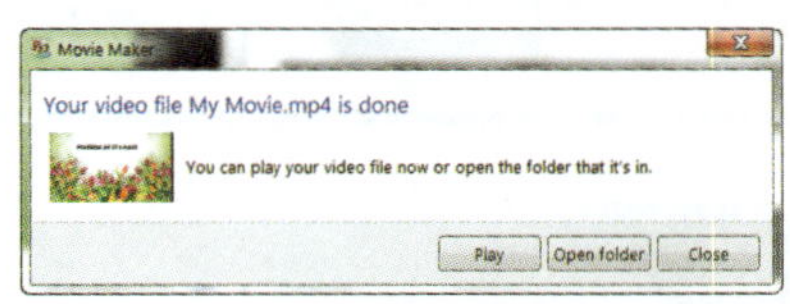

Fig. 10.20: Confirmation dialog box

8. Click the **Play** button in the dialog box to view the movie in any of Media Players. Press **F11** to view the movie in full screen.

Quick Way

You can click on the arrow below the **Save movie** command on the **Home** tab to save the movie in the video format.

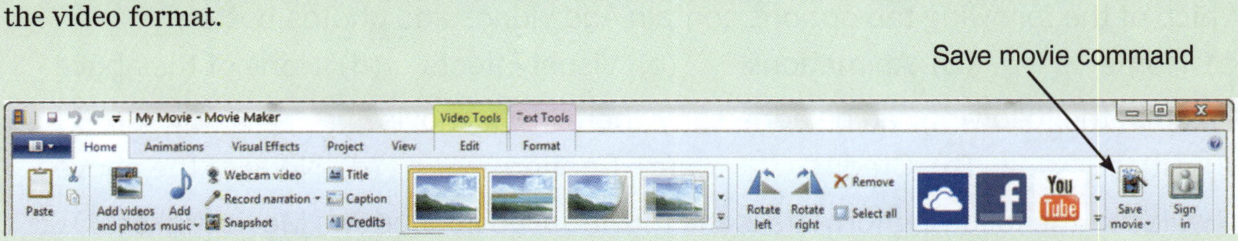

Quick Recap

1. Windows Movie Maker is a software which allows you to capture, import, add and edit audio and video content to create movies.
2. The home page of Windows Movie Maker is known as Windows Movie Maker User Interface.
3. The Monitor is used to preview individual photographs, video clips, titles and credits or an entire movie project.
4. The Playback Control buttons help you to navigate through the movie project. You can play, pause, rewind or forward the movie through these buttons.
5. The Seek Bar below the monitor is used to check the progress of the movie when it is played. You can start playing the movie from any place by clicking on the Seek Bar.
6. The timer below the monitor displays the time elapsed and the total duration of the movie in hours:minutes:seconds.hundredths of a second (h:mm:ss.hs).
7. The Preview Full Screen button, next to the Timer is used to preview the movie in full screen.
8. The Storyboard is used to add, view and rearrange the sequence of clips and/or photographs in your movie. The Storyboard is also called the Mounting Area.
9. The Status Bar displays information of the current movie project like total number of items (video clips and photographs) added to the movie and the currently selected clip's/photograph's number.
10. When the movie project that you are working on is saved as a movie, it is saved in a video format (for example, MPEG-4, MOV, etc.) that can run on any media player like Windows Media Player, VLC Media Player, etc. Such a process is also known as rendering a movie.

EXERCISE

A Choose the correct option for each of the following.

1. Which of the following is a menu option in Windows Movie Maker icon?
   (a) New project (b) Save project as (c) Save movie (d) All of the above
2. In which format is the time duration of the movie displayed?
   (a) h:mm:ss.hs (b) mm:ss:hs (c) h:mm:ss (d) None of the above
3. Which of the following tab options contain Add videos and photos button?
   (a) Home (b) Animations (c) Visual Effects (d) None of the above
4. Which of the following can be added anywhere in the movie?
   (a) Titles (b) Credits (c) Caption (d) None of the above
5. In which of the following formats is the movie saved in Windows Movie Maker 2012?
   (a) *.ppt* (b) *.doc* (c) *.mpeg-4* (d) *.wlmp*

B **Fill in the blanks using the words given below.**

Windows Movie Maker User Interface   Video Tools Edit   Seek Bar   F11   Spacebar

1. The home page of Windows Movie Maker is known as ________________ .
2. You can start playing the movie from any place by clicking on the ________________ .
3. The shortcut key to start playing the movie on the monitor is ________________ .
4. The shortcut key to preview the movie on full screen is ________________ .
5. As you add any of the photographs or video clips, the ________________ tab gets added to the Ribbon.

C **State whether the following statements are true (T) or false (F).**

1. Windows Movie Maker can be downloaded from the Internet without paying any cost. ☐
2. Before downloading Windows Movie Maker, you have to check out the operating system installed on your computer. ☐
3. You cannot rearrange the order of video clips and photographs once it is added to the Storyboard. ☐
4. The Video Tools Edit tab on the ribbon helps to edit only the photographs. ☐
5. Credits can be given at any place in the movie. ☐

D **Give one word for each of the following.**

1. It helps to view the list of collections of clips of the movie. ________
2. This can be used to review or modify the timings of the clips in your movie project. ________
3. These buttons help you to navigate through the movie project. ________
4. This button is used to preview the movie on full screen. ________
5. Another name of Storyboard. ________

E **Answer the following questions.**

1. What are the main components of Windows Movie Maker User Interface?
2. List the steps to create a movie.
3. Write steps to include titles and credits in a movie.
4. Write steps to save a movie as a project file.
5. Define rendering a movie file.

FA

Lab Activity

Visit your school computer lab and try the following.

1. Leena is going for her friend's birthday party. She wants to gift her a movie that showcases their friendship over the years. She has collected some pictures and videos to create the movie. Help her to create the movie and give the title of the movie as 'Our Priceless Friendship'.
2. Tarun went on an excursion to Nainital with his friends as part of the school excursion. His teacher has asked him to create a movie showcasing what all they did during the trip. Give suitable titles and credits to the movie.
3. On Mother's Day, Koel wants to gift her mother a movie showcasing their relationship right from her birth till date. She has collected a lot of pictures and videos for the same. Help her to create the movie and give suitable titles and subtitles to the movie.

FA

Research Project

Other than Windows Movie Maker which other software can you use to make movies? Find out at least two other commonly used movie-making software and list out their main features.

Teacher's Notes

(a) Discuss why movie making is considered user-friendly.
(b) Discuss the difference between saving the movie as a project and saving the movie in a video format.

WORKSHEET

A Choose the correct option for each of the following.

1. Which of the following is the shortcut key to use Free Transform tool?
   (a) P (b) Q (c) F (d) T
2. To which tool does the Eyedropper tool change to when you copy the Stroke of an object?
   (a) Brush Tool (b) Paint Bucket Tool (c) Ink Bottle tool (d) None of the above
3. What in Flash is referred to as changing the size of the object?
   (a) Scaling (b) Masking (c) Both (a) and (b) (d) Neither (a) nor (b)
4. By clicking on which of the following you will be able to compare the previous and next frames?
   (a) Insert Layer button (b) Onion Skin Outline button (c) Onion Skin button (d) None of the above
5. On which of the following, filters cannot be applied?
   (a) Movie clips (b) Buttons (c) Graphic symbols (d) All of the above
6. In which tab of Windows Movie Maker User Interface, will you find the Titles option?
   (a) Home (b) Visual Effects (c) Animations (d) Clip
7. Which of the following tabs are added to the ribbon of Windows Movie Maker User Interface when any photograph or video clip is added?
   (a) Video Tools Edit (b) Text Tools Format (c) Both (a) and (b) (d) Neither (a) nor (b)
8. Which of the following is a component of the Windows Movie Maker User Interface?
   (a) Monitor (b) Ribbon (c) Storyboard (d) All of the above
9. Which of the following components contain the Save project option?
   (a) Home tab (b) Storyboard (c) Movie Maker icon (d) None of the above
10. Which of the following formats are supported by Windows Movie Maker 2012?
    (a) *mov* (b) *mpeg-4* (c) *wmv* (d) All of the above

B Unscramble the words to fill in the blanks.

1. An ______________ is a non-Flash item that you import and store for future usage. (SETAS)
2. A ______________ is a multicoloured fill in which one colour slowly changes to another. (DTGAIREN)

3. The central handle of the selected object in Flash is also called ______________ of the object. (RMNRSATFAONOIT TPONI)
4. In Flash, using ______________ feature, the object can be animated along a definite path. (NTMOIO UEGDI)
5. The movie project is saved with the extension ______________ . (PMWL)
6. To review or modify timings of the clip, use the ______________ option. (ETMLIENI)
7. The clips of the selected collection are displayed in the ______________ on the right side of the Movie Maker interface. (OYSRTDBRAO)
8. To remove a picture from the Storyboard, you press the ______________ key. (ELTDEE)
9. Click ______________ button below the monitor to preview the movie on full screen. (WIVEERP LULF NSEECR)
10. ______________ is a streamlined video-editing application. (SDWNIOW EMVIO KREAM)

C State whether the following statements are true (T) or false (F).

1. If you click the filled area, the Eyedropper tool automatically changes to the Paint Bucket tool with its Lock Fill modifier turned on. ☐
2. The shortcut key to import a picture to Flash is Ctrl+R. ☐
3. The Free Transform tool cannot transform symbols. ☐
4. Flash 8 allows you to add multiple layers. ☐
5. By default the Onion Skin feature is turned off. ☐
6. You cannot delete a Flash layer. ☐
7. You can delete a portion of the video clip while creating a movie. ☐
8. In Windows Movie Maker, you can play the movie from any point by clicking on the Seek Bar. ☐
9. The time duration of the movie in Windows Movie Maker is displayed as hours:minutes:seconds (h:mm:ss). ☐
10. In Windows Movie Maker, the File tab contains Titles and Credits commands. ☐

D Give one word for the following.

1. This tool helps to copy fill and stroke from one object to another. ______________
2. This feature gives the best effect in frame-by-frame animation. ______________
3. Click this button to view relative position of an object over successive frames. ______________
4. These are built-in visual effects for text in Flash. ______________
5. Default name of first layer in a Flash document. ______________
6. This helps to preview the movie project in Windows Movie Maker. ______________

7. The sequence of photographs and video clips can be rearranged in this component of Windows Movie Maker User Interface. ______________
8. This is the process of saving the movie in *.mpeg-4* format. ______________

E Label the following in the figure given.

Onion Skin button, Insert Layer button, Lock Layer button, Start Onion Skin Marker, Delete Layer button

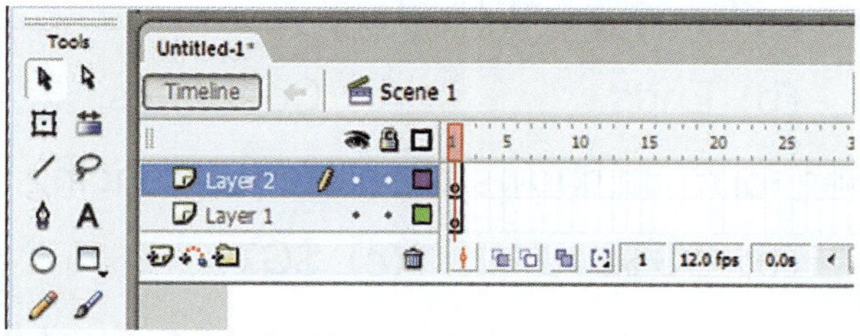

F Application-based questions.

1. Create an animated movie in Flash that shows a butterfly coming from one end of the screen and sitting on a flower.
2. Create a movie in Windows Movie Maker 2012 that shows the achievements of your school in various interschool competitions. Also, put the photographs of the teachers involved in the competitions. Give appropriate title, credits and captions in your movie.

G Answer the following questions.

1. Write steps to change the centre point and width of a gradient.
2. Write steps to create a new gradient.
3. Write steps to modify the instance of a symbol.
4. What is the use of Start–End markers on the Timeline?
5. How can we implement the Filter feature in a Flash movie?
6. In what situations will you prefer using an Onion Skin feature of Flash?
7. What is the use of Storyboard in Windows Movie Maker 2012?
8. While creating a movie in Windows Movie Maker, how can you add and delete a video clip to/from the Storyboard?

Projects

1. In the course of your study, you have learnt to create both animated movies using Flash and motion pictures using Windows Movie Maker 2012. Form a comparative report on both the software. You can include the following in your report:
   - Key features
   - Advantages/Disadvantages
   - Versions available
   - Situations in which you will prefer one to the other

ASSESSMENT 1

Chapters 1-6

(Maximum Marks: 40)

A Choose the correct option for each of the following. **(6 × 1 = 6)**

1. Initialization is the value from where the loop ______________.
   (a) Starts (b) Ends (c) Continues (d) None of these
2. Which of the following formula shows absolute referencing of cells?
   (a) G1 (b) $G$1 (c) $G1 (d) 1$G
3. In which of the following forms will you find text on a chart in MS Excel?
   (a) Legends (b) Titles (c) Data (d) All of the above
4. Which of the following is an invalid step value in the context of looping constructs in QBASIC?
   (a) 0 (b) 1 (c) -1 (d) 100
5. If the loop doesn't terminate, it is called an ______________ loop.
   (a) Endless (b) Never ending (c) Constant (d) None of these
6. Which of the following falls into the category of E-Commerce?
   (a) B2B (b) C2B (c) C2C (d) All of the above

B Fill in the blanks. **(6 × 1 = 6)**

1. Using ____________________ feature in MS Excel, you can display data in a particular colour or style depending on a particular condition.
2. In a 3D chart, the base area constituted by the XY plane is known as ____________________ and the vertical areas, that is, the YZ and XZ planes are known as ____________________.
3. ____________________ is the vertical axis used to plot the value of each data point on a chart.
4. The ____________________ loop in QBASIC is executed till the condition is False.
5. ____________________ is the use of electronic media and ICT to provide education anytime and anywhere.
6. ____________________ of the loop refers to the statements that are to be executed repeatedly.

C State whether the following statements are true (T) or false (F). **(5 × 1 = 5)**

1. A formula results in a new value from an existing range of values. ☐
2. When you bring the mouse pointer over a filter, the filtering criteria is displayed. ☐

3. Plot area of a chart does not include data series. ☐

4. FrontPage is an example of IDE environment. ☐

5. E-governance is of no help to people of the country. ☐

D Give one word for each of the following. **(5 × 1 = 5)**

1. Button to remove filter in MS Excel
2. A type of chart which is used to display graphically quantitative data and is based on a line chart.
3. This is the point where the loop ends.
4. Most widely used security technology by web browsers.
5. Buying and selling on the Internet.

E Give one point of difference between each of the following. **(4 × 1 = 4)**

1. AutoFilter and Sorting
2. Bar chart and column chart
3. WHILE...WEND and DO...WHILE
4. B2B and B2C in the context of E-Commerce

F Give the shortcut keys for the following. **(2 × ½ = 1)**

1. To filter data in MS Excel
2. To create a chart instantly

G Identify the error in the following QBASIC code: **(1)**

```
X = 10
DO WHILE X < 45
    X = X + 1
    PRINT X
WEND
PRINT X
```

H Answer the following questions.

1. What can be the reason if you see a couple of #s in a cell? How will you resolve the problem? **(2)**
2. Define sorting in MS Excel. **(2)**
3. What is an endless loop in QBASIC? How can you stop the execution of an endless loop? **(2)**
4. Write a program in QBASIC to accept ten numbers and display the message 'WELL DONE' every time a multiple of 8 is entered. **(3)**
5. ICT is considered as an indispensable part of our lives today. Give any two points of justification. **(3)**

FA ASSESSMENTS

ASSESSMENT 2

Chapters 7–10

(Maximum Marks: 40)

A Choose the correct option for each of the following. **(6 × 1 = 6)**

1. In which year was HTML 5 released?
   (a) 2009 (b) 2010 (c) 2011 (d) 2012
2. Which of the following is a container element?
   (a) <title> (b) <hr> (c)
 (d) None of these
3. Which of the following always has to be a part of an HTML document?
   (a) <font> (b)
 (c) <hr> (d) <title>
4. Which of the following feature in Flash is used to move an object over a given path?
   (a) Onion Skin (b) Masking (c) Motion guide (d) Breaking
5. Which of the following statements are not true in case of Flash?
   (a) Flash 8 allows you to add multiple layers.
   (b) By default the Onion Skin feature is turned off.
   (c) You cannot delete a Flash layer.
   (d) You cannot have both motion and shape tweening in a single flash file.
6. Which of the following sections of Windows Movie Making User Interface is used to set the order of video clips/pictures in a movie?
   (a) Movie Tasks Pane (b) Storyboard (c) Toolbar (d) Monitor

B Fill in the blanks. **(6 × 1 = 6)**

1. The first version of HTML was ________________ .
2. A ________________ is a piece of code that instructs the browser how to display a particular text or image.
3. The ________________ element is used to place the text in the horizontal centre of the web page.
4. The ________________ tool in Flash is used to copy the properties of one object to another.
5. The home page of Windows Movie Maker is called ________________ .
6. There are ________________ ways to save a movie in Windows Movie Maker.

C Match the following. (6 × ½ = 3)

Column A	Column B
(a) Storyboard	(i) Ctrl+R
(b) <b>	(ii) Draws a horizontal line
(c) <hr>	(iii) Q
(d) Pixel	(iv) Mounting Area
(e) Import a picture in Flash	(v) 72 points
(f) Free Transform Tool	(vi) Physical markup tag

D Give one word for each of the following. (5 × 1 = 5)

1. Name of the person who invented HTML
2. This bar gives the title of the web page
3. An attribute of <hr> tag that gives solid line
4. A tool used to change the multicolour fill of objects
5. A feature that shows relative position of the object in successive frames

E Give one point of difference between each of the following. (5 × 1 = 5)

1.
 and <p>
2. HEAD and BODY section of an HTML document
3. Layering and Masking
4. Flipping and Scaling an object in Flash
5. Linear and Radial Gradient

F Give one characteristic each of the following. (4 × 1 = 4)

1. <html> element
2. Web browser
3. Storyboard in Windows Movie Maker
4. Gradients in Flash

G Application-based questions

1. Create a web page that contains your resume, that is, your name, address, date of birth, contact number. hobbies and interests, class in which you are presently studying and the name of your school. Do the following on the web page you create: **(4)**

   (a) Background colour: Yellow (b) Title of the page: Myself

   (c) Details (name, address, DOB, etc.): Green colour, size 4, bold
2. Write the steps to animate the text ASSESSMENT in Flash. **(3)**
3. Write the four main steps to create a movie in Windows Movie Maker. **(2)**

H Answer the following questions.

1. Name any two versions of HTML. **(1)**
2. What is the use of Start and End markers on the Timeline? **(1)**

REVISION QUESTIONS

Suggested Questions for SA

(Maximum Marks: 100)

A Choose the correct option for each of the following. **(10 × 1 = 10)**

1. Which sign always precedes the formula?
   (a) * (b) % (c) # (d) =
2. Which of the following menu items are not added in the Menu Bar when a chart is inserted in an Excel sheet?
   (a) Layout (b) Insert (c) Design (d) Format
3. What is the shortcut key for AutoSum in MS Excel?
   (a) Alt+= (b) Ctrl+= (c) Shift+= (d) None of these
4. Which of the following is NOT an option in the AutoSum drop-down menu?
   (a) Count Numbers (c) Average
   (b) Count (d) Max
5. Which of the following is a Date & Time function?
   (a) TODAY (b) LEN (c) MAX (d) LCM
6. Which of the following is an umbrella term?
   (a) E-commerce (b) E-governance (c) ICT (d) None of these
7. Which of the following commands in QBASIC is used to stop further execution of the program?
   (a) QUIT (b) BYE (c) EXIT (d) None of these
8. What are the components of the loop?
   (a) Initialization (b) Termination
   (c) Body of the loop (d) All of these
9. Which of the following is not an attribute of <font> element?
   (a) Face (b) Align (c) Color (d) Size
10. Which of the following tool buttons is used to hide/unhide a layer in Flash?
    (a) Lock Tool (b) Hide Tool (c) Eye Tool (d) Eyedropper Tool

B Fill in the blanks. **(10 × 1 = 10)**

1. Filter on the selected range of cells is reapplied by clicking on the ________________ button.
2. The conditional formatting command is in ________________ tab.
3. ________________ displays information about data points on an Excel chart.

4. The HTML files are saved with an extension ____________.
5. The default value of size attribute of <hr> element is ____________.
6. There are ____________ types of gradients in Flash.
7. The shortcut key to Break Apart the text is ____________.
8. In Windows Movie Maker User Interface, an icon for all video clips and pictures being used in your movie can be seen in the ____________ pane.
9. In Flash, ____________ gives special visual effects to the text on the Stage.
10. In Windows Movie Maker User Interface, the command to add video clips and pictures to your movie can be seen on the ____________ tab.

C State whether the following statements are true (T) or false (F). (10 × 1 = 10)

1. Formula in MS Excel can only be given in the Formula Bar. ☐
2. Auto-editing feature of Excel automatically changes the formula in MS Excel. ☐
3. The formulas in MS Excel are case sensitive. ☐
4. A step value of a loop in QBASIC can never be negative. ☐
5. You can do arithmetic operations on a text value in MS Excel. ☐
6. E-learning facilitates the learning and delivery process only for students and not for teachers. ☐
7. You cannot use still pictures in Windows Movie Maker. ☐
8. You can save a file in Windows Movie Maker through a File Save Wizard. ☐
9. The file in Windows Movie Maker is saved with an extension .Imwp. ☐
10. Keyframe helps to preview the movie. ☐

D Answer the following in one/two word(s). (10 × 1 = 10)

1. Adding one string after another
2. Predefined formulas to perform certain operation
3. This tab has Function Library group of buttons in MS Excel
4. Output of the following statement = "Break" + "Free"
5. The chart that is used to plot data for a single data series
6. The mounting area of Windows Movie Maker
7. The command in QBASIC that can be used to exit the loop prematurely
8. HTML was invented by whom?
9. A type of element having only ON tag
10. The feature of Flash that helps to show the objects of a layer beneath it through a window

E Give any one point of difference between the following. (8 × 1 = 8)

1. C2B and C2C with respect to e-commerce
2. Sorting and Filtering
3. E-commerce and E-governance
4. BGCOLOR and background attribute of <body> element
5. Audio and Video formats
6. Masking and Layering
7. Credits and captions in Windows Movie Maker 2012
8. Save project as and Save movie option in Windows Movie Maker 2012

F Write any two features of the following. (6 × 2 = 12)

1. ICT
2. Loops in QBASIC
3. Headings in HTML
4. Layers in Flash
5. Onion Skin feature in Flash
6. Titles and credits in Windows Movie Maker

G Give one example for each of the following. (5 × 1 = 5)

1. Shortcut key to break an endless loop in QBASIC
2. A category of e-commerce where consumers put up their items on sale through auctions
3. Filter in Flash
4. A value of align attribute of <p> element
5. The application software used to create and edit photographs and video clips

H Application-based questions (5 × 3 = 15)

1. Write a program in QBASIC that accepts a number and checks whether it is a prime number or not.
2. Write a program in QBASIC to display the following series

   49 36 25 16 9 4 1
3. Write a program in QBASIC to print first 20 multiples of a number entered by the user.
4. Create an animated movie in Flash in which a car is seen climbing a hill. Please note that a defined path is made for the car to move.

5. Create a movie named Tribals of India using Windows Movie Maker in which pictures and video clips of Indian tribals are used.

I Answer the following questions. **(10 × 2 = 20)**

1. What is the benefit of AutoSum feature of MS Excel?
2. How can sorting be done on multiple columns?
3. What are two ways to remove filtering?
4. What is Secure Sockets Layer?
5. List any two advantages of e-governance.
6. How has e-learning benefited students?
7. What do you mean by 'hypertext' and 'markup' in HTML?
8. What do you mean by comments? How can you give comments in HTML?
9. In how many ways can you align a paragraph in HTML? Name them.
10. Write the steps to change the center point and width of a gradient.

SOF
SCIENCE OLYMPIAD FOUNDATION
Inspiring Young Minds Through Knowledge Olympiads

DO NOT OPEN THIS BOOKLET UNTIL ASKED TO DO SO

Roll No.:

Total Questions: 50 Time: 1 hr.

CLASS 7

SET-A

NCO
14TH SOF NATIONAL CYBER OLYMPIAD

Guidelines for the Candidate

1. You will get additional ten minutes to fill up information about yourself on the Answer Sheet, before the start of the exam.
2. The Question Paper comprises three sections: **Logical Reasoning** Section (15 Questions), **Computers and Information Technology** Section (30 Questions) and **Achievers Section** (5 Questions)

   Each question in Achievers Section carries 3 marks, whereas all other questions carry one mark each.
3. All questions are compulsory. There is no negative marking. Use of calculator is not permitted.
4. Write your **Name, Roll No.** and **Class** clearly on the **Answer Sheet** and do not forget to sign it.
5. There is only ONE correct answer. Choose only ONE option for an answer.
6. To mark your choice of answers by darkening the circles in the Answer Sheet, use **HB Pencil** or **Blue / Black ball point pen** only. E.g.

Q.16: Which of the following is a type of printer?

A. Cathode Ray Tube B. Light Emitting Diode
C. Thermal Flatbed D. Liquid Crystal Display

As the correct answer is option C, you must darken the circle corresponding to option C in the Answer Sheet.

16. Ⓐ Ⓑ ● Ⓓ

7. Rough work should be done in the blank space provided in the booklet.
8. Return the Answer Sheet to the invigilator at the end of the exam.
9. Write your Roll No. on the Question Paper too and take it home for future reference.

1. Select a figure from the given options which will continue the series established by the Problem Figures.

Problem Figures

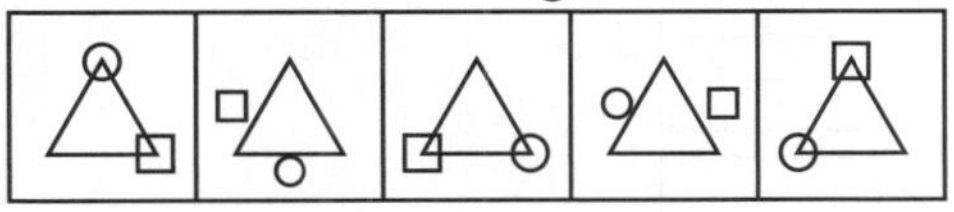

A. 

B. 

C. 

D. 

2. If the first and second letters in the word DEPRESSION were interchanged, also the third and the fourth letters, the fifth and the sixth letters and so on, which of the following would be the eighth letter from the left end?

A. R
B. O
C. S
D. I

3. Two different positions of the same dice have been shown below. If digit 1 is at the bottom of the dice, then what digit will be at the top?

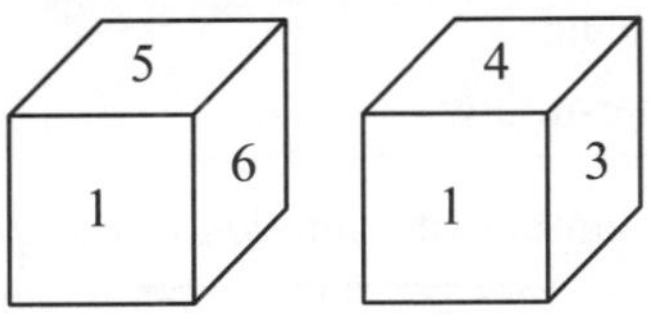

A. 3
B. 4
C. 2
D. 6

4. There is a certain relationship between Fig. (i) and (ii). Establish the same relationship between Fig. (iii) and (iv) by selecting a suitable figure from the given options which will replace the (?) in Fig. (iii).

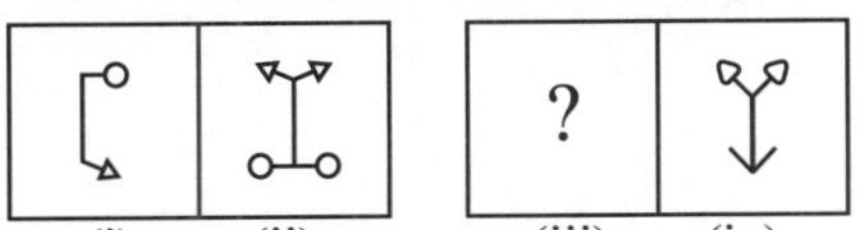

(i) (ii) (iii) (iv)

A. 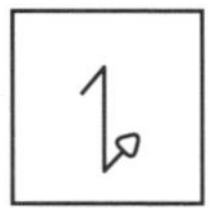

B. 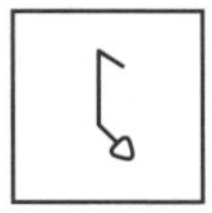

C. 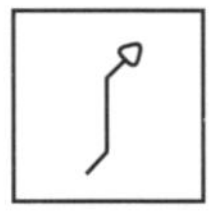

D. 

5. If BOTTLE is coded as YLGGOV, then how will MOPED be coded as?

A. MNKUW
B. MLLVX
C. NMKUX
D. NLKVW

6. Select a figure from the given options which will complete Fig. (X).

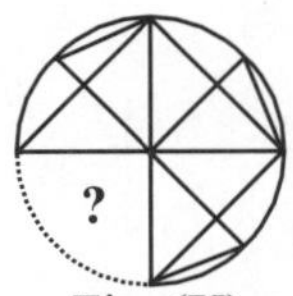

Fig. (X)

A. 

B. 

C. 

D. 

7. Find the missing number from the given options, if the same rule is followed in the three figures.

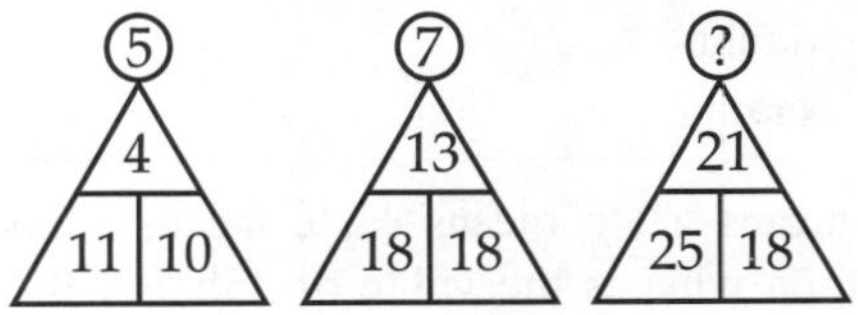

A. 4
B. 8
C. 6
D. 9

8. Which of the following Venn Diagrams represents the relationship between "Mobiles, Televisions, Electronics"?

A. 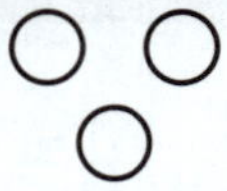

B. 

C. 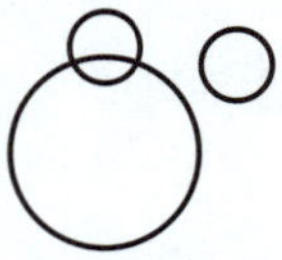

D. 

9. Select a figure from the given options, which will continue the series established by the Problem Figures.

Problem Figures

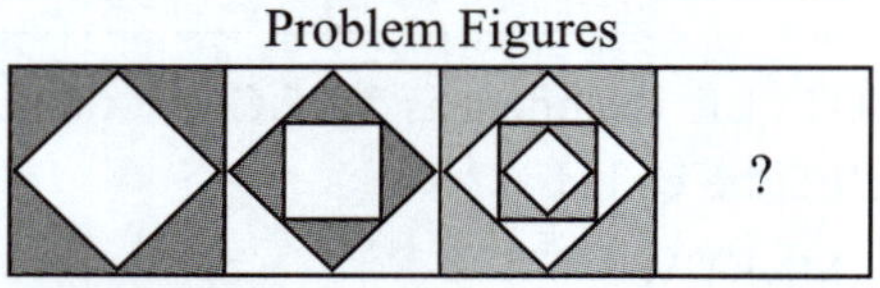

A. 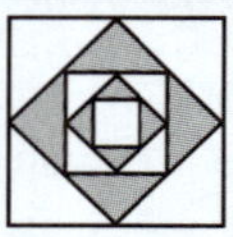

B. 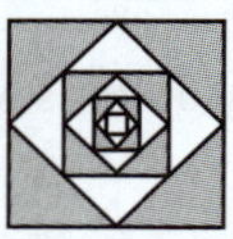

C. 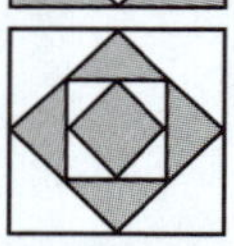

D. 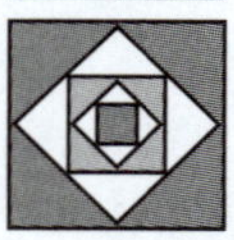

10. Madhu and Shefali are good in Dramatics and Computer Science. Amita and Madhu are good in Computer Science and Physics. Amita, Pratibha and Namita are good in Physics and History. Namita and Amita are good in Physics and Mathematics. Pratibha, and Shefali are good in History, Dramatics.
Identify who amongst these is good in Physics, History and Mathematics, but not in Computer Science?

A. Pratibha
B. Amita
C. Madhu
D. Namita

11. If 'a' means '×', 'b' means '÷', 'c' means '+' and 'd' means '–', then what is the value of 35b7a9c50b10d70b5?

A. 36
B. 40
C. 42
D. 46

12. Which of the following figures in the given options is embedded in Fig. (X)?

Fig. (X)

A. 

B. 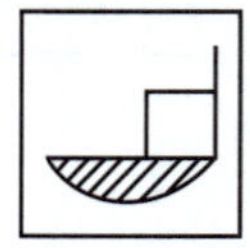

C. 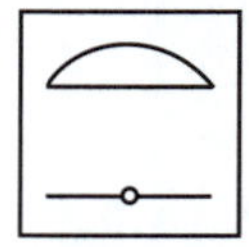

D. 

13. Rahul travels 10 km to the North, turns right and walks 5 km. He then turns right again and moves 10 km forward. How many km is Rahul away from the starting point?

A. 26 km
B. 19 km
C. 13 km
D. 5 km

14. Mohit, introducing a girl in the party, said, "she is the wife of the grandson of my mother". How is Mohit related to the girl?

A. Father
B. Grandfather
C. Husband
D. Father-in-law

15. Find the number of triangles in the given figure.

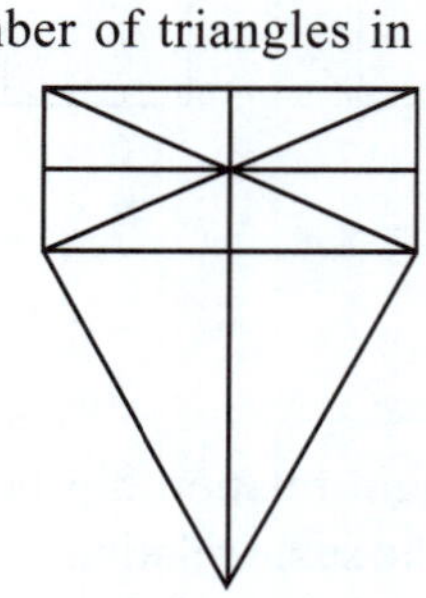

A. 14
B. 18
C. 21
D. 24

16. What is the output of the given QBASIC code?

```
CLS
x = 5
IF (x >= 5) THEN PRINT “x is greater than or equal to 5”
IF (x <= 5) THEN PRINT “x is less than or equal to 5”
IF (x <> 5) THEN PRINT “x does not equal 5”
```

A. x does not equal 5
B. x is greater than or equal to 5
C. x is greater than or equal to 5
x is less than or equal to 5
x does not equal 5
D. x is greater than or equal to 5
x is less than or equal to 5

---

17. This is a centralized place to view all maintenance and system messages. It is displayed by a flag like icon in the taskbar. It is called the _________.

A. Action Center
B. Media Center
C. User Account Center
D. Update Central

---

18. In which of the following options, the access time vary according to the storage location?

A. Random access storage devices
B. Sequential access storage devices
C. Primary access storage devices
D. Secondary access storage devices

---

19. Which of the following I/O devices use CCDs, PMTs or CISs to record the light reflected off an object?

A. 

B. 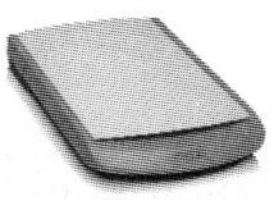

C. 

D. 

---

20. Which of the following statements about the given logo is correct?

parc

A. It stands for Palo Alto Research Center Incorporated.
B. It is a research and development company in California.
C. It is well known for the important development as laser printing, ethernet and GUI.
D. All of these

---

21. Rohit has purchased a new computer system, but he has not purchased an Antivirus software yet. Before purchasing a new licensed antivirus, he decides to try some trial based antivirus software from the internet. To which of the following categories does this software belongs?

A. Shareware
B. Freeware
C. Open Source
D. Open Content

---

22. Which of the following steps is correct to open Navigation Pane in MS-Word 2010?

A. View tab → Window group → Click on Navigation Pane Checkbox
B. View tab → Zoom group → Click on Navigation Pane Checkbox
C. Insert tab → Links group → Click on Navigation Pane Checkbox
D. View tab → Show group → Click on Navigation Pane Checkbox

---

23. The given options come under Picture Tools of Format tab in _____ group. They get activated when you select any picture in MS-PowerPoint 2010.

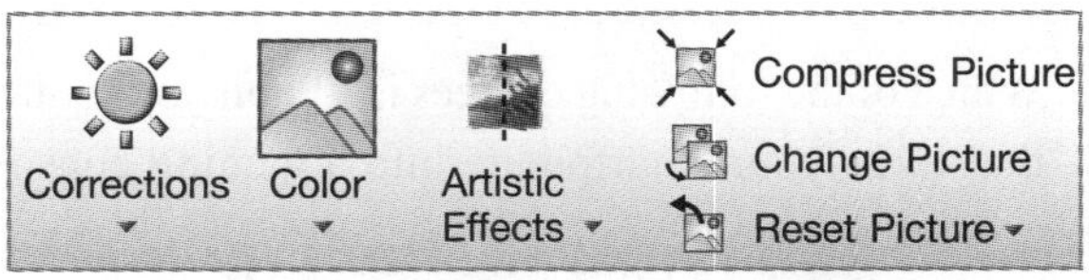

A. Picture Effects
B. Picture Styles
C. Adjust
D. Picture Artistic Tools

---

24. Which of the following hardware technologies is/are used in fourth generation computers?

A. Larger capacity hard disks
B. VLSI technology
C. Microprocessors
D. All of these

25. Which of the following options helps you to capture a screenshot of anything on the desktop in Windows 7?

A. Screenshot Tool
B. Snipping Tool
C. Cropping Tool
D. Imaging Tool

---

26. Which of the following is a drum plotter?

A. 

B. 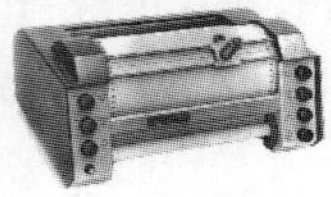

C. 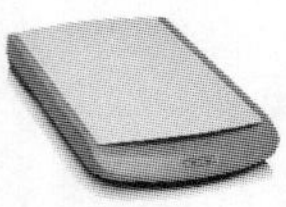

D. 

---

27. Which of the following in the given options converts Text 1 into Text 2 in MS-PowerPoint 2010?

NCO
Text 1

N
C
O
Text 2

A. 

B. 

C. 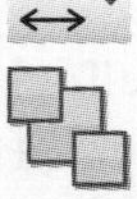

D. 

---

28. Which of the following devices is a Phonejoy controller that turns your smartphone into a gaming console?

A. 

B. 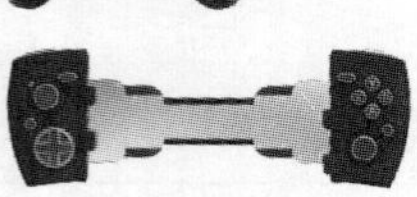

C. 

D. 

---

29. Which of the following supercomputers of PARAM series has been ranked first in India, among the most power-efficient computer systems as of Jan 2014?

A. Padam
B. PARAM 1000
C. Yuva II
D. PARAM 9900/SS

---

30. Which of the following options adds or changes the border around a page in MS-Word 2010?

A. 

B. 

C. 

D. 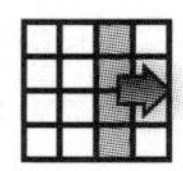

---

31. Which of the following statements is correct in context of Dynamic RAM (DRAM)?

A. It needs to be refreshed on a regular basis in order to maintain its data.
B. It is a volatile memory.
C. It is a type of RAM used in desktops and laptops.
D. All of these

---

32. Match the following keyboard shortcuts given in Column-I with their tasks in Windows 7 given in Column-II.

Column-I / Column-II

(a) 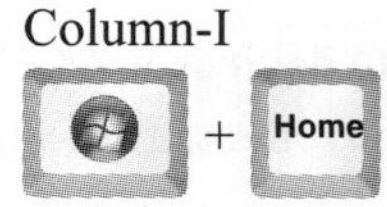

(i) Preview Desktop

(b) 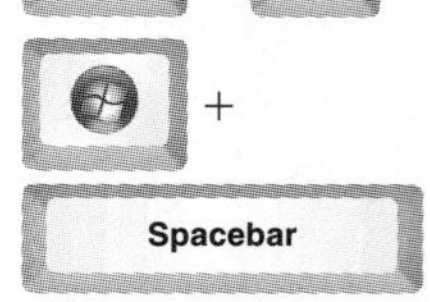

(ii) Turn full page view on/off

(c) 

(iii) Minimize all windows except active window

A. (a)-(iii),(b)-(i),(c)-(ii)
B. (a)-(iii),(b)-(ii),(c)-(i)
C. (a)-(i),(b)-(ii),(c)-(iii)
D. (a)-(i),(b)-(iii),(c)-(ii)

---

33. "Father of personal computer", who designed the first microcomputer Altair 8800 is _____.

A. Ed Roberts
B. Charles Babbage
C. Johan Backus
D. Steve Jobs

34. Select the INCORRECT match of MS-PowerPoint 2010 icons given below with their functions.

A.  - Shows the Animation pane to add effects and custom animation.

B.  - Allows to choose an animation effect to add to the selected objects.

C.  - Plays the animation after certain number of seconds.

D.  - Copies the animation from one object and applies it to another.

35. Match the following computer data storage units given in Column-I with their capacities in Column-II.

	Column-I		Column-II
(a)	1 Geopbyte	(i)	1024 Exabytes
(b)	1 Brontobyte	(ii)	1024 Zettabytes
(c)	1 Yottabyte	(iii)	1024 Brontobytes
(d)	1 Zettabyte	(iv)	1024 Yottabytes

A. (a)-(iii),(b)-(iv),(c)-(ii),(d)-(i)
B. (a)-(iii),(b)-(ii),(c)-(i),(d)-(iv)
C. (a)-(iv),(b)-(iii),(c)-(ii),(d)-(i)
D. (a)-(i),(b)-(ii),(c)-(iii),(d)-(iv)

36. Yahoo is an acronym for ________.

A. Yet Another Highly Officious Oracle
B. Young and huge Official Output
C. Yet Another Hierarchical Officious Oracle
D. Yet Another Hierarchical Object Output

37. Sheet 1, Sheet 2, and so on are the default sheet names used in MS-Excel. You can provide a meaningful name to your worksheet. Which of the following sheet names is INVALID in MS-Excel 2010?

A. ;NCO
B. #NCO
C. :NCO
D. $NCO

38. Web pages are stored on a _____.

A. Client
B. Server
C. Both A and B
D. None of these

39. Select the odd one out with respect to QBASIC.

A. FOR
B. DO WHILE
C. INPUT
D. WHILE

40. What would be the output of the given QBASIC code?

```
a = 50
b = 20
add = a + b
PRINT "add"
```

A. add
B. 70
C. add 70
D. No output

41. ______ is an expansion card that connects a computer to a computer network.

A. MAC
B. NIC
C. IMAP
D. MIC

42. Which of the following companies introduced the Compaq Portable computer?

A. IBM
B. HP
C. Osborne
D. Apple

43. Which of the following output is correct, if you type a formula =COUNT(A1:C3) in the active cell, of the given screenshot of MS-Excel 2010?

	A	B	C
1	56	89	78
2	45		12
3	100	abc	
4			
5			
6			
7			

A. 7
B. 2
C. 6
D. 5

44. Identify the following :

- It is a boot sector virus that was first detected in 1986.
- It runs on IBM-PCs and is considered to be the first computer virus for MS-DOS.
- It infected the first sector of floppy disk with a copy of the virus.

A. Brain
B. Blaster
C. I LOVE YOU
D. Sunday

45. Match the following shortcut keys given in Column-I with their corresponding tasks in MS-PowerPoint 2010 given in Column-II.

	Column-I		Column-II
(a)	Alt + A + C	(i)	Copies animation from one object to another
(b)	Alt + Shift + C	(ii)	Copies text formatting from one place to another
(c)	Ctrl + Shift + C	(iii)	Animation Pane

A. (a)-(ii),(b)-(iii),(c)-(i)
B. (a)-(i),(b)-(ii),(c)-(iii)
C. (a)-(iii),(b)-(i),(c)-(ii)
D. (a)-(ii),(b)-(i),(c)-(iii)

ACHIEVERS SECTION

46. A string of characters, usually longer than the password used in creating encrypted messages for extra security.

A. Passprotected
B. Passphrase
C. Longpass
D. Elabordpass

47. Which of the following options is true?
Statement-1 : Griefer is a player of an online game, who harasses other players.
Statement-2 : Flamer is a person who makes degrading or insulting remarks on a forum or other internet message boards.

A. Statement-1 is true but statement-2 is false.
B. Statement-1 is false but statement-2 is true.
C. Both the statements are true.
D. Both the statements are false.

48. What does the error #REF! in cell D3 represents in the given screenshot, in MS-Excel 2010?

	A	B	C	D
1	56	89	78	
2	45	78	12	
3	100	96	0	#REF!
4				

A. Cell referred in formula in cell D3 has been deleted.
B. Cell referred in formula in cell D3 is not suitable for the calculation.
C. The formula entered in cell D3 is divisible by zero.
D. None of these

49. What will be the output of the given QBASIC program?

```
CLS
x = 15
IF (x = 5) THEN
INPUT a$
PRINT a$
ELSE
PRINT x * 3
END IF
```

A. 5
B. 15
C. 45
D. 5 ,15

50. People with disabilities, who have difficulty in holding two or more keys at a time on the keyboard use sticky keys. For example, if they have to print a document, and are required to press a shortcut Ctrl + P, Sticky keys allows them to simply press one key at a time, instead of pressing them together. Which of the following shortcut keys turns ON the Sticky keys in Windows 7?

A. Pressing Shift key 5 times
B. Pressing Ctrl key 3 times
C. Pressing Ctrl key 5 times
D. Pressing Alt key 2 times

SPACE FOR ROUGH WORK

ANSWER KEYS

1.	D	2.	C	3.	C	4.	B	5.	D	6.	D	7.	B	8.	B	9.	A	10.	D
11.	A	12.	C	13.	D	14.	D	15.	C	16.	D	17.	A	18.	B	19.	B	20.	D
21.	A	22.	D	23.	C	24.	D	25.	B	26.	B	27.	A	28.	B	29.	C	30.	A
31.	D	32.	A	33.	A	34.	C	35.	A	36.	C	37.	C	38.	B	39.	C	40.	A
41.	B	42.	A	43.	C	44.	A	45.	C	46.	B	47.	C	48.	A	49.	C	50.	A

SOF SCIENCE OLYMPIAD FOUNDATION

Head Office: Plot No. 99, Sector 44, Gurgaon - 122 003 (HR) | Email: info@sofworld.org | Website: www.sofworld.org

Regd Office: B-8 Taj Apartment, Ring Road, New Delhi - 110 029

Note: Please address all communication to the Head Office only.

WINDOWS 8

You already know that Windows 8 is an improved version of the Windows 7 operating system. It provides all of the basic features that Windows 7 has. The focus of Windows 8 is on optimizing the operating system for touchscreen-based devices (such as tablets) and cloud computing. The most common editions of Windows 8 are Windows 8 Pro and Windows 8 Enterprise.

The new features specific to Windows 8 include the Start screen with semantic zoom, live tiles, Windows Store, Google Chrome, connected standby, Microsoft account integration, the Windows desktop, etc. You can customize the looks of the Start screen according to your needs.

Fig. 1: Start-up screen of Windows 8

The interface also has a taskbar on the right side of the screen known as the 'charms', which can be accessed from any application or the desktop by sliding from the right edge of a touchscreen or compatible trackpad, moving the mouse cursor to one of the right corners of the screen or pressing ⊞+C. The charms include Search, Share, Start, Devices and Settings charms. The Start charm begins or dismisses the Start screen.

Windows 8 introduces a new form of start menu called Start screen, which resembles the home screen of Windows Phone. The Start screen serves as the primary method of launching applications and is shown in place of the desktop on startup. The Start screen consists of a grid of tiles which can be arranged into columnar groups. The Start screen can uninstall applications directly.

Windows 8 does not have the Start button on the taskbar but it has other ways of beginning with the Start screen. Windows 8 also shows the Start screen on logon, unlike other versions which directly show the desktop.

Windows 8 also has a new lock screen, which includes a date and time display, and a feature to display notifications from other applications. Two new login methods are also available for logging in to the system. You could either set a four-digit PIN or set a 'picture password'. This allows the user to use certain gestures performed on a selected picture to login. However, the shapes and gestures are limited to tapping and tracing a line or circle.

MS EXCEL 2013

It can often be difficult to interpret Excel workbooks that contain a lot of data. Charts help in creating quick graphical representation of data to visualize comparisons and trends.

To Insert a Chart

Follow the steps given below to insert a chart in an Excel worksheet:

1. Select the cells for which you want to create a chart, including the column titles and row labels. These cells will be the source data for the chart. Here, we have selected cells A1:F6 (Fig. 2).

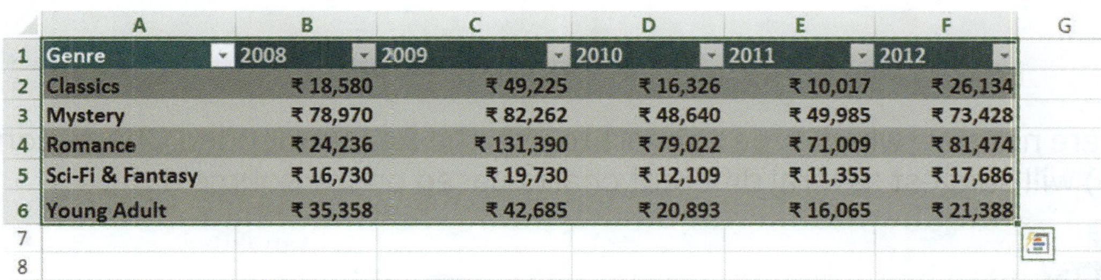

Genre	2008	2009	2010	2011	2012
Classics	₹ 18,580	₹ 49,225	₹ 16,326	₹ 10,017	₹ 26,134
Mystery	₹ 78,970	₹ 82,262	₹ 48,640	₹ 49,985	₹ 73,428
Romance	₹ 24,236	₹ 131,390	₹ 79,022	₹ 71,009	₹ 81,474
Sci-Fi & Fantasy	₹ 16,730	₹ 19,730	₹ 12,109	₹ 11,355	₹ 17,686
Young Adult	₹ 35,358	₹ 42,685	₹ 20,893	₹ 16,065	₹ 21,388

Fig. 2: Selecting cells A1:F6

2. From the Insert tab, click the desired Chart command. Here, we have selected Column chart command (Fig. 3).

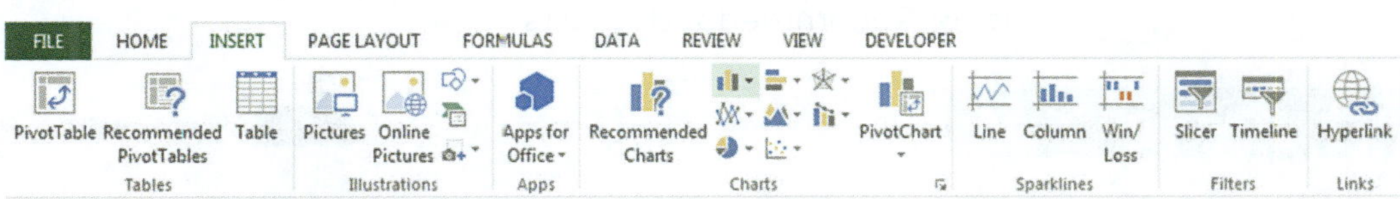

Fig. 3: Click the Column chart command

3. Choose the desired chart type from the drop-down menu (Fig. 4).

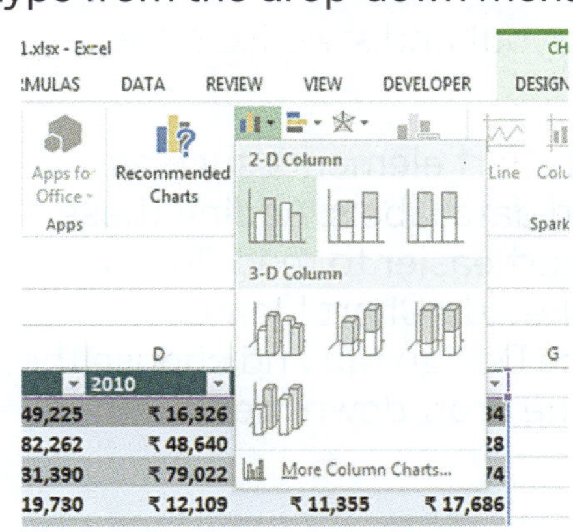

Fig. 4: Choosing a chart type

4. The selected chart will be inserted in the worksheet (Fig. 5).

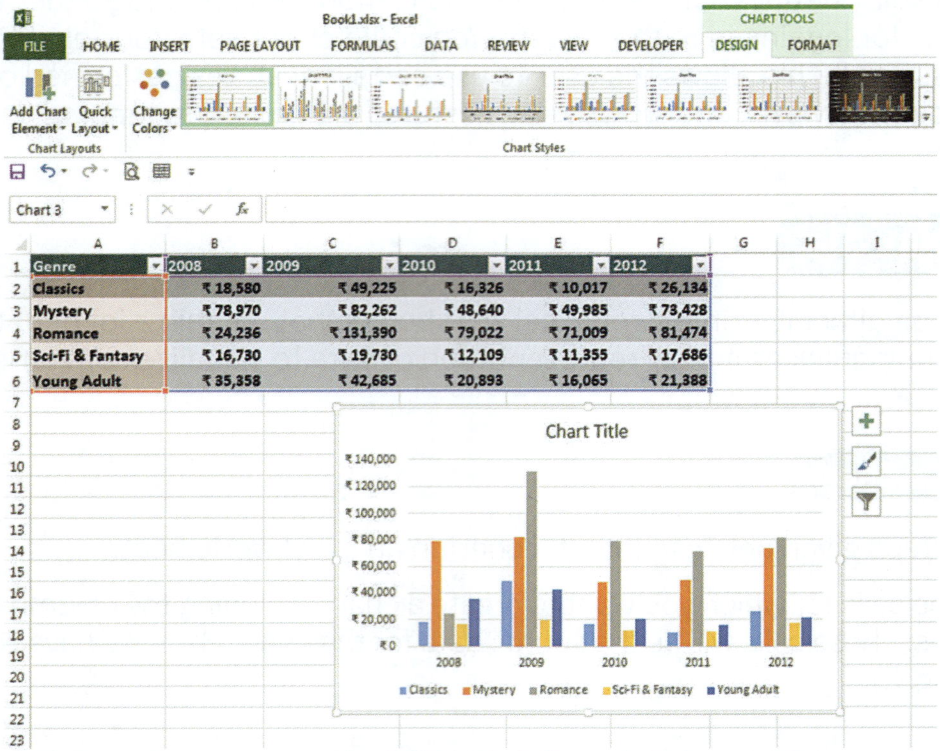

Fig. 5: The inserted chart

If you are not sure which type of chart to use, the Recommended Charts command (Fig. 6) will suggest several different charts based on the source data.

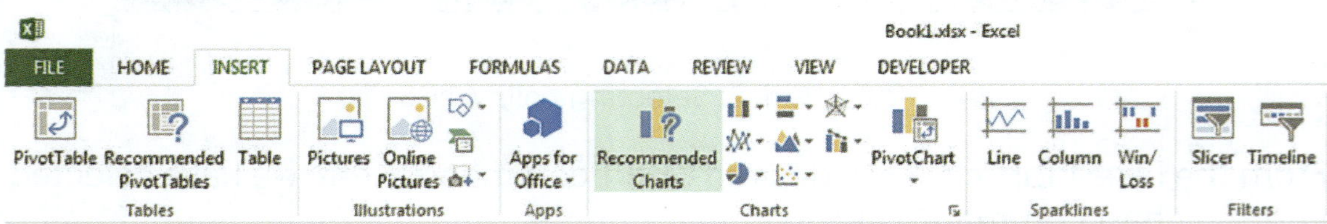

Fig. 6: Recommended Charts

Chart Layout and Style

After inserting a chart, there are several things you may want to change about the way your data is displayed.

It is easy to edit a chart's layout and style from the Design tab.

- Excel allows you to add chart elements such as chart titles, legends and data labels. Adding these elements make your chart easier to read. To add a chart element, click the Add Chart Element command (Fig. 7) on the Design tab and choose the desired element from the drop-down menu.

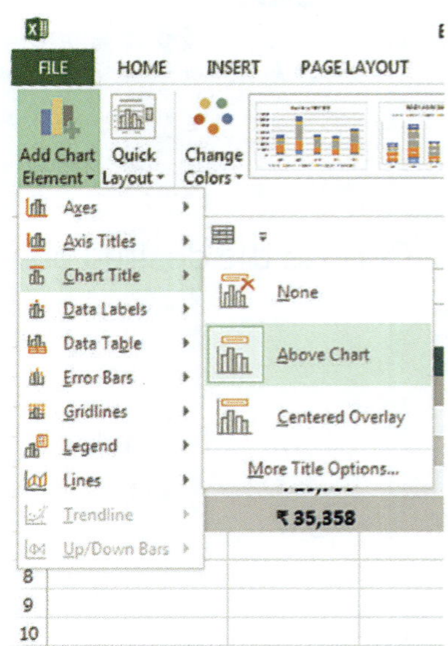

Fig. 7: Adding a chart title

- To edit a chart element like a chart title, simply double-click the placeholder and type the new name (Fig. 8).

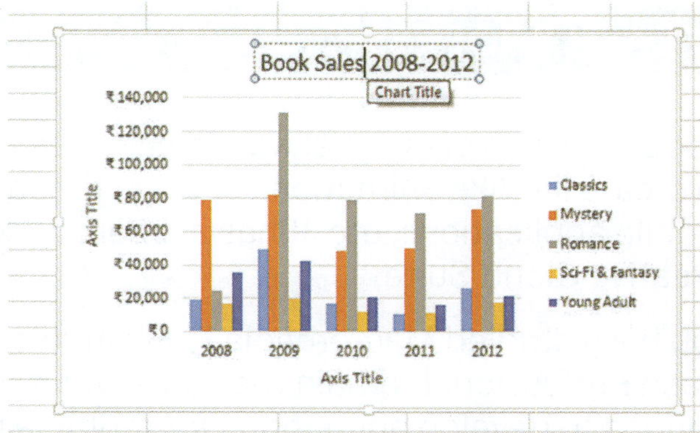

Fig. 8: Editing the chart title placeholder text

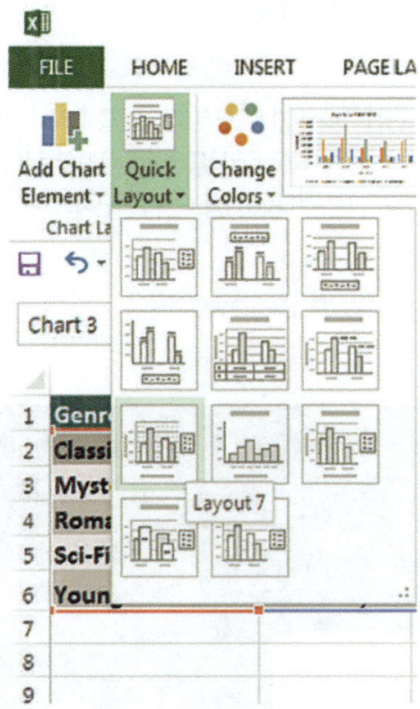

Fig. 9: Choosing a chart layout

- If you do not want to add chart elements individually, you can use one of the predefined layouts. To add a predefined chart layout, click the Quick Layout command and choose the desired layout from the drop-down menu (Fig. 9).

- Excel also includes several different chart styles, which allow you to quickly modify the look and feel of your chart. To change the chart style, select the desired style from the Chart Tools group (Fig. 10).

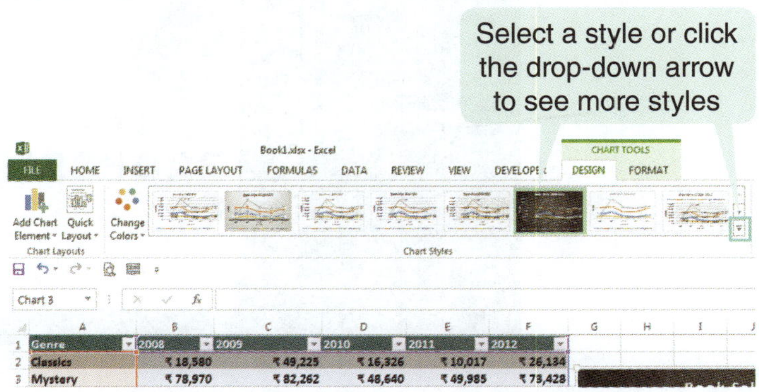

Fig. 10: Choosing a chart style

You can also use the chart formatting shortcut buttons to quickly add chart elements, change the chart style and filter the chart data.

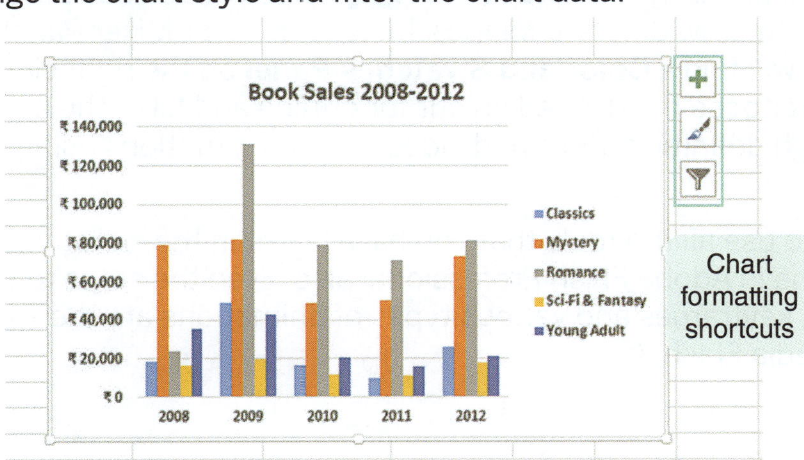

Fig. 11: Chart formatting shortcuts

FLASH PROFESSIONAL CC 2015 UPDATE

Adobe Flash Professional was released as part of Adobe Creative Cloud Suite and is used to create life-like animations and multimedia content for web applications, games, movies, mobile applications, etc. It has a smart dark interface as the rest of the applications of Creative Cloud Suite.

You have studied Macromedia Flash in this series. Although the basic features of Adobe Flash Professional remain the same, yet it gives you a wide range of additional tools and options to develop animations for multiple platforms including desktops, Smartphones (Android & IoS), Tablets, etc.

The User Interface of Adobe Flash Professional is shown below:

Flash Professional CC 2015 has additional tools that help you to build 3D animations. For example, the **3D Rotation Tool** in the Tools Panel helps you to three dimensionally rotate the objects. Similarly, the **Width Tool** helps you to alter the width of the lines and strokes so as to draw different shapes. Instead of Color Mixer Panel in Macromedia Flash 8, here you will find a **Color and Swatches Panel** on the right side of the Interface that helps you to choose the desired colour for outline and fill of the selected object. You can insert high definition audio and video in your animations using Adobe Flash Professional.

The basic steps to use all the tools that you have learnt in the chapters of Macromedia Flash are the same in Adobe Flash Professional also. Even the steps to create and insert symbols, frames, keyframes and various types of animations are the same as you have done in Macromedia Flash 8.

Notes

Notes

Notes

Notes

Notes

Notes

Notes

Notes